D0504095

EATING THE
BIG FISH

EATING THE
BIG FISH

How Challenger Brands Can
Compete Against Brand Leaders

SECOND EDITION

ADAM MORGAN

WILEY

John Wiley & Sons, Inc.

Published by John Wiley & Sons, Inc., Hoboken, New Jersey
Published simultaneously in Canada

For general information on our other products and services or for technical support, please contact our Customer Care Department within the United States at (800) 762-2974, outside the United States at (317) 572-3993 or fax (317) 572-4002.

Wiley also publishes its books in a variety of electronic formats. Some content that appears in print may not be available in electronic books. For more information about Wiley products, visit our website at www.wiley.com.

Library of Congress Cataloging-in-Publication Data
Morgan, Adam.
    Eating the big fish : how challenger brands can compete against brand leaders / Adam Morgan. – 2nd ed.
        p. cm.
    Includes bibliographical references and index.
    ISBN 978-0-470-23827-1   (cloth)
1.   Product management. 2.   Brand name products–Management.
3.   New products. I. Title.
    HF5415.15.M67 2009
    658.8'27–dc22   2008022827

Printed in the United States of America.

10 9 8 7 6

For Ruth

Contents

The task facing a Challenger in competing strongly against a Market Leader is more intimidating than we might have imagined. This chapter explores the scale of the advantages their superior size—and the fact of leadership—brings, and points to why we need as Challengers to consider a different kind of strategic approach in order to succeed.

Marketeers step into this new business world equipped with a set of basic assumptions about their business that have by now become dangerously flawed. The fundamental premises underlying everyday marketing vocabulary such as consumer, audience, and category require careful reexamination, and the implications of their weaknesses need to be understood—in particular, the consequent need for ideas, rather than communications, as the new currency of growth.

This chapter offers an entirely new kind of brand model for second-rank brands finding themselves threatened by the Brand Leader—the model of the Challenger brand. A Challenger brand is defined through three attributes: a state of market, a state of mind, and a rate of success. This chapter concludes by explaining how the core brands considered in Part 2 came to be chosen, and gives

*an example of how the book attempts to turn each significant
Challenger case history into a relevant exercise that can be
valuably applied to the marketeer's own brand.*

*What marketing characteristics do the great Challenger brands
and companies of the past 15 years share? If we could identify those
characteristics, how could we apply them to our own situation
to generate a source of personal business advantage?*

*This section identifies and discusses the common marketing
strands these brands have shared and devotes eight chapters to
discussing each in turn.*

*The great wave makers in any category are those who are new to
it—like Jeff Bezos, who came out of finance to change the
way books were sold, or Eric Ryan of method, who left advertising
to reinvent the household cleaning business. This chapter looks at
the need for marketeers to break free from the clutter of little pieces
of knowledge that are the basis of their strategic thinking in order
to see the real opportunities for radical growth. It also offers ways for
those already deeply experienced in a category to achieve this vital
innocence.*

*Once you have explored the potential opportunities available to
you as a Challenger, it is time to be clear about what your challenge
to the category or another category player is going to be.
This chapter explores a structure for thinking about that central
challenge and discusses the key options open to us; this clarity
is also a key part of laying the foundations for the strategic thinking
that follows.*

*Success as a Challenger comes through developing a very clear
sense of who or what you are as a brand/business and why—and
then projecting that identity intensely, consistently, and saliently*

*to the point where, like a lighthouse, consumers notice you
(and know where you stand) even if they are not looking for you.
This chapter looks at the roots, source, and nature of such identities
and how successful Challengers have built them.*

7 The Third Credo: Take Thought Leadership of the Category

*Marketeers tend to talk as if there is one Brand Leader in every
category. In fact, there are two: the Market Leader (the brand with
the biggest share and the biggest distribution) and the Thought
Leader—the brand that, while it may not be the largest, is the one
that everyone is talking about, that has the highest "sensed
momentum" in the consumer's mind. In this chapter the nature of
Thought Leadership is analyzed, and the methods of achieving
it are explored.*

8 The Fourth Credo: Create Symbols of Re-evaluation

*Successful Challengers are brands in a hurry: they desire (and need)
to puncture the consumer's autopilot and create reappraisal of
themselves and their category swiftly and powerfully. To do so,
they create big, impactful acts or marketing ideas that capture the
indifferent consumer's imagination and bring about a rapid re-evaluation
of their image in the consumer's mind, and role in the consumer's
life. This chapter discusses some of the most striking of these
symbols, what specifically it was about them that achieved the
results they did, and what set them apart them from being just
another publicity stunt.*

9 The Fifth Credo: Sacrifice

*Challengers have fewer resources in almost every aspect of the
business and marketing mix than do the Big Fish—what they
choose not to do, that is, what they choose to Sacrifice, is therefore
as important to their success as what they choose to do. The
nature of this Sacrifice and some of its key dimensions are the
focus of this chapter.*

10 The Sixth Credo: Overcommit

*The converse of Sacrifice is Overcommitment: the idea that, following
the process of Sacrifice, if the marketeer or businessperson has*

When you're only No.2, you try harder. Or else.

Avis can't afford to relax.

Little fish have to keep moving all of the time. The big ones never stop picking on them.

Avis knows all about the problems of little fish.

We're only No.2 in rent a cars. We'd be swallowed up if we didn't try harder.

There's no rest for us.

We're always emptying ashtrays. Making sure gas tanks are full before we rent our cars. Seeing that the batteries are full of life. Checking our windshield wipers.

And the cars we rent out can't be anything less than lively new super-torque Fords.

And since we're not the big fish, you won't feel like a sardine when you come to our counter.

We're not jammed with customers.

Preface

"Everybody pulls for David, nobody roots for Goliath"
—Wilt Chamberlain[1]

In the beginning was Avis. The little fish, aiming to reverse the food chain.

And Avis begat the Pepsi Challenge.

And the Pepsi Challenge begat Apple 1984.

And they all had a love child together called Richard Branson. Who was then knighted by Her Majesty the Queen for services to The Underdog.

And that was the way we thought Challengers went, really. All doing the same sort of thing, all very successfully. All plucky underdogs, all asking us to take a position. All creating the impression that this hugely crowded category was in reality simply a matter of a two-horse race and asking us whose side we were going to take: Were we with the little guy or the big guy here?

And from then on, every decade there seemed to be one new iconic battle between Challenger and leader. And those iconic battles always seemed to take essentially the same form: Small Challenger makes public challenge to Market Leader, in open pursuit of column inches, news footage, sympathy, and sales. A charmingly scrappy David against a visible and, now we realize, strangely sinister Goliath. There was nothing wrong in any of these Challengers and everything right about this stance, of course—but it was always at its heart exactly the same stance. David versus Goliath.

Yet the past 15 years have seen a remarkable new diversity and flowering of Challenger thinking around us, in three important and distinct senses: the number of brands openly adopting a Challenger stance, the diversity of Challenger stances they have taken, and the change that some of the most successful of these Challengers have made to the fundamental way we think about and interact with long-established categories.

THE NUMBER OF BRANDS OPENLY ADOPTING A CHALLENGER STANCE

The first significant recent development in the world of Challenger brands is in the *number* of brands (and other entities—countries and cities, for example) explicitly adopting this Challenger brand stance: Large companies from North America to Singapore to South Africa openly declaring they want and need to think like Challengers, company-wide. And alongside them we find an even larger number of commentators discussing brands through this explicit lens: If you Google "Challenger brand" today, you find people writing about the Challenger brand approach in business from India to Australia to Mauritius, ranging from the fields of politics to education, via soap powder and social networking sites along the way. The concept and language of a Challenger brand has become a mainstream and explicit part of the marketing landscape (whether it is always fully understood or not).

THE DIVERSITY OF CHALLENGER STANCES

The second key development in Challenger brand thinking over the past 15 years lies in the *diversity* of Challenger stances we see taken by Challengers in their chosen marketplace. One of the purposes of the second edition of this book, in fact, is to help us intelligently look at options other than the default Challenger model (which one might characterize as essentially a cluster of attributes around the David versus Goliath theme). Understanding this broader diversity, and how we use it to our advantage, is going to be central to our success.

It is not hard to see why there has been this overarching focus, historically, on "David versus Goliath" as to what it really means to be the Challenger. It is undoubtedly partly the influence of the four iconic Challengers we noted earlier, and how well that stance has worked for them.

And may well also be to do with the implicit influence of military metaphor that underlies so much of the language of marketing (*targets, share battles,* etc.). For what has been the most influential thinking on how a Challenger succeeds within military conflict? The doctrine of guerrilla warfare, whose philosophical authors and successful practitioners in the real world—Che Guevara, Mao, the Viet Cong, Lawrence of Arabia—have made this perhaps the most famous military strategy in the world.

But of course there is a much wider range of Challenger stances one can take than this. For a long time the real scope of the diversity of stances available to us seemed more genuinely visible in the spectrum of political, rather than business Challengers. At either end of the tonal range, for example, one might put the open confrontation of the rioting Paris students of 1968 on the one hand, and the gentle (but more effective) challenge by Gandhi to the British on the other. In between we have seen political Challengers combine the strident with the charming, the steel with the velvet glove: look at the self-styled "Raging Grannies" who doorstepped President George W. Bush over Iraq, for instance, or the smiling Katharine Hamnett, chatting cordially with Mrs. Thatcher in Downing Street while simultaneously wearing a T-shirt that screamed "58% don't want Pershing" (the cruise missiles scheduled to be sited in the United Kingdom). What a brilliant combination of charm and stiletto each wielded—and how intriguing to wonder, we thought, how we as Challenger brands might achieve that kind of potent combination.

But in the recent brand world, too, we are finally coming to see a far richer range of Challenger attitudes, natures, and tones. JetBlue, Red Bull, flickr, Zara, Linux, innocent—each of these has taken a very different approach in order to succeed. They have had to—for, of course, the stance you take as a Challenger is of necessity heavily influenced by the cultural and category context in which you find yourself. (So, for instance, if there are 150 drinks in the energy drink category, and they are all being irreverent mavericks, then one thing a genuine Challenger to Red Bull is *not* going to try to be is yet another irreverent maverick. It will need to find a different way to challenge the conventions of the category or the culture around it.)

And with this fresh diversity from both the physical and digital brand worlds has therefore come the ability to better define the potential choices available to us of the different kinds of stances a Challenger can take in their chosen marketplace. For instance:

i) The Missionary—like Dove, as an agent of change in the beauty category

ii) The Visionary—exemplified by method's vision of a relationship with cleaning that transcends functional germ kill

iii) The Enlightened Zagger—typified by Camper's championship of "slow" in a fast world

iv) The Real and Human alternative—personified by Ben & Jerry's

v) The People's Champion—a torch famously carried by Wikipedia and Linux

vi) . . . As well as, yes, of course, the stance of the feisty little David

These six different stances, and six others are discussed in detail in Chapter 12. In that chapter we will also go on to explore how the nature of this diversity may shed some insight on how long-lived Challengers successfully and continually renew their relationship with the consumer. It will suggest, in fact, that perhaps the whole notion of how one maintains Challenger longevity lies in intelligently evolving across this Challenger typology.

THE CHALLENGE TO THE FUNDAMENTAL WAY WE THINK ABOUT LONG-ESTABLISHED CATEGORIES

The third key development in the centrality of Challenger thinking to marketing and business is the way in which some of the new Challengers are not simply gaining share or changing brand rankings, but threatening to fundamentally overturn entire categories and our frameworks for thinking about them. Twenty years ago, we saw Establishment brands threatened by new Challengers (IBM); now we see the fabric of entire industries and the behavioral cultures we attach to them threatened by this new generation.

Let's briefly consider some obvious examples. While YouTube is evidently a Challenger to television in terms of offering its own live TV channels as well as being an alternative source of entertainment, it has also in the process in effect redefined our notion of quality entertainment. Quality in visual entertainment, one could argue, is no longer about wonderful production values or compelling narrative—post YouTube, it is now simply about how good or fresh the idea is and the emotional effect it has on us (and the person we pass it on to). Wikipedia challenges not only the way we receive authoritative information (Microsoft's Encarta and Encyclopedia Britannica are casually brushed aside by a site that now accounts for one in every 200 online visits), but also our long-held notions regarding credible sources of it (the "amateur versus expert" debate). The foundations have been pulled out from under the conventional music business by iTunes. Game changes such as the Tata Nano and the $100 laptop look as though they will come to create a profound shift in the automotive and computer businesses. Will social networking sites bring down conventional e-mail? What will the Kindle e-book reader do (if anything) to the book business? Will we see a generation of consumers used to "free" Challengers (free music, free entertainment, free texts, free search, free software, free newspapers, free gaming, free calls) question the whole value and transaction model more broadly in every aspect of their lives? (And could this translate into packaged goods?) What will be the impact of environmental Challengers not just on the way we vacation, but on the whole way we think about packaging and what we really need and don't need in that packaging?

And all this structural change before, of course, we have really begun to explore the intimately related future of communications.

A STRATEGIC MODEL, WITH SOME CONSISTENT PRINCIPLES

While this broad and multifaceted emergence of Challenger diversity has been taking place, our context for it—the context of the marketing, consumer, and brand landscape—has obviously also been changing enormously. In our marketing world, some things are new (social everything), some things are back (product performance), some things are wrongly written off (TV), and some things are trumpeted and then forgotten. And the socio-digital economy has currencies all its own that we are having to learn, even as they flex and evolve themselves.

While we might disagree on this implication or that implication of the changes around us, one thing is clear to everyone, it seems: Marketing, or rather the transition that marketing is making, is now to be seen as a journey without maps. We know, because influential CMOs have told us, that the old marketing model is broken, and certainly we have all lost confidence in it. What we *don't* yet know—because it is in a state of continual emergence and experimentation—is what the nature of the new model is that we are supposed to replace it with.

So, at one level, a thorough understanding of successful Challengers is ever more interesting and important to us. Even if we yet lack a coherent model, we can at least take some consistent principles with us. And perhaps these principles should be Challenger principles, for in a very real sense this new world will make necessary Challengers of us all.

It is these principles—which we'll come on to call the *Challenger credos*—that the book offers for us as a framework as we move forward. A constant way of thinking for us and our team to help us steer our brand into a dynamic and rapidly evolving future.

CHANGING CRITERIA

Discussing Challengers in this new world is not without its difficulties, though—it is obviously often hard to be entirely clear who is challenging what. Who and what is Facebook challenging, for example? MySpace? Google? E-mail? Basic human concepts of what it means to be friends? What are we to make of the new brands from India and China—that Tata Nano, for instance (a four-seater car costing $2,500)? It is not going to be sold in Peoria or Paris any time soon, but it will significantly affect the shape and nature of car purchasing and thinking in emerging markets. Infosys, Wipro, and China's Lenovo—are they Challengers? Or still, in effect, products and services with logos (to the Western world at least)? What of the new brands to Africa, such as One Laptop per Child (OLPC)? Not yet a threat to Dell's sales, but it certainly challenges our conceptions of what can be done with technology in poor economies—and it certainly stops and makes me think about exactly what I need from a highly overspecced computer that I am going to buy for my 13-year-old sons in London.

So I have modified in one significant way over the past 10 years my definition for Challengers to include in the study. When we researched the book originally, my partners and I wanted to see three to five years of success before writing about any of the brands we considered. Now, if we were to wait and give each brand the five-year test, we'd either be risking many of the more famous ones becoming clichés, or perversely ignoring some of the most profound potential shifts any of us as marketers have to consider. So let us, with our eyes wide open, embrace a slightly different approach in this edition. Let us look at well-established Challengers, for the main part, but accept that we will need to consider some of the more important new contenders before it is yet clear what their real mid-term trajectory is going to be. And we accept as we go along that there are some much larger challenges posed to the fundamentals of the world around us, and we explore these toward the end of the book.

AN OVERVIEW OF THE FLOW

After exploring some of the key challenges facing us as number two, three, or four brands and reviewing the argument about why we need to think differently from a Market Leader, the book then goes on to discuss the key commonalities Challengers seem to share in terms of *Attitude, Strategy,* and *Behavior.* (See the following page.)

Once we have looked at each of these principles in turn, we go on to look at what it means to be a Challenger brand driver (or Lighthouse Keeper) today, and close by discussing the "ghost in the machine" for all of this: how Challengers manage and indeed lean into risk.

For those of you familiar with the first edition, each of the credo chapters has been substantially updated and considerably revised, and there are two wholly new chapters (Chapter 5, "Monsters and Other Challenges," and Chapter 14, "The Scope of the Lighthouse Keeper").

Finally, the book is designed to be practical, and a series of exercises towards the end is intended to provide stimulus when applied to your business. In addition, you can see some of the interviewees talking on video by following relevant links to a web site for the book; these links are indicated at the end of each chapter. This is not simply to be digitally current; it is because in many ways it is the *way* Challengers talk, as well as what they say, that is the crucial factor in understanding the underlying Challenger mindset we will need in order to succeed.

The Challenger Strategic Approach

Stage 1: Attitude & Preparation

Stage 2: Challenger Strategy

Stage 3: Challenger Behaviour

Stage 4: Sustaining Challenger Momentum

Foreword

T he true test of an idea, a model, an organization or a brand, is whether it can withstand the test of time. There has never been so much testing in such a short period of time as in the last nine years.

Nine years ago, Google and YouTube did not exist; the iPod was one idea, of many, in Steve Jobs's head, and the founder of Facebook was not even allowed to drive. Cable fragmentation and consumer zapping were the issues marketers dealt with, not streaming, downloading, or a la carte and on-demand viewing and listening. We had desktops and laptops then, but no BlackBerries or Treos to check at midnight or before brushing our teeth in the morning. The world seemed to have more *curvature;* now it feels it is virtually flat with competition for goods, services, and labor coming from anywhere and everywhere. Nine years ago, there was no 9/11 and institutional data mining for surveillance and consumer journalism were the subjects of only fiction books and movies.

Eating the Big Fish was also published nine years ago. At the time, Adam Morgan made waves describing the philosophy, profile, and behavior of a Challenger brand trying to dethrone "The Big Fish," perceived to be infallible and invincible. He was clear in articulating the amplified challenges of a Challenger brand within the changing consumer dynamics of the time. He spoke of: a consumer who was not listening, believing, or consuming like she used to; the fluidity and permeability of categories that would no longer fit within the well-defined segmentation boxes of a marketer; and the ineffectiveness of communication that could not capture consumer's imagination in a world where no one was actively listening.

Adam described the Challenger mind-set as "An ambition that exceeds conventional marketing resources and the preparedness to accept the marketing implications of the gap." Challengers can break through by understanding their Big Fish and radically simplifying consumer choice, or by creating new criteria for evaluating a category, or by dramatically changing the sand box. It is all about making tough choices; not about focus, but about Sacrifices. It is about letting go and saying "no" to the existing multiplicity of marketing options; to concentrate energy on the ones that matter the most. Within this framework, Adam created the Lighthouse brand concept. Lighthouse brands have a clear and unapologetic point of view and invite consumers to navigate around them. They are not afraid to flaunt their values even at the expense of alienating some consumers. And they live to consistently delight and surprise consumers, using every possible angle at their disposal, especially the nontraditional. Brands like the Mini Cooper, Harley Davidson, The World Wrestling Federation, Mountain Dew, and Unilever's Axe have lived by the Challenger principles for many successful years.

I read *Eating the Big Fish* in the year 2000 as I was beginning my journey as Chief Marketing Officer of PepsiCo Beverages International. Leading the marketing efforts for the quintessential Challenger brand company in its most intense category and its most competitive market gave me the playpen to bring Adam's concepts to life. I have been a believer ever since.

But times change, thinking evolves, and in nine years, the winds of change have been transformed into the typhoon of change. *Wired* magazine called our times the Petabyte age, an age where infinite information can be stored, processed, and organized to drive innovation in every field and every industry and provide more customized choices than ever before. In this world of algorithm-based thinking there is sometimes the tendency to eliminate or discard the models of the past, even when the past is measured now in months or years instead of decades. As marketers then, one of the toughest questions we will face before embracing new options is: "Within this ocean of change, what are the key principles and process that we must maintain?" I will submit to you that in a world where information overflows our capability to absorb it and the foundations of science and marketing are challenged by it, where consumers are wired 24-7 and are blessed and cursed by choice, where institutions, leaders, and brands are exposed by the vigilant and omnipresent eye of consumers, Adam's Challenger brand and Lighthouse Identity principles are more vital and vibrant than ever.

I was very happy when Adam told me that he was going to revise *Eating the Big Fish* and was truly honored when he asked me to write its foreword. I have enjoyed this assignment thoroughly. In this revised edition, Adam confirms the principles of his 1999 book but brings them to life through new and up-to-date examples of Challenger brands behaving as such within the new world order. Like a lighthouse itself, there is *semper aliquid novi,* or always something new, but the book is firmly grounded within the bedrock of the original Challenger brand essence.

My journey through this book was different from the first time, though. Life has taken me into new adventures and now I am blessed to manage a truly phenomenal Big Fish. So I have reread his book from a very different point of view. In spite of my eternal agnostic mind and my firm belief in constant evolution, I was still able to confirm its concepts. In fact, I now firmly believe that the new world order requires a Challenger brand mentality even when you lead. Categories are constantly being restructured and competitions have been amplified by the steroids of technology and the democratization of media. Megacategories like personal computers, software, music, beverages, and financial services are being resegmented every day, opening the doors to new leader-Challenger discussions. This forever changing environment, where consolidation and fragmentation coexist, implies that potentially every David could play Goliath and every Goliath could play David in any aspect of a broad-based business.

Importantly, as the pressure for returns on investment continues for companies and their marketing investment, affordability, and predictability of available media will force everybody to break with convention. Therefore, breaking and transforming needs to be not only the privilege of the Challenger but also, the obligation of the leader.

For overexposed, overinformed and overwhelmed consumers, a brand with Lighthouse Identity can truly be more relevant than ever. It can be an aid for navigating the storm of choice, a trusted haven to satisfy all her needs within a defined space. The new order requires that any brand with aspirations, Challenger or not, relies on a solid rational bedrock, is enhanced by a strong and authentic emotional connection, but is also inspired by a true sense of mission in the world. All of this guided by a thorough understanding of its history and DNA coupled with a genuine and authentic sense of purpose. Within this model, the Lighthouse Identity brand understands the need for total transparency and consistent dialogue with its consumer, without forgetting its self-referential and unapologetic essence.

Finally, Adam's Challenger mind-set presents three timeless principles of universal appeal. First, "Intelligent Naivety" will encourage any business to consistently embrace doubt and ask the tough transformational questions required for constant innovation and rejuvenation. Faith is, after all, an active exercise in doubt. Second, to have a self-referential and unapologetic point of view, the brand will have the obligation to answer to itself its big questions first. This means big questions cannot be delegated to consumers because consumers "do not know what they do not know" and their opinions are always grounded on what is and not in what can and must be. Third and last, the Roman poet Lucretius's call for *Semper Aliquid Novi*, or always something new, reminds us of the need to constantly delight and surprise but always within the essence of the lighthouse.

As I said, this is a timeless book and its principles transcend market share position. To transcend, we must challenge, especially when we lead!

Antonio Lucio,
Global Chief Marketing Officer, Visa, Inc.

PART 1

THE SIZE AND NATURE OF THE BIG FISH

1

THE LAW OF
INCREASING RETURNS

A t one level, we know all about the benefits for a Market Leader of critical mass—the advantages at consumer, company, and competitive levels the Brand Leader enjoys over every other player in the game due to their size advantage. And these are of course enviable advantages: Who would not want the distribution power of Anheuser-Busch over the trade, or the ubiquitous consumer visibility of Coca-Cola, or the research and development resources of Procter & Gamble?

But this is not the key point we are going to recognize here. Nor is the preference given to the social acceptability of the brand leader by the uncertain consumer (whatever Wilt Chamberlain thinks); nor indeed the formidable trust and reassurance it enjoys; nor yet the power of its monstrous marketing budget relative to ours. These are odds we know and understand. These all merely lead us as Challengers to talk generally about "trying harder" and "differentiating in our advertising," and "focus." Everything we are already trying at the moment.

What we are going to look at first is how, even knowing all this, we are still underestimating the difficulty of the situation facing us: The true dynamic is actually worse than this. For it is not just that Brand Leaders are bigger and enjoy proportionately greater benefits: The evidence we are going to consider suggests that the superiority of their advantage increases almost exponentially the larger they get.

THE LAW OF INCREASING RETURNS

The simplest illustration is that of the relationship between share of voice and share of market. We all know, from theory and experience, that there is a strong correlation between the two: that your share of market will usually correspond strongly with your share of voice, and if you want to increase your share of market you will have to increase your share of voice. John Philip Jones's work has shown clearly that smaller brands need to spend proportionately more than larger brands simply to maintain equilibrium. Recent analysis confirms this to be true of *growth* as well: If one analyzes brands that have sought to grow, smaller brands have to disproportionately increase their share of spend ahead of share of market in order to grow, while larger brands, conversely, have to make relatively smaller increases in share of voice to derive those same market share increases.

This is illustrated in Figure 1.1. This graph examines the data of almost 900 growing brands where the growth was proven econometrically to

FIGURE 1.1 Small brands need greater excess SOV to grow.

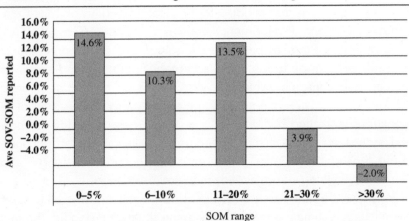

Source: Les Binet and Peter Field, "Marketing in the Era of Accountability," part of the IPA Datamine series.

come from the way they used communications. The horizontal axis on this graph groups the brands by their share of the market: the left-hand column, for instance, represents brands with 5 percent share of their market or lower, while the one on the far right represents brands with more than 30 percent market share. The vertical axis represents the percentage they have had to spend in share of voice *ahead* of their share of market to achieve that growth—the taller the bar, the *more* they have had to spend ahead of their share of market to achieve their growth. And what we see is that once you reach a certain size as a brand—20 percent—you start to have to spend proportionately much less to increase your share of market.

We can go on to see that this "law of increasing returns" plays out in a very similar way in four other key dimensions that are relevant to us. The easiest way to illustrate these differences is to map out the brand-consumer relationship into three stages (albeit rather crude ones) and look at the relative performances of the Brand Leader at each stage relative to a second- or lower-ranked brand in the same category. We then come on to look at the impact on profitability.

STAGE ONE: CONSUMER AWARENESS

First, awareness. Who does our target think about first?

Top-of-mind awareness, sometimes called *salience*, is the proportion of consumers for whom a certain brand comes to mind first when they are thinking about your category. An acknowledged key driver of purchase in lower-interest or impulse markets, like burgers and snacks, top-of-mind awareness is also an underestimated factor in shopping higher-interest categories. General spontaneous awareness, on the other hand (the proportion of people who are aware of your brand at all without prompting), is obviously important at some level to a brand's success—people rarely buy an unfamiliar brand—but tends to reflect brand size and share of market: It often corresponds roughly to market share.

The assumption marketeers generally make is that the relationship between the two is a linear one—one's total spontaneous awareness and top-of-mind awareness will rise in roughly equal proportions. Figure 1.2, however, taken from analysis of the relationship between the two among

FIGURE 1.2 Top-of-mind awareness versus total spontaneous awareness.

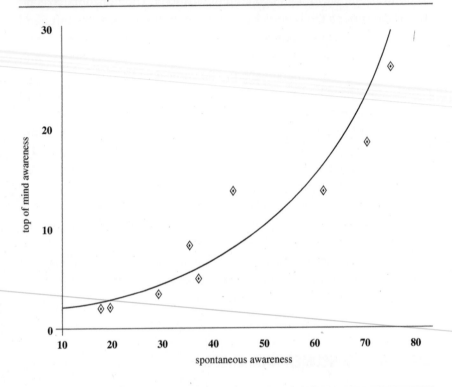

Source: U. van de Sandt/Lintas (now Lowe)

packaged goods brands in France by the advertising agency Lintas (now Lowe) in 1990, shows otherwise.[1]

What is striking here is that top-of-mind awareness increases quasi-exponentially in relation to total spontaneous awareness. That is to say, if I as Brand Leader am twice as big as the Number Two or Three, and spontaneous awareness is linked to market dominance, my top-of-mind awareness is on average close to four times as great. By the same token, if I as Brand Leader starting from a higher base increase either of these, my return will be almost exponentially greater, gain for gain, than that of a Challenger making the same gains lower down the scale.

Not only, it seems, do Brand Leaders have more muscle and resources to start with, but it earns them almost twice as much top-of-mind awareness in return. Udo van de Sandt, the French strategic planner whose work this was, found the same relationship existed between "spontaneous brand awareness" and "usual/preferred brand." We may have to differentiate more sharply than we thought.

STAGE TWO: SHOPPING

What happens when the consumer leaves the house?

What happens is that this law of increasing returns is translated directly into shopping behavior. Imagine our consumer is shopping for a truck, for instance. Well, from a marketing point of view, you would expect that the more you advertised your new truck, the more footfall in-store you could generate compared to the competition. And this is true, up to a point. If one takes the U.S. compact pickup market, for instance, and plots the relationship between advertising spend and shopping across three consecutive years for each brand (Figure 1.3),

FIGURE 1.3 Hypershopping in the truck market.

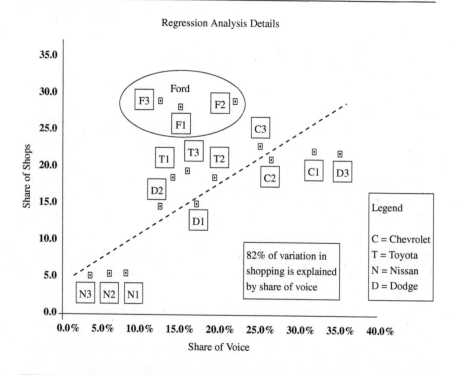

Regression Analysis Details

82% of variation in shopping is explained by share of voice

Legend

C = Chevrolet
T = Toyota
N = Nissan
D = Dodge

Source: Cindy Scott/Allison Fisher

there will be a close fit along a straight line for every brand—except the Ford Ranger. It alone did not obey the normal laws of proportionate returns.[2]

Why? Because the Ranger was the compact pickup segment leader and as such enjoyed a dramatically higher share of shopping, even when supported by a comparatively low share of voice. And we see all around us Market Leaders playing this card, knowing the strength of it for an important group of consumers, from Clarins talking in its advertising about its being "The European Leader in Luxury Skin Care" to a Singaporean bus side informing us that "Seoul Gardens is the world's largest chain of Table Barbeque Restaurants." If you are looking for a recommendation for somewhere to eat this evening, you can't argue with that, it seems.

It looks as though, then, as an ambitious Number Two we will need to offer a greater source of differentiation, not just in our image, but in a way that genuinely impacts the entire shopping process. We cannot compete effectively with the brand leader under the existing rules.

STAGE THREE: PURCHASE AND LOYALTY

A picture is emerging. It translates even into purchase and loyalty, albeit in a less dramatic fashion.

Double jeopardy is a brand phenomenon that has been studied and modeled by researchers in marketing for over 45 years across a variety of markets in cultures as diverse as the United States and Japan. It refers to the combined effects of two benefits that high-share brands profit from relative to low-share brands. The first of these benefits is the obvious one: High-share brands enjoy higher penetration (i.e., simply have more buyers) than low-share brands. The second, more interesting observation is that the buyers of high-share brands buy them more often than the buyers of low-share brands purchase those low-share brands (e.g., see Figure 1.4).

The cumulative effect of these two factors taken together leads to relative scale of increase in the number of purchases tending toward the exponential effect observed in the work on salience shown in Figure 1.2. (Some researchers, indeed, have claimed to observe variances for very high share brands greater even than this.)

FIGURE 1.4 Annual penetrations and average purchase frequencies (leading brands of U.S. instant coffee in their market-share order).

Instant Coffee (USA, 1981)	Market Share	Penetration	Average Purchase* Of Brand	Average Purchase* Of Any
Any Instant	100%	67%	—	7
Maxwell House	19	24	3.6	9
Sanka	15	21	3.3	9
Tasters Choice	14	22	2.8	9
High Point	13	22	2.6	9
Folgers	11	18	2.7	9
Nescafe	8	13	2.9	10
Brim	4	9	2.0	9
Maxim	3	6	2.6	11
All other brands	13	20	3.0	9
Average Brand	11	17	2.8	9

*purchases per buyer of the brand

Source: MRCA/Professor A.S.C. Ehrenberg/R & DI[3]

THE CONSEQUENCE: PROFITABILITY

What, of course, all this leads up to is Brand Leaders making more damn money than we do. Figure 1.5 is taken from the Profit Impact of Market Strategy (PIMS) database; it shows the return on investment for a Brand Leader (split into two different kinds—dominators and marginal leaders) compared to second- and third-ranked brands.

FIGURE 1.5 Return on Investment % (average over four years).

Market Rank	United States	Europe	Industrial	Service	Consumer Durables	Consumer Non-durables
Dominator	32	40	30	46	32	45
Marginal Leader	21	27	20	34	22	33
Rank Two	18	26	17	33	16	29
Rank Three	12	12	13	17	7	11
Follower	8	7	8	15	6	5

Source: PIMS database of performance of 3,679 businesses, 2007, www.pimsconsulting.com

Look at the overall figure for the United States (the left-hand column): While a second-rank brand makes half as much profit again as a third-rank brand, a brand leader that dominates the category makes almost triple that. Or take durables: A second-rank brand makes twice as much as a Number Three, but a dominator doubles that again. I bring this up not just as a stockholder issue, but as a further compounding of the difference in resources between us. Those with an aversion to data tables may find the profitability of a market dominator illustrated a little more vividly by the remuneration of Roberto Goizueta, the late CEO of Coca-Cola, who became the first CEO to earn $1 billion in salary and bonuses alone. That has yet to happen at PepsiCo or Dr. Pepper.

If profit allows a company to make choices, to invest resources in finding sources of future competitive advantage, then this disparity serves to widen the discrepancy between the chips the Brand Leader has at its disposal and the pile we have to play with. As we have seen, each of a Brand Leader's chips seems to win for it twice as much as ours.

Which is one of the reasons why so many Brand Leaders in fast-moving consumer goods (FMCG) markets, for instance, are exactly the same brands that were Market Leaders 60 years ago.

So what?

The point of all this is not to suggest that it is difficult for second-rank brands to catch the Number One; as we will come to see, that is rarely their objective anyway. Nor is the point that at a crude level we as second-rank brands are outgunned more comprehensively than we thought (though we are). And we have not even come to talk about the kind of aggressive business practices pursued by Market Leaders to diminish the impetus, will, and opportunity for their lesser competitors.

What the law of increasing returns means is that we have to swim considerably more vigorously than the Brand Leader just to remain in the same place. Up to now, this has largely translated itself into conversations about relevance and focus: decisions about communication strategy and customer targeting.

But what if staying where we are in the future will not be enough? What if profitable survival in our category requires the achievement of rapid growth, in a probably static market, in the face of three new kinds of competition? Knowing that to follow the model of the Brand Leader is to help it increase its market advantage?

It would mean that we would need to abandon conservatism and incrementalism and start thinking like a Challenger just to survive healthily. It would mean we would have to behave and think about the way we marketed ourselves in a completely different kind of way. Find a different way of thinking about our goals and strategic objectives. Require, in fact, a different kind of decision-making process altogether.

A financial analyst was quoted approvingly in *Financial World* for commenting, "There is a certain trust associated with the McDonald's brand name." Continued the magazine, "Of course, [the analyst] has paid McDonald's the ultimate compliment a service brand could hope to receive."[4]

A service brand? Any service brand? A Brand Leader, maybe, but certainly not a Number Two or Three looking for growth. Of course trust is important—perhaps more important than ever before. But the currencies of quality, reassurance and trust, though they may well have been adequate until relatively recently for dominant Establishment brands, are woefully inadequate as the only basis for the kind of relationship we are going to need with our consumer. Facing the Law of Increasing Returns, Number Two brands are going to need to deal in altogether more potent currencies: those of curiosity, desire, and reevaluation. To succeed, they are going to have to create an emotional identification, a strength of belief in the brand, a sense that we are one to watch or explore—active expressions of choice and loyalty that will make someone walk by the big, convenient facings of the Brand Leader and lean down to pick out the little blue can at the side. As a second-rank brand, we don't just want to create desire, we want to create *intensity* of desire.

This demands a different kind of marketing altogether, a different approach. We will come to see that it will demand a change, in fact, not just in strategy but in the attitude that precedes that strategy and the behavior that follows. Fundamental to each decision taken and each way of thinking will be the concept of *mechanical advantage*—the physical principle describing a machine that manages to create greater output from the same or lesser input. Getting more results, in short, from fewer resources. Not only is this going to be the framework for our entire way of thinking, but it is also going to be the brief for the way we rethink the internal working structure, processes, and behavior of the company and people behind the brand.

And at the heart of mechanical advantage in marketing—its currency, in fact—are ideas.

SUMMARY

There are considerable advantages in being a Challenger: We don't have to be all things to all people; we can choose a place to stand and something to believe in; we can focus on brilliantly delivering that and that alone—even if, while some people love us, others sail right on by.

But let us go into this challenge with our eyes wide open. The reality is that the middle ground will be an increasingly dangerous place to live—it is not for nothing that Wal-Mart talks dismissively about "the mush in the middle." To allow yourself to continue to be just another second-rank brand is, by default, to put yourself into the mouth of the Big Fish and wait for the jaws to close. Caught in the new food chain between the new hunger of the Brand Leader, the speculative sharks from other categories crossing over into ours, and the crocodile smile on the face of our retailer, the only path to medium- and long-term health is rapid growth. We are not necessarily seeking to be Number One; there is a perfectly healthy living to be made as Number Two or Number Three in our market (or large market sector). But to be one of those brands, we have to put some air between ourselves and the competition. We cannot be just another middle-market player; we have to be a strong Number Two.

And we can't get there by behaving like a smaller version of the Big Fish.

2

THE CONSUMER ISN'T

I rarely go out to lunch. I consider it an interruption in my workday.
I review news clippings during my lunch minute.

Donald Trump[1]

If consumerism were a brand, we would say that the person on the street had developed significantly different usage, attitudes, and behavior toward that brand over the past three decades—and yet the vocabulary we still use to talk about it remains essentially unchanged. The old underlying structures and concepts that we still refer to implicitly every time we use words like *consumer* and *audience* and *category* are thus now left fundamentally flawed. These were concepts, after all, coined at the beginning of the packaged goods mass market, when families watched television together and being a consumer meant something because—certainly in the United States—consumerism was embraced by the general public as a healthy sign of being part of, or aspiring to, the middle class. But although our vocabulary fails to acknowledge it, the world is very different today. Consider what has happened to just those three basic concepts—audience, consumer, and category—over the past 30 years.

THE AUDIENCE ISN'T

Ant Farm was a radical collective of American architects/artists, best known for two pieces of installation and performance art. One, called *Cadillac Ranch*, consisted of a row of Cadillacs buried nose down in

Texas. The other, *Media Burn*, was more of a polemic performance piece, where, in 1975, in front of an invited crowd in a small arena in the Cow Palace in San Francisco, a car accelerated up to and crashed through a stack of 42 burning televisions. The meaning of the event was introduced by the self-styled "Artist President," who addressed the crowd before the car set off on its last run. "Who can deny," he asked the crowd with feeling, "[that] we are a nation addicted to television and the constant flow of media?"[2]

Ant Farm's prescient cri de coeur was, of course, in vain. More than 35 years later, the addiction to a constant flow of media is one of the defining qualities of modern life across the developed world. To the point, of course, where consumers, particularly the younger generation of so-called digital natives, are experiencing and interacting with many of those media flows simultaneously.

Figure 2.1 is a chart from a piece of research by OMD and Yahoo!, looking at how an average global citizen (specifically a family-based citizen) spends time during an average day. You can see that if you add together all these units of activity with the time individuals spent on each one, they cumulatively add up to 43 hours of activity per person in what

FIGURE 2.1   What does the average global citizen do in a day?

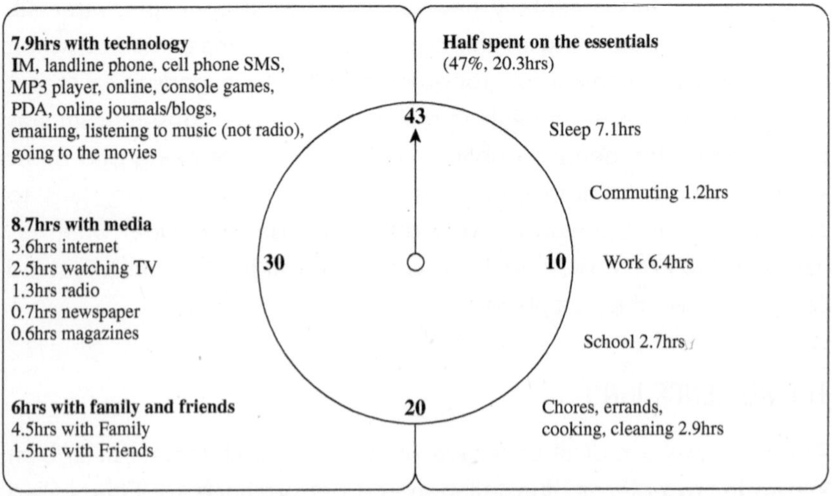

7.9hrs with technology
IM, landline phone, cell phone SMS,
MP3 player, online, console games,
PDA, online journals/blogs,
emailing, listening to music (not radio),
going to the movies

8.7hrs with media
3.6hrs internet
2.5hrs watching TV
1.3hrs radio
0.7hrs newspaper
0.6hrs magazines

6hrs with family and friends
4.5hrs with Family
1.5hrs with Friends

Half spent on the essentials
(47%, 20.3hrs)

Sleep 7.1hrs

Commuting 1.2hrs

Work 6.4hrs

School 2.7hrs

Chores, errands,
cooking, cleaning 2.9hrs

43

30

10

20

Source: Yahoo! and OMD study[3]

we would have historically thought of as a 24-hour day (including 7 hours of sleep). The reason, of course, is because people are doing a number of these key activities at the same time.

And of course this rate of activity is operating at a time when many consumers feel—in part because of this multiplicity of stimulus—more stressed than ever before. So much has been written about the consumer's sense of being time-poor and stressed today that it has become a cliché. But the fact that it has become a cliché should not blind us to the fact that it is profoundly true and is having a considerable effect on the way that consumers interact with marketing activities, communications, and ideas. One of the most important shifts that has resulted, from our point of view, is the relationship that people are looking for in the media they use.

In a poll a few years ago, 94 percent of all American adults stated that a primary use of their free time was to recuperate from work. If true, this is one of the most important pieces of marketing data to have emerged in recent years, and it describes a profound shift in the way consumers use one of the principal marketing tools at our disposal, namely, the television. It implies that there has been a profound shift in our society, from a work/leisure society (i.e., one that self-consciously divides itself between two basic types of activity, work or leisure) to one that divides its time between three: a work/recuperation/leisure society.

Why is this important to us? Because recuperation is a very different thing from leisure. You use recuperation time in a different way, and you look for different kinds of experiences. Look at yourself. Exhaustion is, in every sense, a great leveler. At a very profound level, the consumer is yourself on a Thursday night after a tough four days. What kind of advertising do you want to watch, or have pop up on your screen? The answer, of course, is none at all. At nine o'clock on a Thursday night, all you want to do is escape a little. Relax. Eat peanuts and scratch your stomach.

It is not simply a question of boredom thresholds or tolerance levels decreasing—even in serious relationships (with a local divorce rate running at 68 percent, one county in the American Midwest has been considering compulsory prenuptial counseling before granting a marriage license). It is a question of the pace at which we live profoundly impacting quite basic levels of human need. We live in a world in which companies are monitoring the amount of bathroom tissue that is used to demonstrate that people go to the bathroom less often when they are working more intensely. We take less time between activities—we constantly hurry on to the next. We show no surprise when we read the CMO of Quiznos saying, entirely seriously (based on their research), "The average lunch hour has shrunk to 23 minutes."[4] Well, it used to be an hour, but we take less than half that now, before we propel ourselves on to the next task we need to achieve today. If individuals, social animals with physical needs, are cutting down on such basic requirements in order to get through the day, what slack are they going to cut us, the people trying to communicate with them? In this context, when their prime evening motivation is recuperation and escape, advertisers have moved beyond being clutter. They are no longer in the communication business, they are in a new kind of business altogether: the nuisance business. And our brilliant response to this as communicators has simply been to increase the number of different ways we try to throw our messages at them. Gas pumps, post office queues, ATMs—is it any wonder that the mayor of São Paulo has now banned all outdoor advertising as visual pollution? Are we not pouring kerosene on the problem rather than genuinely addressing it? And if we think São Paulo is a little extreme, let us at least consider Figure 2.2.

FIGURE 2.2   Annoyance with TV Advertising is increasing.

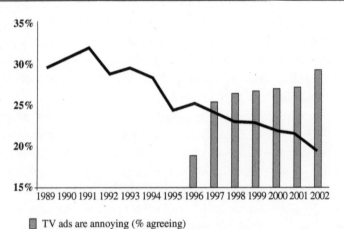

    ■ TV ads are annoying (% agreeing)

    — Enjoy ads as much as TV programmes (% agreeing)

Source: Target Group Index © BMRB 2008

They have less energy to give to us, they are doing more things at the same time, and the relationship with much of conventional advertising is slowly and insistently degrading.

Which means that the audience is not an audience. To call them an audience presupposes they are listening. In fact, we, the brand, are merely one of the three or four acts that are on stage simultaneously, each vying for the attention of the potential audience. Children, conversation with one's partner, food, magazines—video research of consumers watching television shows that they are anything but a captive audience, even when the programming is on. In the UK, for instance, 36 percent of texting takes place in front of the television, while in the United States one study suggested that 23 percent of golf programming *plays to an empty room.* So an audience's attention to advertising is getting even more selective (see Figure 2.3).

Referring to *audience,* then, although that word is used almost interchangeably to refer to our target, is fundamentally flawed. Our target is not an audience, for that would presuppose they were watching or listening. While it may have more usefully described our target at the beginning of the intersection of mass marketing and television (and even this is arguable), it certainly does not do so now. The audience isn't.

FIGURE 2.3   "Do you recall seeing any commercials while watching the program (*American Idol* or *Desperate Housewives*)?"

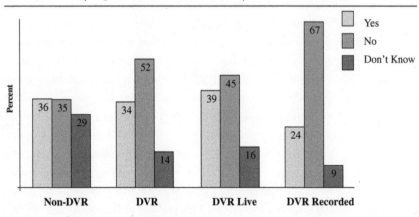

Source: OMD Proprietary DVR Study 2006

And neither, in fact, in any very useful sense, is it a consumer.[5]

THE CONSUMER ISN'T

Implicit in the idea of a *consumer* is someone who is engaged in an activity—namely consuming. Basking in this, as marketeers we eagerly add rational information for consumers to absorb and inform themselves with our packaging, brochures, in-store material, and direct mail. Don't put it in the body copy, we say, confidently—we'll get our consumers to pick it up in the nutritional information.

In fact, consumption for the vast majority of our target of anything other than the product itself is passive at best, and with very rare exceptions, it is centered around the actual moment of purchase or use—people don't have the energy or inclination to be continuously engaged with regard to a product. They are simply using your product and getting on with their lives. In most cases, the smaller the interaction—the less they have to react to—the better. There is evidence to suggest that people want fewer nutritional claims, less choice, and less information to have to deal with in the things they buy every day, whatever they actually tell you in groups.

Furthermore, to say they are willing consumers of a product is *not to say they are necessarily open-minded consumers (or even consumers at all) of its marketing.* It is well-known that the happy coexistence between marketeer and consumer of 30 years ago has been strained by the cynicism toward institutions of all types (from the government down)—to the point where they have become inoculated against many of the marketing claims in each category. It is not simply that people are marketing-aware in concept and vocabulary (the knowledgeable contemporary consumer is the exact antithesis of Vance Packard's unprotected innocent), it is that as victims of hype and oversell by flagging players in maturing or overmature markets, they don't intend to trust anyone but themselves. One might forgive them for scoffing at advertising images of smiling flight attendants pouring drinks, when the evidence of experience has denied the gloss for so long; more startling is the disbelief when a genuinely superior product comes onto the market. This is not new: Even 10 years ago, when Sony PlayStation at launch in the United States tried, as a possible communications route, to talk about its

FIGURE 2.4   Trust is eroding.

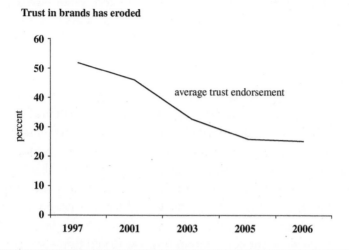

Trust in brands has eroded

average trust endorsement

Source: Y&R/Brand Asset Valuator USA 1997, 2001, 2003, 2005, 2006[6]

genuine product advantages (360-degree movement, 3-D graphics, and higher resolution), the teenage target exposed to these concepts simply sneered—not because these were not things to be desired, but because Sega and Nintendo had tried to sell their ailing 16-bit technology on such claims and lied. Burnt once, twice, the target was not about to be fooled again. And, as Figure 2.4 shows, this weak trust in brands has further halved since then across all categories.

So, how much of your marketing does your consumer *really* want to consume? I suggest to you that your consumer isn't consuming in any really useful sense. The consumer, in fact, isn't.

And neither, perhaps, is your category.

THE CATEGORY ISN'T

To begin with, we are all much too close to our own categories: Consumers simply don't see them in the clearly defined way that we see them. If one lays out 16 products in front of focus group respondents and asks them to sort the products by which criteria they—the product users—regard as being the same and which as being different, one frequently finds that what we would regard as the "category" groupings are the least interesting, least useful (and often emerge surprisingly late) in the different ways the products can be sorted. Where we as marketeers see each product category as being substantially different from another, the target very often doesn't. Consumers are making comparisons of relative use and value across categories that transcend the crude ways we ourselves divide them. A woman asked in a focus group to sort out female toiletries divided them into two piles: one she called "Pretties," and one she characterized as "Things you throw in the basket with the frozen chicken."[7] Quite apart from being a more accurate portrayal of her relationship with, for instance, underarm deodorants than our own physical description of what the category offers, this is also a far more revealing and useful way of thinking about the problems and opportunities for your brand. Instead of considering minor package changes for relative standout compared to the competition, for instance, our time might be better spent considering how we would turn something that was just for "throwing in the basket with the frozen chicken" into a "pretty."

In any case, the most powerful brands have an emotional role that transcends their historical category usage—and in the digital space much of the point is that people are finding their own applications for what brands are giving them. For instance, a traveler recently going to Hawaii researched a hotel he was considering staying at (the Fairmont Orchid), by using other people's photographs on flickr, postings on YouTube, and comments on TripAdvisor because he wanted to avoid the glossy unreality of the hotel's own website.[8]

Does this make flickr a photo sharing site, or a travel research tool? It is whatever its consumer wants it to be: We are limiting the potential of our own brand by thinking purely in terms of our own category.

Furthermore, what boundaries they do draw are not always the ones we ourselves live by; they are in fact being encouraged by product development within even apparently complementary categories to break down the walls even further. Technology is an obvious example—if one offers the consumer a machine that is simultaneously a phone, a camera, an e-mail device, and an Internet browser, which category are we in? But this blurring is not limited in any way to technology. Historically, for instance, you would have said that the hotel business and the luggage business were complementary—greater use of one encouraged greater need of the other. But as Samsonite reinvigorated its product range for the travel-jaded road warrior a few years ago, making it lighter, faster, more convenient to carry and stow, the Four Seasons Hotel in Chicago introduced "No Luggage Service," where, far from needing to minimize your luggage, you can in principle travel with *absolutely no luggage at all*—you can have the clothes you walk in wearing cleaned while you put on one of a range of men's or women's apparel that the hotel lends out. The Four Seasons realized, it seems, that the question one typically asks of consumers in luggage focus groups—"What kind of bags do you really want?"—is in a very real sense starting too far downstream: People these days simply don't want to have to deal with the hassle of carrying bags *at all*.

Besides, in certain key respects, consumers don't *want* to see categories as being entirely different; in many ways, they want their service aspects, for instance, to have more in common. Twenty or so years ago, every service category had developed its own rules of engagement with its consumers—car dealers treated you one way, fast food treated you in its own fashion, airlines were airlines, and so on. And the consumer, in turn, generally accepted this. But today, consumers have become aware of what is possible—and indeed what they should be expecting for their money—in *any* category. Educated by quality of service or experience in one business, they transfer those expectations to every category in which there is a service transaction. A respondent at a focus group on airlines put the case with some verve:

> You know, I have a dry cleaner at the end of my street. It's just a little Italian guy doing his own thing, no big company or anything. I took him a work blouse on Monday, and I needed it in a hurry. "No problem," he says. So on the way home I picked it up in the evening and it turns out it's missing a button and he's replaced it with another just the same, without even making a big deal about it. Doesn't charge me anything extra; like it's all just part of the service.
>
> Well, then on Wednesday I get on the flight to New York, and I ask for an extra packet of peanuts because I haven't eaten any lunch, and the flight attendant tells me I can't have any more because she only has one bag of nuts per passenger to give out.

And that doesn't hold up for me. When I look at how much more money I give the airline each year than my dry cleaner, and how many more people they have working for them, and the infrastructure and everything, I just don't understand how they can hold their heads up and say stuff like that.

Ask them in focus groups in Des Moines what the blueprint for a new camera company would be like, and they answer the name of a computer/media/electronics company: Apple. Today, quality of experience and the expectations that it engenders travel beyond the category in which they were first experienced.

Our category, in summary, isn't.

In conclusion, then, the language that we use every day in our jobs is a legacy from a past that is no longer relevant, leaving that same vocabulary and the concepts it represents fundamentally flawed premises for the new world in which marketeers say they are beginning to find themselves. Implicit in those concepts are numerous assumptions that may have been correct when the language was first coined but that are dangerously misleading today. Now, I am *not* going to attempt in the rest of this book to pursue this caution into the invention of a replacement vocabulary—it would make for tiresome reading, besides distracting us from the principal thrust of the book, which is the study of Challenger brands. For the moment, it will serve to remain keenly aware of those implicit pitfalls and think of the old marketing language we still use as like a rotten wooden floor—it will take our weight as long as we realize we have to walk gingerly and understand the nature of the drop beneath.

Which brings us back to the imperative of mechanical advantage and the importance of ideas.

COMMUNICATION DOESN'T

The shift in the way we need to think about the category, the audience, and the consumer suggests that we should not be thinking of our marketing goal as communication. The sum of all this is that communication doesn't, or rather, that communication doesn't *necessarily*. Communications suggest active listening, but our target doesn't want to be communicated to, isn't waiting for a further message. Put bluntly, therefore, anyone who talks about "communications" or "integrated communications" is again using a flawed concept in the current business environment. The only business to be in is the *ideas* business (integrated or otherwise); for implicit in the ideas business is not simply the idea of communication, but also that of *engagement*—seizing the audience's imagination.

The combination of category blurring and the consumer's changed relationship with television has significant implications for advertising: In a very real sense, our competition in this new world, particularly this new world of recuperation is now *all* advertising, not just our principal competitor's share of voice. If total ad spending in the United States was $210 billion in 2006, and we are a brand that spends $21 million on advertising a year, our real share of voice is 0.01 percent. If we are in the laundry detergent business, our competition is not the appalling commercials our competitors deploy for laundry detergents but the other commercials our target are engaged by, and respond to, across *every* category: pizza, online dating, cola, beer. A competitive advertising review must be all the competitive advertising the target sees: our action standards measured in terms of which of those—*whether within or outside what we call "our category"*—the consumer finds relevant and appealing.

Which is why, as a Challenger, we need ideas. Implicit in the concept of ideas, quite apart from the content, is that they are engaging, provocative, and self-propagating. The unexpected pairing that an idea consists of seizes or engages the attention and imagination of the target rather than assuming what ears are already waiting to hear; it provokes a response rather than allowing the listener's indifference to be maintained; and it is self-propagating in that, once seeded, it does not require constant external feeding to flourish.

This concept of ideas will run throughout the book. Indeed, most of the Eight Credos have at their heart the development and implementation of ideas.

3

WHAT IS A CHALLENGER BRAND?

I'm going to upset the whole world.

Muhammad Ali, 1964

N ot least among the difficulties in abandoning, as we are attempting to, the natural reactions we fall back on in times of marketing adversity is the daunting prospect of facing a journey we have not made before—a journey that seems almost by definition to be one for which there is no map or precedent. It takes more time, energy, and effort to create something new than to mimic something old, and these are the three commodities of which we feel most deprived. We need new brand models to guide us, to give us an overall sense of direction—an intuitive marketing compass we can fall back on in the fog of war. We look enviously at the precedents of the legal world; would that we had new precedents of our own to help shortcut decision making.

Well, we do. They're just not the precedents we used to use—the Brand Leaders. Instead, we have to look to another kind of model—from a type of brand that is far more relevant to us. The criteria for a brand we (as, at best, a Number Two in a category) should be looking to emulate are three:

1. They should be *at best* a second-rank brand themselves.
2. They should have demonstrated a period of sustained and dramatic growth.
3. They should be from a category other than our own.

It is these kinds of second-rank brands we shall call Challenger brands.

WHAT IS A CHALLENGER BRAND?

The expression *Challenger brand* may be thought to simply evoke a Number Two or Number Three brand that is up against a much bigger and more muscular Brand Leader—the *Establishment brand*. Images of David against Goliath come again to mind: attitude and a single shot against confidence and power. And isn't the Challenger naturally the Number Two to the Establishment brand rather than any rank lower? Can one really challenge from the position of fourth, fifth, or sixth?

One might have agreed with this up until the 1960s. But when Avis, which explicitly introduced the whole concept of the Number Two brand to modern consumer and marketeer alike, launched the celebrated "We're Number Two, so we try harder" positioning, the brand wasn't quite in the close second place its advertising suggested; it was certainly in the following pack, but at some distance from Hertz. The brilliance of the strategy was that its *claimed* position took it out ahead of the chasing pack, apparently snapping at the heels of the gigantic Hertz. One would get the impression from the advertising, in fact, that they were the only two players of any significance in the market at all. Two decades later, Richard Branson's Virgin Atlantic played the same game with British Airways in its home market. Although there are a huge number of choices of carriers to cross the Atlantic, Virgin has created the impression for the domestic consumer that there are only two choices on the routes it flies: itself and British Airways.

The classification of brands we examine throughout the rest of the book are consequently deliberately broad, both in the ranking of the Challenger within its market (if it has one—Second Life, for example, effectively created an entirely new market) and indeed in the definition it embraces of what is and is not a brand. The reader immediately comfortable with New Zealand and Daniel Radcliffe alongside Burger King and method as brands, and the Blue Man Group and Dubai alongside Lexus as Challengers can move directly to the First Credo (Chapter 4). For those who prefer greater preliminary clarity, the rest of this chapter looks to define exactly what we mean by the term "Challenger brand."

THE THREE CRITERIA FOR A CHALLENGER BRAND

There are three criteria for a Challenger brand: a state of market, a state of mind, and a rate of success:

1. *State of Market.* Challengers are by definition not the Number One brands, nor are they niche.

2. *State of Mind.* This is what really characterizes all these players—being Number Two (Number Six, or 18) is simply an accident of birth. Challenger brands have a mind-set that encompasses two key differentiators:

- Ambitions that exceed their conventional marketing resources, and,
- A preparedness to accept the marketing implications of the gap between their ambition and their marketing resource.

The latter is an important distinction—ambition in a marketing plan is not enough; being smaller and hopeful, without a preparedness to behave *in whatever way is necessary* to fulfill that ambition will lead to nothing but being small and disappointed. And note that in talking about a "Challenger mind-set" we are not necessarily talking about aggression. Taking a historical perspective, both the Sex Pistols and Gandhi were Challengers, but only one of them was aggressive; a determination to change the status quo doesn't necessarily require a full frontal attitude.

3. *Rate of Success.* The final criterion for a Challenger has to be, for our purposes, success. There is no point in imitating an aggressive brand that has failed—this is not challenge, merely arrogance or misguided ambition. We shall require of all our brands that they have enjoyed significant and sustained growth through their marketing actions. This is not to say that they are *still* always growing at the same rate (e.g., Oakley), but that there is a period of their life we can learn from, a period in which they enjoyed *rapid* growth. This is what Challengers can offer us over the Brand Leaders—an illustration of how to do it *quickly*.

The antithesis of the Challenger brand is the Establishment brand. The most dominant example of this is the Brand Leader, but other brands—even long-standing Number Two brands—can fall into this category if they lack either the ambition or the acceptance of the marketing implications.

THE PRINCIPAL CHALLENGER BRANDS CONSIDERED HERE

I have chosen brands that I have been able to get good primary or secondary data on, or have worked on myself. Although, therefore, not a scientific study in the sense that the brands can be said to be a representative sample of all brands, I have attempted to include a broad mix of the following:

- Launches (method, Facebook) versus relaunches (Burger King, Dove)
- U.S. brands versus international brands
- Challengers that continue to enjoy strong growth (innocent) versus Challengers that have displayed strong growth in the past, even if recent performance has plateaued (the Schrager hotels)
- Categories as diverse as, for instance, packaged goods, services, fast food, cities, automotive, online retailers, and entertainment

I have included some brands the reader may not be familiar with, either because they are regional brands within the United States (Umpqua Bank) or because they are brands from countries and markets with which the reader may be unfamiliar (e.g., South Africa). These are included not simply to leaven their more familiar costars, but because each has an enviable growth rate that has strikingly outperformed the category—and the Brand Leader—they compete against. method, for instance, may be at some level relatively small ($150 million in sales in 2007), but it is at once the seventh-fastest-growing company in the United States and the world's largest eco-cleaning brand. Equally, innocent is a UK smoothie brand that, though it began without any advertising support at all, has grown to become the UK's fastest growing packaged goods brand, and in the process has redefined much of the way the British marketing world thinks about the role and power of packaging. These are brands I have felt it is worth trading a small amount of explanation for in order to reap the rewards of their experience.

Category aside, these fall into four groups, as shown in Figure 3.1. Each of the four sections of the grid represents a different kind of Challenger. Most of the discussion in the book centers on group A; these are launches or relaunches that have challenged the Brand Leader in the category. Group B includes brands that have either created their own category or succeeded by moving outside what had been thought

FIGURE 3.1   Different kinds of challengers.

A. Challenger Brands	B. "Challenger" Brands
Launches or re-launches into a category with an established Brand Leader (e.g. Dyson, Target)	Challengers that have succeeded by inventing their own category (e.g. Red Bull)

C. Challenger "Brands"	D. Historical Challengers
Challengers that are not brands as such (e.g. Bikram "hot" yoga, soy)	Historical Challengers (e.g. Gandhi, America 1776–1941, The Sansculottes)

of as their "natural" category altogether. They accomplished growth in slightly different ways from group A—if growth is caused either by increasing their market share or increasing their market, then brands in the top right of the grid increased their market: Cirque du Soleil, for instance, redefined its competition from other circuses to be "every other show in town" and aimed to attract the occasional show-goer by being one of the two things they went to see that year. Brands in the group A, on the other hand, were as likely to take share from the Brand Leader as they were to grow the market.

WHAT'S A SEARCH ENGINE GOING TO TELL ME ABOUT SELLING SHEET METAL?

The problem with marketing case histories such as the list of Challengers we have just mentioned is this: If they are in our category, we already know all about them, and they have long since lost the ability to stimulate or inspire (far less offer an opportunity to derive competitive advantage). If, conversely, they are outside our category, we don't know what to do with them. Take the most discussed Challenger (and now dominant leader, in search at least) of the past 10 years: Google. Much featured, much feted, but what do we make of it if we don't sell search? Or how do we apply the learnings from Zara? The clothing market is fascinating, but it's an image market, and I'm competing on service. Oh, and don't talk to me about New Zealand—my distribution system is nothing like the tourism business. Like looking through a piece of textured glass, one thinks one grasps the application of the point the author is trying to make, but it doesn't really seem to match the lines and structures we actually live with every day. And so we put this other marketing world down and forget about it, the bridge unfinished between them and us.

Yet a key thrust of this entire book, and the strategic process we are going to create, is that there is at least as great an advantage to be gained from watching the players in other categories as in analyzing the players in one's own. In order to flourish under the dynamics of the new, more voracious marketing food chain, the new brand models we should be watching and learning from are not the other brands in our own category. They are instead:

- Second-rank brands (or people who were at the time second-rank brands)
- Brands outside our category
- Brands that have demonstrated rapid growth

If this is to work, we have to find a way of constructing a bridge from an apparently unrelated marketing category to our own in a way that is genuinely useful. Let us try to construct a bridge between two such businesses, and in doing so derive the first of a series of exercises that will form the building blocks of the Challenger strategic process later in the book.

Google is an interesting case for a number of reasons. When one reviews studies of the world's favorite brands, Google almost always lands in the top 10 of all brands and almost always comes in the top 3 favorite technology brands—and yet it has one very unusual characteristic compared to the other brands it finds itself in the company of in such lists: As a company it has an aversion to marketing. It is worth just lingering on this point, because it is so striking: Google has grown, as a Challenger (and then as a leader), to become one of the world's favorite brands *without actively marketing itself at all*. Although Google is now one of the world's largest companies, you as a consumer will never see any form of conventional advertising for it. Yet people love it.

How has it done this?

The answer is a very simple one. The reason that people love Google so much is that it is startlingly useful. It delivers this startling usefulness in less than a second. It helps people do things they didn't think possible (answer any question, see who has the biggest garden in the neighborhood, send all the wedding guests a map of how to get from the church to the reception), and it offers them ways of exploring their world and their potential with tools (from Ad Manager to Google Earth) that are easy or dramatic—and sometimes both. And it does all these things for free (or free to us, the user), with a simple and unassuming interface. And from the combination of these it comes across as a genuinely generous, giving brand. What's not to love?

So, what can we learn from this if we are selling cars? Well, first things first. In one key regard, of course, Google *is* using marketing. Whether you are a student of the 4Ps or the 7Ps, one of those Ps is product. And Google is using the combination of three of these Ps in particular (*product, price,* and *place*) to deliver this sense of startling utility—it just isn't using brand building in the "visible marketing" sense of brand building. But the product in this case is not an object, it is a service.

But the key thing we can learn from this is the value people place on a brand being startlingly useful to them—so, applying this, what would it mean for a car brand, or perhaps a car dealership, to be startlingly useful to people? Well, perhaps we would have to offer a whole range of information or services that we don't currently offer. Perhaps, for instance, we would offer information about brands and models other than our own. This information would not be in the form of leaflets out on a table or even accessed via the Internet. Nothing startlingly useful about that. Perhaps we would offer our own version of Apple's Genius Bar, with a resident techie who would be prepared to help them answer any question they liked, not just questions about car specs. This would not be our lead salesperson, perhaps all smiles and suavity in a sharp suit; this would be someone who wasn't trying to sell us anything at all. Just help. To be startlingly useful, he or she could offer to tell us ways to reduce our commute to work by 10 minutes each way every day. They could be the center for neighborhood carpooling services or school ride shares. Perhaps our equivalent of Google Earth might be to offer additional services like "great car journeys of the world," wonderful drives in which to enjoy our cars, beautifully rendered, with places to stay along the way and the kinds of small boutiques, hotels, and cultural museums that reflect our particular brand sensibility. Or family picnics—places to take the kids, to get them away from the game console, so the family could all just mess around together. Bike trails within a 40 minutes' drive. Guides to how to teach your son or daughter fishing, and places to do it together. And all done in a way that, as your customers unfold it, makes them gasp slightly at the drama of its unfolding.

Second, this new service would be very simple to use and enjoy. No forms to fill in, no clutter. No one trying to doorstep you on the way and sell you stuff. Very approachable and accessible.

Third, we would do this for free. We would recognize that there is a consumer response to generosity that we will recoup in other ways. That, in our case, word of mouth is the best advertising, and certainly as people shop for their next car, this would be a unique reason for them to come and see us while they are going around their three or four options. And if they come in and want to talk to the salesperson on the way out, then that would be wonderful. (If we are concerned about the cost, we could in fact let the publishers pay, like Google—those little hotels, boutiques, and fishing rod stores.)

And we would have a magic ingredient at the heart of all of this. Google has its mythical algorithm, which it is constantly improving (450 times last year alone). So what would be our magical ingredient, the one that renders us both better and unable to be copied, at least in the consumer's mind? Is it our techie? Is it the way we brand that person and their service? What is the thing we would be constantly and publicly improving, every day of every year?

In other words, the relevance of the Google case to us has nothing to do with whether we are in the search category or not. If we identify the points of emotional value that Larry Page and Sergey Brin created, and then look for how we would create exactly those same points of emotional value in our offer, even in this entirely different category, the relevance is not hard to find. In fact, we will go further. We will create the first of a series of exercises that turn a key point of relevance from the brand outside our category into an exercise we can apply to any category, regardless of the superficial differences and anomalies. These exercises take the form of intransitive verbs. The first such verb is this (and we are going to deliberately change the conventional meaning of this verb here):

To Google *vb:* to make ourselves *startlingly useful* to our user.

If we can translate each key case history discussed within each of the Eight Credos in this way, we will begin to develop a group of exercises that allows us to apply profitably the breakthroughs in thinking from other categories to our own and thus replicate their challenge and growth.

As second-rank brands, of course, we need rapid growth, whether we want to challenge or survive. The middle ground, as we saw earlier, is going to be an increasingly dangerous place to live.

THE EIGHT CREDOS

We shall start with a series of observations about what these brands all seem to be doing and then construct a new kind of strategic process and series of exercises we can apply to our own brands.

It will, of course, be something of a postrationalization. None of the people behind the brands we are discussing consciously sat down and said, "Okay, team, I think I've worked out the Eight Credos we have to follow." They did it instinctively, often because they had to, rather than of their own volition. But that doesn't matter for our purposes; we are learning from their experience curve. And in some cases, of course, they will be Challengers whose mistakes are as valuable as their successes.

Finally, at the heart of being a Challenger is precisely the fact that marketing is not a science, but rather informed judgment—there is opportunity in there being no marketing absolutes anymore. In the spirit of that informed judgment, then, while I have substantiated the core hypothesis as rigorously as possible throughout, at certain points I leave the tarmac road and offer a point of view about the future of marketing and the consumer; I telegraph these more subjective observations as clearly as possible when they occur.

PART 2

THE EIGHT CREDOS OF SUCCESSFUL CHALLENGER BRANDS

4

THE FIRST CREDO: INTELLIGENT NAIVETY

Experience is what gets you through the door, but experience also closes the door. You tend to rely on memory and stick with what has worked before. You don't try anything new.

Twyla Tharp[1]

THE VITALITY OF INEXPERIENCE

Looking at the list of the great Challengers that have really impacted their individual markets, the first thing that strikes one is how many of them are launches: that is to say, how many of them (and more specifically, the people behind them) lack any previous experience in their chosen category.

Even in the days when companies were still being started in garages rather than dorm rooms, it is striking how many of these founders knew relatively little about the categories they were launching into, and how beneficial that freshness proved to be. Both method and innocent, arguably the most influential packaged-goods brands of the moment in the United States and the UK, respectively, were started by people with no experience in cleaning products or smoothies. The most influential Challenger soft drink in mainland Europe (Bionade) was started by a brewer who had never made nonalcoholic drinks before. Jeff Bezos of Amazon was in fact a hedge fund manager when he determined there was an opportunity to go into online book retailing, and start up in a two bedroom house in Seattle. Richard Branson famously used the money he made from selling rock albums to start an airline business. George Hickton, the CEO of Tourism New Zealand, which has become perhaps one of the most admired and successful country brands of the past 20 years, had no experience in tourism or marketing: He was an expert in turning around businesses. James Dyson (who had studied furniture and interior design, rather than engineering, in college) had no experience in vacuum cleaning—his previous invention was a new kind of wheelbarrow. Jimmy Lai of *Apple Daily* came out of clothing to start a newspaper. And of course, a whole new generation of entrepreneurs—who have never worked anywhere at all very much before—is changing forever the media, social, and information landscape. This last group is so successful they clearly don't need the reassurance of any predecents, but they find one anyway in Michael Dell, who was himself a college student in Austin, Texas, when he realized he could beat both IBM and Compaq by focusing on the delivery system rather than on the product; by 2007, Dell Computers had a revenue of $57 billion.

So what's the point here? The point is that we are taught that category experience is valuable, perhaps essential. There is a natural tendency in a company to think of its sphere of business or category as being special, with its own rules, intrinsically different from everyone else's. And whenever one changes jobs or moves within the same job into another category of business, there is always that grimly predictable moment when the old hand leans across the table and explains over the course of an hour or two (rather patronizingly, in my experience) why this business is like no other business you have ever worked for. Our enthusiasm and fresh thinking are understandable, it seems, but misplaced—and when we know the business a little better, we'll understand why.

And in some rather limited respects, of course, they are sometimes right. There are often lead-time differences, or distribution structures, or union agreements, or even (very occasionally) consumer purchase cycles that shade things a little differently here or there—if one knows a great deal about the subject and thinks about it from the manufacturer's point of view. (And in the digital world, the business model might indeed be very new.)

But the consumers haven't had the benefit of working on the business for a number of years, either. They don't think that what they enjoy about the *experience* in one market has to be necessarily any different from what they like in another. Indeed, in many ways they'd *like* the experience they get in some categories to be more like those they get in another. If they could find an airline that treated them like their favorite local restaurant, they'd fly it every time.

Which is exactly why people have responded so strongly to many of the Challengers on our list. Far from category inexperience being a drawback, it has proved to have a vitality that has allowed the new players to envision fresh possibilities in the category, possibilities that those who have worked for years in the category are unable to see because they have grown too close to the status quo.

And the same is true, I would suggest, of you and me. After all, do we not really feel underneath that we understand the possibilities of a market better in the first month we work in it than we do three years in? In those first few weeks, we are absorbed by and focused on the questions and opportunities, uncalcified by the category shibboleths and uncluttered by the petty details and manufacturing perspective that obscures our judgment later on. It all seems so wonderfully simple and clear; we open up the market instead of closing it down. We ask "Why not?" and not simply "Why?" We see no real reason why the questions our five-year-old daughter would ask of the category are any less valid than those we pay our research department to ask: "Why are vacuum cleaners all so gray and ugly?" "Why can't you rent a car for an hour, instead of a whole day?" "Why do healthy products have to be so dull?" "Why are banks such cold and silent places?" And this beginning is the time, if at all, when we tend to change things. Look at Branson, Dyson, Dell: Innocence, intelligently applied innocence, has changed the face of the categories around us more profoundly than all the MBA expertise in the world.

This goes beyond marketing. My English literature teacher used to claim that the finest writers in the English language in the past 200 years were Conrad and Nabokov—neither of whom had English as their first language. It was indeed, he contended, the very fact that both of them started from another culture, another tongue, that the possibilities of the English language opened to them in such striking and unusual ways. So, too, the creative breakthroughs of the 1960s, the golden age of U.S. advertising, were credited by some New Yorkers at the time in strong part to an influx of minorities with strong cultures of their own into a profession historically dominated by WASPs. Creative thinkers from strong Italian and Jewish cultures, the theory went, were able to bring fresh insight to familiar categories that those in more mainstream U.S. culture were too close to see. The photographer Robert Frank, whose 1955 masterwork, *The Americans*, a visual study in 83 images of all levels of American society, has been hailed as the photographic equivalent of the Great American Novel, wasn't an American at all; he was a Swiss. The only artist to really capture the light in California was an Englishman, David Hockney. And so on.

In other words, it is what we will call "Intelligent Naivety," a questioning and insight creation born of dynamically applied inexperience, rather than rich familiarity with the category, that has changed the face of the categories around us in the most profound way. That has opened up new business models, introduced new dimensions of appeal for potential consumers, found new ways to build premiums and drive loyalty. It might seem easy to confuse Intelligent Naivety with simply flying in the face of conventional wisdom, and in truth one does see some Challengers espousing exactly such a philosophy. Larry Ellison of Oracle has consistently remarked that he got to where he is now by doing the opposite of what people expected of him. Patagonia's Yvon Chouinard has said of his approach: "I would never be happy playing by the normal rules of business. I wanted to distance myself as far as possible from those pasty-faced corpses in suits I saw in airline magazine ads. . . . I wanted to be a fur trapper when I grew up."[2] Yet while the idea of exchanging our normal office attire for beaver pelts is in many ways an intriguing one, we might, as Challengers wanting to take a larger group with us, need something a little more systematic in our approach from a strategic point of view. And by *Intelligent Naivety* we mean in reality something more than "do the opposite of what everyone else is doing." We mean, very specifically, to bring a fresh and dynamic set of questions to the category, a set of questions that deliberately breaks with the immediate past of the category (and our brand, if we are an established player) and looks at what we can learn from other categories—both in terms of what we can bring that is new, and also in terms of which bits of so-called wisdom we need to *unlearn* in order to break through.

Which is why the preparation, the mental preparation of approaching or reapproaching the category with a little Intelligent Naivety, is the First

Credo for Challenger brands. Let us first explore in more detail what its value is and then turn to how we might do it.

ASKING UPSTREAM QUESTIONS

The first, and most obvious benefit of Intelligent Naivety is that it allows us to step back and ask those upstream questions that brands and brand owners more immersed in the category have lost the ability to pose. Why does the category have to be all about *this*? Why could it not be about *that* instead? I understand why people don't care about anything but functionality at the moment, but does it really have to be that way? What would make them change that? Why do they always talk about this particular dimension of the category first when we do focus groups— why couldn't we get them to see it in a wholly different way?

In 1999, Eric Ryan was a strategic planner, working in San Francisco. He knew he had always wanted to start his own company, create his own mass-market brand, and, as he began to look for opportunities across the variety of categories in front of him, he was clear in his own mind that design was going to be a key part of the way the marketing world was going to develop and that the use of design would be a strategic element in whatever he started. He found himself thinking about cleaning products, and was struck by how "problem-solution"—focused it all was—all the existing players were competing on *needs*, and none were even attempting to compete on *desires*. Ryan recognized that they were all much too powerful to go up against on their own terms—that is on needs, on effectiveness of germ kill, for instance—and asked himself how one could therefore create a very different kind of relationship, a higher level of emotional bond between consumers and brands in the household cleaning market. So he stepped back and looked at the broader context for these cleaning products.

He looked at homes, the environments these products lived and worked in, and observed that your relationship with your home is perhaps, after your family, the highest-involvement relationship you have— so why couldn't cleaning products be part of that high-involvement relationship? He looked at the television programs people were making and the quantity of programs about home makeovers, and he recognized that, with even MTV producing a home show (*Rock the House*), this heightened relationship with home was now part of mainstream media and consumer culture. Why couldn't he connect these two things—this huge interest in making your house look more beautiful on the one hand, and cleaning products on the other? He sat in the park with his girlfriend, looked at a Snapple Elements bottle in his hand, and asked himself: Why couldn't pine-scented cleaning products come out of a bottle like this? He looked at higher-involvement markets, like hair care, and saw that they were driven not by segmentation by product function, like cleaning, but by systems, approaches, and regimes, each with a philosophy at its heart. So why could one not create a master brand with a philosophy at its heart, one that would span all areas of home care? And when he shared his emergent thinking during a car journey with his old college roommate, Adam Lowry, a chemical engineer, Lowry realized he could create a naturally derived, environmentally friendly product that would deliver both the kind of product Ryan was looking for and perhaps premium differentiation as well. Which is how they came to create method, a premium home-care brand and now the seventh-fastest-growing packaged goods company in the United States.

Ryan's approach to thinking about the market and exploring the potential to create a powerful new Challenger in it is very different from the approach used by most large companies to look for insight about where to develop their offers. While he starts by thinking about the consumer's relationship with the category, for instance, he does not start to develop his hypotheses by asking consumers *how they feel about* the household cleaning market; instead, he starts by asking himself *how one could change the relationship they have with the market as it currently stands*. He does not, as one might at Clorox, for example, ask how to increase the germ kill efficiency or improve the pine fragrance delivery (important though both of those things might be within the current parameters of the market). Giants of the industry tend to become too close to their own business to become wave makers; the more we work on a piece of business, the more we become trapped in midstream thinking, particularly if that business becomes quietly successful. But Ryan is asking a completely different level of question here: How one could create a much higher degree of emotional involvement with a brand in that category? And the process from then on is not a linear one, with verbal concepts being developed and sequentially tested. He goes on to answer this key upstream question of his by subsequently asking a lot of different questions about the category and its relationship to other categories around it—some of those other categories being relatively close to his (home makeover programs) and some very different (skin care). This exploratory questioning is a continual process for Ryan: He is as likely to try to find an answer in the soft drink bottle in his hand on a Saturday afternoon as he is at his desk on a Monday morning. In answering these questions, he is doing just that—trying to find connections by asking "Why not?" rather than ruling out possibilities because they are inspired by what, on the face of it, are very different categories.

And as a consequence, at the end of all this questioning and connection building, it would be difficult to fill in the "What is the key consumer insight?" box on a conventional brand essence form for method as a Challenger. While the insight is about consumers and their potential relationship with the category, it isn't based in a need they could articulate at the moment, and in fact it is as much an insight about *the opportunity* within the category as anything else. And it isn't really a single observation—it is a bundle of answers, intelligently joined, which together provide the answer to the original question.

method is currently, of course, still relatively small compared to the total category—$150 million revenue, in a total market currently worth around $4.6 billion. (See Figure 4.1 for some of the products in its developing range.) But let's look at some of the dynamics that accompany that figure and how the brand is positioned for the future. In terms of growth across its constituent categories, IRI tracks method across 15 different categories: The brand is in triple-digit growth in six of those, double-digit growth in another six, and single-digit growth in the remaining three. How many of our brands can we say that trajectory is true of? In terms of its relationship with its primary customer, Target has given method its own 12-foot branded sets in aisles, allowing it to display its product range in a branded grouping—generating a significant jump in its sales. In terms of profitability, method products sell at a substantial premium to the historic market. And in terms of momentum, the company has established clear Thought Leadership in the market (with an article in *Vanity Fair*, for instance). Which of these four dynamics do we not wish we had ourselves?

FIGURE 4.1   method's range of products.

Or let's look at an entirely different market. When Tom Ford was handed the Creative Directorship at Gucci, he inherited the difficult task of restoring Gucci's credibility after the cliché it had almost become in the 1980s (the sprawling cliché, in fact—at one point it had stamped its name on 14,000 different items). His first show would clearly be pivotal: Although haute couture accounts for less than 10 percent of Gucci's sales, it defines the fashionability of the rest of the brand—and the world's media were waiting to judge the fashionability of Gucci from Ford's first outing.

Fashion works in trends. Almost as a collective, the fashion world tends to create one predominant climate or another, and at the beginning of the 1990s the climate included asexual clothes and political correctness: Clothing styles were becoming almost cerebral. Ford felt dissatisfied with this; instead, he swam upstream. He asked himself the deceptively obvious question—"Why do people wear good clothes?"—and kept coming back with answers that had nothing to do with the fashion climate of the time. Good clothes were, surely, all about attracting people. It wasn't complicated; they wore them to feel sexy. Ford felt this was an opportunity for Gucci, so instead of loose-cut greens and beiges, he produced a look instead that was very aggressive, sleek, sexy, and glamorous. Tough chic. It was an instant hit with both critics and the public.

What unites both of these cases, then, is someone being prepared to step back and ask some really simple upstream questions: the kind we ask at first, but quickly forget, or get beaten out of us. Underlying both cases is clearly an attempt to really understand what consumers want and need, but not by asking them directly. Very often, of course, consumers are as close as the brand is to the preconceptions about the category. They cannot tell you what they want, because the category has effectively defined it for them. In the case of *Apple Daily*, for instance, a newspaper launched in Hong Kong in 1995, they stepped back and asked themselves what people *really wanted* to read in a daily newspaper. And the answer wasn't politics or what the government was doing (the fare of the Market Leader); it was something different. When you ask *Apple Daily* what they mean, they illustrate this with a story.[3]

It is 2003. *Apple Daily* has just launched in its second market, Taiwan, and at this point is number three in that market. One day there is a spectacular bank robbery—complete with machine guns and response units (the army had, in fact, to send in a specialized SWAT unit to deal with the heavy weaponry the bank robbers were using), most of which was covered live on TV. Thousands of rounds were fired, ending with one of the robbers dead and wounded on both sides. *Apple Daily* got its photographers to the scene as fast as it could.

The next day, the top three Taiwan newspapers hit the streets. The Market Leader leads with a public-spirited story about the young men of Taiwan going off to serve in the US Navy. The number two newspaper focuses on a sober pronouncement from the President on economic policy. The number three newspaper—*Apple Daily*—chooses not to lead with either of these stories. Instead, it offers four full-color pages of photographs of the shootout (bloody police officers and all), diagrams of the firefight, plus (for those interested in a little fuel for social conversation) a breakdown of the weapons used by both the bank robbers and the police. A story the Taiwanese man and woman on the street were not simply interested in reading, but in talking about. In showing to their friends. As a consequence, *Apple Daily* is no longer the number three newspaper in Taiwan—it now ties for first place. It has arrived there both by taking share from the incumbents and by attracting a swath of people who previously had been uninterested in reading newspapers.

We hear the same theme echoed by those behind the success of Axe in the United States, Unilever's deofragrance brand that has gone from Challenger to Number One in just three years. Axe's Global Brand Director has observed that it was in fact relatively easy to break through in the United States, even though this was a very mature market. Why? Because the only thing the category had been talking about up to that point was problem-solution—efficacy in the gym, efficacy when riding your bike, and so on. The existing brands treated deodorant more or less like toothpaste—a product that did something functional to your body. What Axe introduced, though, was a dialogue that was hugely interesting to consumers because it went right to the heart of what young guys (or perhaps just guys) spend most of their time thinking about—how to get the girl. If one chooses, then, to ask the question "Why couldn't we occupy *that* space, the high-interest space consumers spend all their time thinking about, rather than *this current space*, which they think about for half a second before they apply it in the morning?" then one very quickly moves into an entirely different kind of dialogue, of relationship, and of impact. Asking this kind of question, then—swimming upstream as a mental preparation for challenging the category and the Brand Leader—allows us to see what business we are really in, or *could* really be in.

So, the first key value of Intelligent Naivety is that it allows us to ask the fundamental upstream questions that the rest of the category is too close to the industry to ask anymore—to question why the relationships with consumers and structures between the groups of constituent brands have to be the way they are—because often the nature of that relationship needs to be changed in order to succeed: to reduce the relevance of the germ-kill credibility of the Market Leader, or of reliable underarm reassurance when you are in the gym, or to overcome years of comfortable familiarity with the country's top political journalist. It is not that Challengers idly amuse themselves with wanting to reinvent categories; it is that they have to find a new way in, in order to make obsolete at least some of the old criteria for choice in the category as a whole. And the very act of asking questions of the category prompts one to move higher, even if those questions are wrong. Tom Ford talks of how he likes to walk the streets and look at people whose clothes combinations he *doesn't* think work—the people whose clothes sense really makes him wince. He then sits in his office and tries to work out why; he finds this as valuable an exercise as starting from what he knows to be aesthetically in tune. Besides asking different kinds of questions, then, we should also be looking for the answers in different sorts of places. The chances are that the company's traditional wisdom has been calcifying because it has been asking exactly the same questions *in substantially the same ways* for years.

We can see that in starting to answer those kinds of questions, to find that fresh way in, Challengers start (often intuitively) to use a number of related techniques to formulate their potential solutions. They start to look to find a currency that the consumer is genuinely interested in rather than the self-regarding fare that the category has historically been serving up. They look to introduce new kinds of emotions into the consumer's relationship with the category. And they see no reason why this category cannot play by the rules of an entirely different category altogether.

Let's now explore the second and third of these.

PUTTING A WHOLE NEW EMOTION INTO THE CATEGORY

One of the key ways that Challengers transform a category, our relationship with that category, and in effect our criteria for choice in that category, is to introduce a whole new emotion into it. And very often it is apparently the dullest and most day-to-day categories that are reinvigorated in this way. We liked Gap, but thought T-shirts and leggings were pretty mundane until American Apparel put sex into our daily cotton. And we are not alone in finding such clothing a little more interesting these days: Lovefoxxx, the bouncy front woman for Brazilian party rockers CSS, when asked if she likes shopping for fashion replies, "I buy American Apparel leggings that I wear every day. Everything else is boring."[4]

Let's continue with some more apparently unexciting categories. A key part of Eric Ryan's answer to the questions he posed to himself was for his new brand method to put (in his words) "lifestyle" into household cleaning products. Who would have thought that the design aesthetic, brand values, and environmental impact of a cleaning product could tranform it into an aspirational, premium brand you are proud to display? Dyson put a different kind of sexiness into vacuum cleaning (which would have meant nothing if the functionality had not been superb, of course). Altoids put "pain" into mint eating. VitaminWater put a rich color (literal and metaphorical) into water consumption. Havaianas has elevated humble $2 flip-flops into a fashion line that has contenders at $100 a pair.

Choosing to look at low-interest categories is simply a test for us here, not a definition of our Challenger universe: this kind of insertion of a new emotion or emotional range into the consumer's relationship with our brand (and thus with the category beyond us) is, of course, not limited to such categories. So Bratz put an urban sassiness into the wholesome blondness of Barbie and Sindy. Puma put lifestyle and fashion into sports shoes, Samsung high design into mass-market consumer electronics. Virgin has always looked to put a new level of entertainment in the airline business—yes, it has always been competitive on price, but at the center of what has made the Virgin experience consistently different has been a less boring, more entertaining flight. This was true with Virgin Atlantic in the 1980s and is still true with the launch of Virgin America more than 20 years later, which will offer highly competitive fares, but also compete on service experience: Virgin America's branded entertainment system, called Red, will offer everything from TV channels to pay-per-view movies to games to a system for ordering meals. Even in more unlikely categories, such as self-protection, we see aspirant Challengers trying to change the relationship with the category by introducing a new emotion via their brand: The brand Pepperface, for instance, is flamboyantly trying to put a new emotion into personal security. In the inimitable words of the *New York Post:* "They put the chic in kicking ass!"[5] How? The pepper spray brand persuaded celebrities to customize individual sprays for a charity auction. While Hilary Duff went for some optimistic daisies on her pepper spray, Lindsay Lohan opted for, perhaps predictably, something a little darker, with a skull and crossbones design. Paula Abdul, meanwhile, took the bling route with a spray fashioned from 18-carat gold, adorned with black Swarovski crystals. The point here is not that Pepperface is using PR to create a splash—it is that it is using playfulness to try to create a new kind of emotional relationship with what is essentially a very serious thing: a weapon for self-protection in some of the most frightening situations a woman can find herself. Pepperface is looking to create a product that does not sit, dripping with foreboding, at the bottom of women's handbags, but is something they take out and show their friends with a smile, while dining on a low calorie chicken salad at Spago.

Is this new emotion always about playfulness, fun, chic, or attitude? A young and irreverent Challenger being a little hipper and sassier than the Establishment brand? Not at all—sometimes the new emotional dimension is a very serious one. Online dating companies, for instance, are also putting something new into the mating game. If I tell you this new dimension is partly mathematical, you might think I am talking about greater percentages (more + faster = greater chance of meeting Ms./Mr. Right, perhaps), but in fact it is the sober confidence of a mathematical algorithm. eHarmony claims that its 258-part questionnaire, created by a psychologist in 1997, uses an algorithm to match people on 29 core character traits. Does it work? eHarmony boasts that it was responsible for 2 percent of all marriages in America last year. And moving nimbly from math to science, the chef Heston Blumenthal has put scientific precision into cooking—what he calls "molecular gastronomy"— which has been one of the key factors in his restaurant, The Fat Duck, being voted the second-best in the world.

As we noted, all of these Challengers are introducing these new emotions, not out of whim, but out of necessity. In a world of choice, where the rate of launches and relaunches far, far outstrips consumers' interest or market capacity (last year saw the launch of 100 superpremium vodkas in the United States alone), our task as Challengers must be to:

(1) Dramatically simplify choice for the consumer by

(2) Creating a new criterion for choice in the category, and . . .

(3) In doing so, give consumers a way of thinking and feeling about the category in a way that they had not before.

innocent, the UK (and emerging European) smoothie brand, illustrates this last point well. At its launch, innocent had (and still has) as an intrinsic part of its mission the desire to help people "do something good for themselves every day." But the founders also knew, when they started in 1999, that health products were a worthy but dull bunch— doing something healthy for yourself in reality involved a certain amount of resolution and self-denial. So creating a playful and chatty personality around the brand and the usage experience was not from a desire to introduce a charming quirk for the sake of charming quirkiness; it was an attempt to introduce a fundamentally new kind of relationship with a product that is "good for you," because that would be the only way innocent could genuinely succeed against its bigger ambition.

All of the examples so far center around launches. Yet one can find oneself with an even greater need to add a new emotional dimension as a Challenger expanding into a more fiercely competitive environment than one did when one was smaller. Target has famously put the chic into cheap precisely because it made a strategic decision, as it expanded into new geographic locations where it would come up directly against the might of Wal-Mart for the first time, that it could not succeed from now on by competing on price alone: It would need to introduce a new element into the shopping relationship with a discount store in order to challenge successfully such a powerful incumbent.

And sometimes, of course, it is in fact precisely in expanding as an existing brand that we start to see the opportunity to really develop the new emotion that will set us apart in the future—but only if we still have our eyes wide open. Costco, now the third-largest grocery chain in the United States, with revenue that doubled between 1998 and 2003, started by being the same as any other warehouse club, selling cheap supplies to small businesses. But as they expanded, they saw an opportunity to sell more—and drive greater differentiation at the same time—by offering their business owners products to buy for themselves as well. What then began as a push into a broader range of goods has now developed into the famous "treasure hunt" concept, where alongside the peanut butter you will find a 42-inch plasma TV at a ludicrously cheap price, and next to the jars of mayo you'll see Dom Pérignon 1995 at $90 a bottle. And it's a treasure hunt with a timer on it: If you don't buy it this time, it may be gone when you come back. "We try to convey a sense of urgency, so if people see it, they better buy it," comments Costco's CEO, Jim Sinegal.[6] With a policy of never marking up beyond 14 percent (tell *that* to your local champagne seller), it is perhaps not surprising that Costco is now the largest wine retailer in the United States. The company has, in short, grown to revenue of $64 billion by putting a new dimension—an urgent treasure hunt—into weekly grocery shopping.

OVERLAY

We noted earlier in this chapter that Challengers often bring no experience to their category, and this can, if used correctly, be an advantage. In reality, though, while they did indeed have no experience in *the category they were entering*, they frequently brought inspiration from their experiences in *another* category, and sometimes this juxtaposition led to the discovery of a fresh opportunity in their chosen new market.

The benefit of this kind of overlay of the rules and codes of one category onto another can simply be one of initial inspiration. The CEO of ING Direct, Arkadi Kuhlman, for instance, knew that people didn't like banks, and found an inspiration for a different kind of bank in what other industries were doing: If IKEA could sell furniture without assembling it, and Southwest could sell plane tickets without assigning seats, he asked, why couldn't you successfully offer a stripped down version of a bank? Perhaps a bank similar in concept to the way McDonald's sells fast food: Offer a few key products, make it easy and quick to get in, buy something, and get out again; be genuinely consumer friendly. We will go on to explore in a later chapter some of the key components of how he and his team turned this into a reality and created the success it has become: ING is now not simply the largest Internet bank in the United States, happily banking just over $45 billion in online deposits, but it is the twenty-eighth-largest bank in the United States, period.

One of Kuhlman's sources of inspiration, IKEA, is in point of fact also an example of learning from an entirely different category. In the early days, when IKEA consisted of just three stores in Sweden (and without one yet even in Stockholm), its founder, Ingvar Kamprad, went to New York. While there, he visited the Guggenheim Museum and found himself struck by a very particular quality about it: They don't give you a choice where you go. They make you go up to the top, then walk down past everything on display (there's no choice), and then walk you out through the shop, past the cash register, and out into the street. "Hmm, this is interesting," Kamprad thinks to himself, "We could do exactly the same thing: When we open in Stockholm, we could be just like the Guggenheim—we could construct it so we won't give them a choice where they go." So when he returns to Sweden, he briefs his architect, and when the first Stockholm IKEA opens (23 years after IKEA was founded), it is indeed just like the Guggenheim, on the outside as well as the inside. And the idea works brilliantly—asking your customers to walk past everything you have does indeed increase the length of their visit to IKEA, yet it also (particularly if you can couple this with the innovative introduction of inspirational room sets) significantly increases the amount of spontaneous purchases in what one might have thought was a considered-decision market. And now, with the exception of a couple of experimental stores in China and the United States, the traffic flow system of every IKEA in the world is essentially the same: You do not have a choice where you go. And spontaneous purchasing is as vigorous as ever.

So let us just stop and note two points here. The first is that this insight about how to grow the IKEA business did not come from an exhaustive study of how other home furnishing retailers sell home furnishings. It came from a key individual looking at *an entirely different category* and overlaying the rules—or one significant behavior from those rules—onto his own. And the second point is that IKEA had already been going, in a variety of different guises, for 23 years at this point. Let us not think that Intelligent Naivety is the province of the inexperienced founder at launch; it is a mind-set that we as Challengers need to be *constantly* applying, certainly at the outset, but *long into the life of our brand.*

Lush cosmetics is instructive in helping us deepen our understanding of why Intelligent Naivety is so valuable. We often hear invocations to push for groundbreaking ideas in marketing. And one of the reasons this seems so intimidating to many of us is that we interpret *groundbreaking* here to mean "ideas that have never been done before"—and that seems a very high bar. Can we possibly achieve that? But in reality groundbreaking doesn't necessarily mean that at all; it usually means, in reality, not ideas that have never been done before, but ideas that have never been done before *in this context.* So take Lush. We are all used to the idea of fresh, handmade things; this in itself is not a groundbreaking idea (it has been around in prepared foods, for example, more or less since Homo australopithecus made the first tool three and a half million years ago), but "Fresh Handmade *Cosmetics*"—the same idea in an entirely different *context*—becomes a very groundbreaking idea. In effect, what Lush is doing here is taking the principles and codes of a delicatessen or a fresh fruit and vegetable shop and overlaying them onto cosmetics and bath products—in the appearance and appeal of the products, in their manufacture (telling us when they were made and the "best-before" date) and in the sensory theater of the stores, laying the products out like enormous cheeses to be sliced, or writing on blackboards in chalk to cue freshness and artisanal manufacture.

This kind of stimulating application of Overlay clearly has a range of different scopes: It is obviously not necessarily going to be a blanket application. We will want to focus on the dimensions that are most relevant to creating a new kind of emotional relationship with our brand and product experience, and perhaps on those that give us a different kind of advantage in our business model. Returning to *Apple Daily*, for instance, there were many who counseled against launching a newspaper at the time. This is the postliterate society, they said, and you will never get people, particularly 18- to 25-years-olds, to really get interested in reading a paper anymore. As we saw earlier, one key way *Apple Daily* overcame that apparent barrier was to choose subject matter that the audience was genuinely interested in. The second was its celebrated use of color. And the third was the way they treated that subject matter and optimized the power of that color—by using narrative techniques that Asian youth are very interested in reading, but from the very different categories of animation and manga. (See Figure 4.2.) The combination of these three elements has created a compelling product experience, even for those not previously interested in reading newspapers.

One last example. Very occasionally, one sees a complete adoption of a set of rules from a different category, because it is in effect *forced* on a Challenger. German soft drink Bionade overlaid beer brewing principles—and more particularly German beer brewing principles—onto soft drinks, because it had no other choice. The flood of imported bottled beers to Germany had dislodged a number of the traditional smaller domestic brewers, and the Privatbrauerei Peter in northern Bavaria was no exception. Facing bankruptcy, the company explored renting out the brewery for parties and events, but realized that this would not be enough—the family-run company would have to create a new kind of future for itself to safeguard its existence. So the master brewer, Dieter Leipold, came up with an idea: What if he were to invent a healthy soft

FIGURE 4.2 *Apple Daily.*

drink for children, one that used only natural ingredients, following the German purity laws historically used to control the quality of beer?

A simple idea, but difficult to do. It took him eight years and $1.5 million dollars, but eventually he found a way to ferment the product in the same way he used to brew beer, but this time turning the ingredients not into alcohol, but into gluconic acid, which carried the additional benefit of accentuating the sweetness of the sugar added, meaning he could put in much less sugar than was contained in the other soft drinks Bionade (as he called his creation) would compete against. And the company put Bionade into the bottles it had—beer-shaped bottles. Or Pilsner-shaped bottles, to be exact (see Figure 4.3).

Interestingly, the last Overlay of beer—hip marketing—was something that came much later. Originally, the product and packaging codes of beer were the only ones the company took on—once it had a healthy soft drink, it first marketed it as a healthy soft drink, and for the first four years of its life Bionade performed as dully as that tag suggests. Then, in 1999, the company redesigned the graphics, appointed a new

FIGURE 4.3 Bionade bottle.

marketing director and, using grassroots marketing and PR (as a new beer would), repositioned Bionade as a cool lifestyle drink that just happened to be healthy.[7] The brand took off: Within seven years the company was selling 70 million bottles a year.

Before we leave the idea of Overlay, let's note one key danger of it. In many ways this is something we do instinctively when starting a new job—we naturally see it through the lens of the old brands and the old segmentations from the category we have just left. But doing this continually through the lens of just *one other category* may not give us the way in we seek; in that search, the value for a Challenger often comes not *just* from thinking about our category from the perspective of software, or *just* thinking about it from the perspective of luxury cars, but from the perspective of a diverse range of other categories in sequence. What about the lens of the products that people love to spend hours talking about socially, like wine? What of brands that have made themselves iconic, like super-premium vodkas? What about the new wave of entertainment brands? What of Cirque du Soleil—how could you make pasta, for example, as fun and unpredictable as a contemporary circus? It may be that we do indeed come to see the future as hinging on overlaying the rules of one other category onto our own, but we want to explore (as we saw Eric Ryan do) a range of other possible categories to find our own "Aha!" moment.

DELIBERATELY BREAKING WITH THE IMMEDIATE PAST: PUTTING EVERYTHING IN PLAY

Challengers see and realize places to stand in the market that other brands have not seen or realized before. *Seeing* them depends on making oneself innocent again. *Realizing* them depends on divesting oneself of all the baggage a brand acquires over the years in terms of all those individual marketing elements that *do not in themselves make a difference* but are thought to be important collectively in differentiating the brand from the competition and maintaining consistency with the past. So, even for existing brands, challenging is about beginning again.

Beginning again when you already have a brand that is substantial and not yet in critical decline is a hard thing to contemplate. Much of what has been written about Brand Management concentrates on consistency over time—recognizing your current equities and maintaining them through your marketing activities. Indeed, our natural human reaction is to protect what we have once we think it has achieved a certain basic value; studies have shown that as human beings we are not so much risk-averse as loss-averse—the more you already have, the more your inclination is *not* to gamble it. Which is why, of course, the risk-taking entrepreneurs tend to be the people who start with nothing.

But if we want to Eat the Big Fish, protecting what we already have for its own sake seems like out-of-date thinking in a Challenger mindset. Challenger brands seem to deliberately break with their own immediate past (if they have one)—they intentionally reinvent key aspects of themselves in order to force rapid reappraisal from the consumer. To do so, they first become prepared to break with every equity, every preconception about the market, and every current marketing strategy for every current marketing tool, and then they need to sacrifice minor equities to create major differences.

Again, this seems counterintuitive; we are taught to protect and nurture marketing and advertising equities. But ask yourself this: If any of them were all that valuable in the first place, why aren't we in a better position now? As we go through the process of reexamination, what is important in our past will rise to the top again; but we won't see it if we're swimming surrounded by the flotsam and jetsam of the immediate past. The question for us about such equities is not "Are they valuable?" but "Are they valuable *enough?*" Are they valuable enough for the change in growth rate we now need to achieve?

The same will be true for practices as much as equities. It is said that when Kraft picked up Altoids as a by-product of the of Jacob Suchard acquisition, it recognized that the brand—this strange, old-fashioned mint in a square tin that cost four times as much as the Market Leader— was going to need a very different approach from the way the company sold cheese slices. In the brand team's first meeting with the agency, they asked for a break with the company's past: "We don't," they said, "want to do anything the way Kraft usually does it."

In launching the Nintendo Wii, Reggie Fils-Aimé asked his marketing department and his agencies to do the same thing: to break with the past, to throw out all the ways they had historically launched a new console, and to think of an entirely new way to bring the Wii to market. "He basically challenged us to rethink not only what we do, but how we do it," said George Harrison, SVP of Marketing, at the time. It wasn't just that they went after moms, for instance, it was *how* they went after moms: with parties in hotel suites serving champagne, and events that were more like "transgenerational Tupperware parties" than conventional hard-core gamer launch parties.[8] By all means, they said, let's look at strategic partnerships, but what about a strategic partnership with cruise lines, deliberately courting an older profile of user?

And we all know the results. (See Figure 4.4.)

Breaking with the immediate past, then, and putting everything in play is not the same as mindlessly throwing everything away. It is simply a way of asking what is genuinely still relevant to your future, of freeing yourself to focus on the questions and possibilities that will make the

FIGURE 4.4 A crude measurement of success.

difference between being a Challenger brand and being an establish-ment brand.

If current marketing equities and practices are in fact still significant, they will float to the surface again as one reenters the upstream/down-stream questioning and listening. But they may be masking something more important that you already have in your past. And the effort and resource consumed in retaining it may dilute the force of the new direc-tion you are about to assume.

NOT KNOWING WHAT IS POSSIBLE AND IMPOSSIBLE

> *Inexperience erases fear. You do not know what is and is not pos-sible and therefore everything is possible.*
>
> Twyla Tharp[9]

The final value of Intelligent Naivety for us as Challengers is that we don't know what is possible and what is impossible, so we are not going to screen out key opportunities on the grounds that "it can't be done." There is an interesting distinction between what the UK marketing press talks about as important in innocent's success, and what innocent talks about as important in innocent's success. If you listen to the marketing press, they celebrate innocent's innovative marketing. If you talk to the founders, they talk about the primacy of getting the product better: The success of innocent, the founders will tell you, is 90 percent the product, and 10 percent the marketing, critical though the latter undoubtedly is. And the story they tell is that they were able to do this only because they didn't understand that what they were doing was impossible. Having had no experience in making smoothies (other than mixing their own in a blender), they set about trying to find someone who could make what they wanted—a pure fruit smoothie with no additives or preservatives. They spent nine months being told this was impossible, until they eventually found someone who came up with a way to do it; they were the first to do it in the category, and that product quality is still central to their success.

It is striking how often this kind of story comes up for Challengers. If you ask Colleen Barrett, President of Southwest, for the defining story that encapsulates for her what makes Southwest Airlines the successful Challenger it is, she will recount to you the time when, reduced to flying a four-plane route with three planes (because legal bills had required the company to sell a plane), Southwest had to figure out how to hit a 15-minute turnaround time (i.e., land the plane, get the luggage and passengers off, clean the plane, and load luggage and passengers on again in just 15 minutes). When Southwest did it, Barrett says, and the rest of the incredulous U.S. airline industry asked how a small airline, with very little experience, had pulled this off, the company responded, "We didn't know it couldn't be done, so we did it."

George Hickton, the CEO of Tourism New Zealand, sees this as a quality of New Zealanders as a whole and why they punch disproportionately above their weight. "I think in a sense that New Zealand is an incredibly young country, and it hasn't really had the risk-taking knocked out of it yet. A New Zealander cracked the atom, a New Zealander climbed Everest, the country became nuclear-free—they're things people said you couldn't do. But we didn't know they couldn't be done . . . and as a consequence for us it seemed obvious: Why wouldn't you do these things; what could hold you back?"

So let's not be too wise about what is possible and what is impossible as we look at these possibilities and ask these upstream questions. Let's not dismiss possibilities because they can't be done. Perhaps that simply means we haven't historically found a way to do them, which is not the same thing at all. Perhaps it simply means they can't be done if we leave everything else the way it is—in which case we will simply have to change something, as Southwest changed having assigned seating, in order to make it work.

GIANTS AND CHILDREN

The famous giant killers of folklore tend to be children. Whether their names are David or Jack, it does not occur to them that a small round stone cannot successfully take on an eight-foot spear. (If you are going up against an eight-foot spear, the one weapon it is foolish to choose is a four-foot spear; if you can't match the length, you need something different.)

The first foundation of challenge, then, is not experience, but innocence: the ability to step back upstream and question all the old assumptions afresh. Challenge them, in fact, and see which can really withstand the inquisition.

Then, if one views strategic thinking in terms of upstream (questions about the fundamentals of the category) and downstream (refinements of product or service offering), it seems that most Challengers have to deliberately attempt to compete either *significantly upstream* or *significantly downstream* of the Establishment brand. The Brand Leader, having established the codes and conventions of the category, does not revisit or attempt to change them in terms of upstream thinking; equally, they are too large and cumbersome to arrive at or implement innovative downstream thinking with any speed. Once one has made oneself innocent, perhaps the first decision to take about eating the Big Fish, then, is whether the real opportunity to attack them lies upstream or downstream: Do we overturn the category basics (as Swatch), or develop the product to a point it hasn't yet reached (JetBlue's seat-back entertainment)?

HOW DO I MAKE MYSELF INTELLIGENTLY NAIVE WHEN I HAVE YEARS OF EXPERIENCE IN MY CATEGORY?

Intelligent Naivety seems deceptively easy for someone new, of course; there is no knowledge there to get rid of in the first place. But how do you make yourself inexperienced in your own category? And how do you create that climate in others?

Andrew Grove fired himself. In 1985, Intel, far from being a Brand Leader (or even a Challenger) and at the time a player principally in the memory-chip business, seemed unable to match the Japanese price/value offer and remain profitable. Grove reached a personal crisis. To demonstrate emotionally to himself the need to wipe the slate genuinely clean, he began again by inviting his chairman to walk out of the Intel building with him as if they had both been fired; they would reenter the building not as Andrew Grove and Gordon Moore, but *as the newly recruited replacements for themselves.*

Sitting down afresh in the boardroom they had just mentally vacated, they looked with new eyes at the business they had been managing for the previous few years and identified immediately the key issue the company faced: namely, that it was in the wrong business. It had to get out of memory and put the entire emphasis of the company behind what had up to now been a secondary priority, namely microprocessors. In one dramatic moment, Grove created the ability to see through innocent eyes the solution to a problem they had both been wrestling with for months.

At this point, then, we invent the second in our new set of intransitive verbs. Taken together, they are intended to collectively define the sequence of actions that will take place in the two-day off-site at the end of this book, actions that will be involved in turning you into a Challenger.

The new verb, then, is this:

Grove *vb:* To fire oneself, reenter the building as one's hard-nosed successor, and identify the core issue facing the company.

In other words, identify the Big Fish. We have talked about it up to now as if it were another major competitor, but in fact it may not be quite as simple as this. It may be that the threat or success of this major competitor is a *symptom* of the problem, rather than the problem itself.

We then have to instill this sense of innocent vitality not simply in the individual but in the whole team around us, or at least enough of them to drive the difference through the thinking of the company.

SUMMARY

Intelligent Naivety, then, has four purposes:

1. To establish afresh the core issue facing the brand or the company (the Big Fish); taking a step back and more accurately defining the problem
2. To help define, therefore, what business we should really be in
3. To free ourselves to see all the possibilities of the category
4. To allow us to see what we may need to break with from the past to enable a stronger future

It is thus both a valuable mental exercise in itself and critical to making a Challenger a brand of action, rather than just a company of talk.

Greg Nugent, the Marketing Director of Eurostar (whose own challenge we will discuss later in the book) sums up both the importance of, and the inherent caveat within the application of Intelligent Naivety: "It is so important because it puts the magic back into a category. It pushes the category forward again, when it starts to become mundane. But you have to remember at the same time that you are keeping one foot in the category, as well as putting one foot outside it. Some brands have got carried away, and completely forgotten they were supposed to be a toothpaste, for instance, and just lost the consumer completely. That's when it becomes just naivety, rather than Intelligent Naivety."

Videolinks for this Chapter:

www.eatbigfishfood.com/etbf/intelligentnaivety

5

MONSTERS AND OTHER CHALLENGES: GAINING CLARITY ON THE CENTER

I am a noble Internet buffoon fighting the giant of celebrity.

Perez Hilton[1]

O nce we have stepped back, broken with our immediate past, and regained a little Intelligent Naivety in exploring the opportunities open to our brand, we will have done a great deal of vibrant and divergent thinking. Now is the time not to close down any of that thinking, but we do need to find the center of it, to serve as the pivotal bridge between clarity on where we are going to redefine the rules of the market in our favor on the one hand, and the foundations of our brand identity on the other. We go on to discuss the second part of this Challenger identity we are building toward in Chapter 6, but first let's begin to find our center by being clear about the answer to this question: Having explored the possibilities open to us, what is the key challenge we are laying down to the category, or even to the consumer? What do all the possibilities we have explored through Intelligent Naivety really represent, at their heart?

Before answering this question, let's be clear on one thing: We are not entering or reentering this market in order to offer consumers more choice. They have more than enough choice already, in almost any category we are in—there are 160,000 trademarks in the United States alone, and 45,000 lines on U.S. grocery shelves (a number that has tripled over the past 15 years). While we may think this degree of choice is inherently to the consumer's advantage, there is substantial evidence that more choice in and of itself actually *drives consumer purchase interest in the category down.* In a celebrated experiment conducted by researchers from Columbia and Stanford universities, while the creation of greater choice in a category significantly increased the people who stopped and *browsed* that category, it dramatically reduced the number of people who *bought* from it.[2] Once you get past a certain— quite finite—level of genuine choice, it seems more choice isn't really in the consumer's interests, and it certainly isn't in ours.

So, we are not here to offer *more* choice. What we are here to do is offer a significantly better choice, and indeed to *radically simplify* choice for the consumer in our chosen category. And a key way in which we are going to do that is by changing the key criteria for choice for a significant body of people in our favor.

DEFINING THE CHALLENGE WE ARE MAKING

One might say that Challengers are, by definition, challenging some quality or dimension of choice in the existing category. How we express that challenge externally in our communications is obviously still some way from being decided, but we will certainly need first to be clear *internally* what that central challenge is going to be, because it will be critical to shaping what we offer, how we behave, and the kind of Challenger brand we want to be. Clarity here will help give us sharpness and energy from the outset.

The range of potential challenges that we can make lie in one of the following:

- Challenging some fundamental dimension or driver of our category
- Challenging some aspect of the way the consumer shops for, experiences, or consumes our product
- Challenging the culture surrounding the category
- Challenging some broader aspect of contemporary culture
- Challenging some dimension or quality of the competition/Market Leader

What we will see, as we start to explore each of these, is once we have a clear sense of what they are, they will then lead to a fork in the road—namely, in whether we choose to be *implicit* or *explicit* in publicly stating the nature of that challenge. That is, we can either use the understanding of what we are challenging simply to shape our nature, offer, product, and personality, or we can take it further and use it to explicitly lay down a public challenge of some kind. We will come on to explore this later in Chapters 11 and 12.

First, let us look at each of these kinds of challenges in turn, devoting most of our time to the first and the last of them.

Challenging a Fundamental Dimension or Driver of Our Category

Often, the initial sense of what you stand for as a Challenger, and the challenge you are going to make, comes from first knowing what you *reject* within the existing category.

Take, for example, the Blue Man Group. What is now a highly successful global entertainment brand, with a number of interesting Challenger qualities, began as three friends working in a New York catering company in the mid-1980s. Interested in moving into the arts, their early sense of what they wanted to do was inspired by an almost visceral *rejection* of everything they saw in the existing category of the 1980s New York art world, namely that it was "an elitist bullshit art-speak scene," in the eloquent words of one of the founders, Chris Wink.[3] Their very first performance was, accordingly, driven by this rejection—they decided that the first outing of the Blue Man in 1988 would be, in a very literal sense, a funeral for the 1980s and everything they hated about it. They filled a wood coffin with what they perceived as all the rubbish of that decade, from effigies of yuppies to Rambo dolls, and carried it on their shoulders through the streets of Manhattan before setting fire to it and burning it in Central Park. Inviting, of course, MTV to film them all en route. (See Figure 5.1.)

Clearly, while still irreverent and creative, the sense of the group's identity has now evolved beyond this initial "hate" into a clear identity and thriving business, watched by millions with no interest in the 1980s art scene, and who would neither be interested in nor perhaps recognize artistic pretension if it smacked them on the nose. In 2007, Blue Man had

FIGURE 5.1 Blue Man's funeral for the 1980s.

simultaneous shows in nine cities, including their permanent installation at the Venetian in Vegas. Their live shows have now been seen by 12 million people around the world. And it was first understanding what they rejected about their category that then gave them the initial step toward understanding who they really were, around which they built their distinct and compelling entertainment offer.

So one way to see this challenge is to ask ourselves very simply: What is the category orthodoxy that we reject? What do we think is wrong, or what will we have to "break" (i.e., *prove wrong*) in order to succeed? And as we explore it, the way the category currently thinks usually yields a very rich variety of potential sources of challenge.

Perhaps we might wish to challenge the mundanity of the way the category thinks about its nature and role—that vacuum cleaners have to be dull gray boxes. Or perhaps there is an inherent and taken-for-granted assumption about what is good and bad that is so hardwired into the category's relationship with the consumer that we have to challenge it to succeed—that water that is good for you has to be colorless and tasteless (VitaminWater).

Perhaps there is an elitism we could take on: the fact that some aspect of the category is available only to the wealthy. As a player who has a key value component, for instance, we can go beyond simply advertising prices and question the value system. So we see a billboard from Daffy's (a U.S. family-run discount clothing chain, whose line is "Clothing bargains for millionaires") showing an item of lingerie, and challenging us with: "At $30 it's sexy, at $125 it's obscene." Here Daffy's is not just selling a value line, but taking on the whole concept of over-priced lingerie, and inviting us to question that with them.

Perhaps there is a *disease* we need to overcome—sometimes one that only we can see, something only we can be the solution to. Recently, we have seen Audi in the United States kicking against traditional automotive luxury before looking to set out its own stall, and JetBlue famously setting out to overcome the dehumanization of domestic air travel in the United States, which has had a "cattle truck" mentality that the existing players were either too close to see or too set in their ways to care about.

Surf detergent challenges the mundanity, the drudgery, and the chore of doing laundry. It complements the vivid sensory fragrances it has introduced by using packaging that is bright, happy, exotic, and projects the spirit it champions; in Latin America, for instance, Surf has deliberately used the cheerful, chatty, and colloquial format of a woman's magazine, rather than a conventional packaging approach, to converse with its users in an entirely different way. (See Figure 5.2.)

So, we have a broad canvas here, but let's not confuse *broad* with *fuzzy*. We need within each of these options to be very clear about where we are, and are not, challenging the status quo.

Challenging an Aspect of the Way the Consumer Shops for, Experiences, or Consumes Our Product

If we are trying to build a new kind of behavior within our chosen category, we are probably challenging *existing habits*, those ways of thinking and interacting with the category that consumers now have and follow almost by rote. These are notoriously difficult to break, so we often have to create from the outset a juxtaposition that jolts the audience.

FIGURE 5.2 Surf packaging.

At their most challenging, these habits can be to do with your chosen consumer simply not thinking about, or engaging with, the category you are trying to sell them at all. So, for example, I am sitting in a yellow cab one day on my way to JFK airport in New York, when a large brown truck pulls up alongside me. It is a Brink's security truck, and on the side of it is a large question in white writing. I read it. It says something like:

"Why throw your business documents away, when you could just mail them direct to your competition?"

Why is this question powerful? Because it doesn't just speak to me about an emotional benefit of "peace of mind," or some other bland cliché—and rightly so: I had been feeling nothing *but* peace of mind about it until then, because the issue simply wasn't a concern for me at all. Instead, this question directly challenges my complacency as a business owner. That very stark "There are only two real choices you have to make here" juxtaposition slips me a burrowing little worm of paranoia, to wriggle around inside me on my plane ride home. It is the beginning of unraveling my unthinking confidence in my company's security; it prompts me to begin to go out and do something about it. And the brilliance of this question is that it gets my options down to *just two choices of action*. At the beginning of the chapter, we saw how a Challenger's role is to create a radical simplification of choice; here, Brinks has presented such a radical simplification to me, when I hadn't previously thought about the choice at all. In this case, the challenge is simply driving Brink's' communication strategy, but clearly you could structure every aspect of your product experience around it. In the case of Nintendo with the Wii (and to some degree the Nintendo DS), the issue had been the same: The brand had deliberately chosen to try to engage a target that wasn't interacting with the category at all. In the words of Satoru Iwata, the President of Nintendo, "We are not competing against Sony or Microsoft. We are battling the indifference of people who have no interest in video games."[4] And as we see in later chapters, everything from product redesign, to game experience, to the nature of games, to marketing strategy flowed from this clear understanding of the challenge.

It may be that the fundamental trend in consumer product usage is going against you, and you need to be clear on whether you are going to accept or challenge this. The United Kingdom was historically a nation of ale drinkers—with a taste for the dark, character-filled, bitter beer traditionally drunk at room temperature. Over the past 40 years, however, the national palate has gradually but profoundly shifted to lighter, much less bitter lagers, and the bitterness levels of even this easier taste profile has, in the past six years, been muted further still by serving lager brands extra cold (which suppresses the taste) or with fruit flavorings, which masks any remaining bitterness entirely. So, what do you do if you are an unreconstructed bitter ale? Hobgoblin is a brand that has chosen to challenge this trend to blandness head on. It recognizes that

FIGURE 5.3 Hobgoblin's challenge.

there are a number of drinkers who have a portfolio of both lagers and ales, and it needs to give them a reason to include itself as an ale in that portfolio, and reinforce the emotional and masculine imagery of ale at the same time. So Hobgoblin does this by putting out a direct challenge: "What's the matter, lagerboy—afraid you might taste something?" (See Figure 5.3.) Hobgoblin uses the trend toward the blandness of lager, in effect, as another surface to grip against.

Sometimes, of course, there are habits in the category that consumers themselves would like to change, but just have trouble actually changing, particularly in the area of health and wellness. Here the opportunity is for the Challenger to own, even to brand, that better habit. Thus LesserEvil snacks describe themselves as being "the antidote to snackcidents."

What is a *snackcident?* The company helpfully defines it for you:
Snack • ci • dent [snăk-si-duh nt] n.
1. The consumption of a snack that leaves you unsatisfied and/or remorseful
2. An infringement on the LesserEvil mission to Stop Bad Snacking
3. Spilling your Krinkle Sticks—(see also: tragedy)[5]

This is a brand, of course, whose entire name and nature is structured to make the most of this position. But that opportunity to take and own, through branding, the behavioral problem we are looking to overcome is an opportunity for us all.

Challenge the Culture Surrounding the Category

Some Challengers recognize that in order to genuinely break through, to genuinely change the criteria for choice in the category in their favor longer term, they need to challenge the *cause* and not the symptoms: the underpinning beliefs and prevailing culture that have been wrapped around that category by Establishment brand and consumer alike.

We might want to debunk this surrounding culture because we think it is simply wrong and not in the consumer's best interests. Fred Franzia, CEO of Bronco Wine and creator of the legendary "Two Buck Chuck," the nickname for the Charles Shaw range wines (essentially offering good-quality drinking for a very low price), is not taking on the category of "other low- to medium-priced wines in the $4 to $10 range," although that is where his volume is coming from. He is waging (in his words) a "war" against pretentious mediocrity, summed up for him by much of what the Napa winemaking region and its most famous sons stand for, with its conversation about soil, and "noses," and all the fancy ritual and language that they wrap around it.[6] This kind of war is not the sole prerogative of Challengers with pugnacious founders: Dove challenged the beauty myth, written up for the past 20 years by the Beauty Giants on that digital blackboard called the television (namely that "beauty = youth" and "youth = no lines or gray hair"). Dove challenged this for the deception they felt it represents, and the pressure it places on women—and it made this challenge not simply because Dove cannot compete by trying to be the same as L'Oréal, for example, but because the people leading the brand fundamentally believed the beauty myth was wrong, and a belief system that needed to be debunked.

It may be much less personal than this, though. It may be simply necessary for us to challenge the existing category culture because as long as the existing category culture is alive and healthy, we will not be able to succeed. When Mini, for example, launched in the United States, in order for such a small car to succeed, the brand team felt they needed to challenge the hardwired belief, underpinning all U.S. car culture, that "bigger is better." As we will see in Chapter 6, its whole identity was then built around this challenge.

The desire to change this culture need not restrict its ambition to simply creating a perceptual shift, which will reframe the criteria for choice in our favor—it can be part of a bigger mission, with very measurable objectives. Zipcar is a U.S. Challenger to the conventional rental car business and business model. Inspired by a new kind of car club the founders had noticed while on holiday in Berlin, Zipcar allows you to rent a car not just by the day but by the hour (and conveniently positions its cars around the city to make it easier for you to do this). The natural assumption would be that in doing this, the company was in fact challenging the rental car category. But in reality the founders of Zipcar don't see this as the challenge they are making at all: They see themselves as challenging *car ownership* itself. And this is not an empty challenge: Almost 40 percent of Zipcar's users either sell their car or halt a purchasing decision after trying Zipcar. The result is that, on average, Zipcar members drive 369 miles annually compared to 5,295 prior to joining. Zipcar's stated long-term mission is in fact to reduce the national population of cars, working on the principle that one shared car equals at least six cars taken off the road.

Challenge an Aspect of the Broader Contemporary Culture

We are seeing that with a paucity of genuine unmet consumer needs to deliver against anymore, Challengers increasingly look to find another surface to rub up against, to give their offer traction in the consumer's imagination and some cut-through in a crowded and noisy marketplace. And, while we do and should explore where this defining "other surface" might lie within the category, and within the culture its inherent beliefs and codes have woven around it, we are also starting to see, with examples like Zipcar, that we need to step back and look at popular culture itself and where the opportunity (or necessity) might lie for us to challenge something bigger.

Perhaps there is something about this cultural context that is directly impacting people's relationship with you and your category. Sometimes the consumer is interested in the category and interested, in principle, in what you have to offer, but has culturally based inhibitors that go beyond the category itself. IKEA, in its global journey, has had to be a profound Challenger in many of its markets to the way people feel about buying new home furnishings, or about buying cheap home furnishings, because of local, deep-seated cultural barriers that it has had to identify and then face head on. In Switzerland, for instance, which IKEA knew was going to be the hardest European market to crack, the Swiss liked the design and the furniture, but felt it was embarrassingly cheap: Could they really put this in their living rooms and hold their heads up, at those sorts of prices? So IKEA faced this head on, campaigning for Swiss consumers to stop being so snobbish (i.e. IKEA took on an aspect of Swiss culture, not just furniture-buying culture). In the UK, where people in research groups liked the furniture but felt it would not go with their current decorations, IKEA consequently challenged them to throw out what they already had ("Chuck out your chintz").

It may be thought that in talking about popular culture, we are inherently talking about trends. And there may be such trends—obesity, for example—that are easy to see and obviously require groups to combat them. But in fact what the brands we are exploring are more commonly doing is not so much riding a trend as identifying a mainstream theme or prevailing current in popular culture, something that is generally thought to be good, and then *deliberately swimming against that prevailing current*. Nextel, before the Sprint merger, had forged considerable success by challenging the notion that "Talk is Good" in telecommunications and in human connection; no, Nextel said to us, we believe "doing" is good, and we are a brand for doers. Club Med for its part talked for years about being the "Antidote to Civilization," a deliberately startling statement, because we had all rather naively imagined civilization to be a good thing. Yet Club Med in effect suggested that there are effectively two ways of seeing civilization (see Figure 5.4).

FIGURE 5.4 Two ways of seeing civilization.

How we saw civilization	How Club Med saw civilization
The pinnacle of human achievement	Bloodless mundanity
The cradle of culture	The stifler of spontaneity
What separates us from the beasts of the field	Suppressing the best of what it means to be alive
Noble, aspirational	Gray and sterile

And of course the brand gets our attention precisely because we had blithely assumed civilization was a good thing: the pinnacle of human achievement, we had thought; the cradle of culture; the thing that separated us from the beasts of the field. Then a Challenger comes along and invites us to question that—because that Challenger has a different view about civilization: as being gray, as being sterile, as bloodless, as a sea of conformity, suppressing all that is good in feeling the breath of life in our face. The establishment the Challenger is questioning is not another brand, but our underlying assumptions about what is good and bad in our culture and the world around us. It is this challenge, and its accompanying point of view, that gives Challengers a freshness and entirely new kind of relevance we want to engage with.

So this kind of challenge lies in explicitly confronting a commonly accepted aspect of contemporary culture and, in doing so, the (in the Challenger's view) unquestioning narrow-mindedness of the status quo and those who adhere to it.

Challenging the Market Leader

Because Market Leaders have very often established the parameters and criteria for choice within their category, they are in effect the embodiment of established thinking about the category—so at one level challenging some aspect of the Market Leader can simply be a different way of challenging a fundamental driver of the category. But the leader's very singularity lends a clearness and focus to our thinking about what we might want to challenge (again, whether we use that Market Leader explicitly or not), and by breaking out the individual elements of what that leader represents, and creating almost a photographic negative of some or all of those dimensions, we can in effect use that negative as a blueprint to define our own identity.

So when the South African fast-food chain Nando's began in Johannesburg in 1987, it was clear that it wanted and needed to do things differently from the Market Leader in chicken, KFC, in every way. Instead of being deep fried, the product would be flame-grilled. Instead of being bland fare, Nando's would offer hot sauces and marinades. It would have a personality that was cheeky and irreverent, as opposed to the stodgy Colonel. It would aggressively use PR rather than depending solely on advertising. In other words, Nando's realized that the way to succeed was in effect to be the exact opposite of what the Market Leader in fast-food chicken stood for; every dimension of the new brand's identity, in effect, was to throw down a challenge to the Market Leader.

Indeed, this kind of deliberately opposed starting point can create Challenger brands whose star continues to shine long after the leader they were born to be a counterpoint to has disappeared. Twenty-five years before Nando's, Andrew Loog Oldham had accentuated the image of the young London rock band he had discovered to be exactly the opposite of the Market Leader, Liverpool's Beatles. The Beatles were wholesome, lovable, and safe, boys you could take home to meet your mum; so Oldham's band would look dangerous, rude, perhaps even a little dirty. They called themselves The Rolling Stones. Forty years on, their "A Bigger Bang" tour became the highest-grossing tour in history.

While this kind of wholesale reversal of what the Market Leader stands for (creating a "positive negative," if you like) might end up being too broad for us, the process of exploring it in such detail does allow us to identify, relatively precisely, the dimensions on which we as Challengers will want to be the same as the leader, and those areas in which we will want to dramatically differentiate. This exploration may lead us to recognize that the center of our challenge to the Market Leader will in fact be confined to one very specific dimension. This might be to do with the leader's product—that it's serving up an inferior, characterless, or unnecessarily complicated offering, for example (the Mac versus PC campaign). Or we can object to the personality, to the impersonality, and to the faceless corporateness of the Market Leader: Aren't there any people in this behemoth who really understand what it is to be a human being, for heaven's sake? We might want to push deeper and question its motives and interests—perhaps we see the leader as having an entirely cynical relationship in its business transactions with the consumer, and in fact being simply a fat cat, lining its own pockets as it pretends to offer the honest hardworking consumer what passes for an overpriced product or a poor service. (This is of course a stance that Virgin Atlantic and Ryanair have both taken against British Airways.)

Whichever we choose, we have to puncture inertia. We have to prompt consumers out of their habitual behavior—at best marching somnolently to the omnipresent beat of the Market Leader's drum, and at worst entirely satisfied with what they are using, and seeing no reason to change.

UNDERSTANDING THE CHALLENGE TO THE CATEGORY AS A PRELUDE TO UNDERSTANDING THE DESIRED IDENTITY OF THE BRAND

Before we move on to discuss in more detail the relative merits of an implicit versus an explicit challenge, let us briefly note two things. First, let us recognize the value of sometimes needing to determine what we *reject* or even *hate* before we can be clear about what we love. Being very clear on what we are *not* can be an important prelude to establishing what we are.

Second, let's bear in mind that even if we are (as we will usually be) working on a specific brand, there can sometimes be real value in first determining our overall stance vis-à-vis the category. As a practical example of how the value of recognizing what you stand *against* can help you identify what you stand *for* within a category, consider the following example.

We were working on an ice cream brand within a large, multi-brand company. The company was understandably interested in moving into a health and wellness agenda, in line with the consumer macrotrend, and at some level in this regard had a little yogurt-envy. Yogurt represented health, well-being, fitness, modernity, compared to ice cream's role as an indulgent treat. And this yogurt-envy was an issue: While we might aspire to yogurt, we were in reality selling ice cream. So in order to find out how we might best start to come up with a place for our ice cream brand to stand, we set out to explore what it would mean to deliberately juxtapose ice cream with yogurt, in particular by identifying what we *hated* about yogurt (thereby also starting to surface what we *loved* about ice cream). We talked about it much of the afternoon, and then one member of the group working on the project sat down with a glass of wine at midnight and wrote this:

Ice Cream Philosophy versus Yogurt Philosophy

Ice cream people always answer the question "How are you?" with "Great" or "Fine." Yogurt people always answer the question "How are you?" with "Well, since you ask . . . "

Ice cream people see the world through a glass half full.

Yogurt people see the world through a glass of cabbage juice.

Ice cream people get upset if they forget your birthday.

Yogurt people get upset if you forget theirs.

Ice cream people always let you out in traffic.

Yogurt people never let you out; it's as if those crucial few inches will determine the success or failure of their day.

Ice cream people exercise when they can.

Yogurt people ride exercise bikes for 20 minutes a day (except for the third Sunday of the month when they make love to their partners).

Ice cream people often drop in on their friends on the spur of the moment.

Yogurt people make plans to see their friends months in advance.

Ice cream people listen to their iPods.

Yogurt people listen to Enya.

In meetings, ice cream people make sure they say what they think.

In meetings, yogurt people make sure they say pertinent things in order to make a contribution.

When you go into a yogurt person's office, there is always a sign on the wall, saying something like this: "Every morning a lion awakes. It knows it must run faster than the gazelle or it will not eat. Every morning a gazelle awakes. It knows it must run faster than the lion or it will be eaten. Every morning when you awake, it does not matter if you are a lion or gazelle, it is enough that you start to run."

Ice cream people don't have signs on their walls. In fact, ice cream people are sometimes in their office, sometimes not. Sometimes they're at home having a duvet day.

It was a brilliant juxtaposition, using all that was "wrong" about yogurt to help define ice cream's virtues. Suddenly, as he read it back to us the following morning, we no longer had yogurt envy; we felt actually that, although we didn't always behave in these ice cream ways, we wished we did—because if you looked at it this way, then it was ice cream, not yogurt, that was aspirational. We had started to identify what was true and important about ice cream that we could build on. We felt that ice cream was important, full stop. We had started to identify a kind of person that we were for and not for. We personally felt like, and wanted to be, ice cream people ourselves. We were on the way.

So we need two surfaces to give us a grip on the consumer's imagination. One will be a clear sense of what we stand *for*. The other will be the surface that we will deliberately rub up *against*, in the category or in popular culture.

Explicit versus Implicit Challenge

Now let's return to the nature of the challenge. As we noted previously, in each of the cases we looked at, our challenge can be an explicit one or an implicit one. If implicit, it will guide very strongly and clearly our identity and activities, but not be directly visible to the consumer. The retailer Urban Outfitters, for example, had as part of its starting DNA the thought that it was the "anti-Banana," that is, the opposite of Banana Republic. The public never saw this manifested in any way—it just drove the way Urban Outfitters designed its clothes, store, and experience. In terms of communication, the mask of the "King" for the relaunch of Burger King in a sense represented the "anti-clown" to McDonald's, but it was never presented to us explicitly in this way.

In a deliberately explicit challenge, on the other hand, we are obviously going to make it clear that we have this aspect of the category or other player clearly in our sights. Our desire is to create more conflict, more drama, and change in some way the narrative of our category in doing so.

We look more fully at how to do this kind of explicit challenge well and badly in Chapter 11, but in order to give us half an eye on one of our possible destinations as we start to develop our strategic thinking, let us briefly explore the fertile territory of wars, enemies, and monsters before moving on.

Wars and Monsters

There is much that we have forgotten from English classes (what *is* the difference between a gerund and a gerundive, exactly?). But among the things we do remember, of course, are the basic constructs of a good story: the need for a hero, a conflict, and, more often than not, a monster.

Monsters have a number of important values in stories. They raise the stakes; they create drama, emotion, and conflict. They throw up a hero (oh, look, that's us). They give the hero a very visible adversary and clearly position the hero as being on the side of right. They highlight what his or her virtues are—there is nothing like a little darkness to give definition to light. And, perhaps most important from our point of view, monsters *unite the community against them*. This is one of the important differences between a monster and an enemy: An enemy is a threat to *you*, but a monster is a threat *to the larger community*. This is what brings the community together. However disparate, divided, or simply indolent the community had been up to that point, the presence of a monster brings them together in unity against it. In modern storytelling and popular film, the nature of the monster ranges from real monsters (*Jaws, King Kong*) to conceptual monsters like big business and large corporations (much of John Grisham's oeuvre) to particular people (*Dodgeball*). And one of the key narrative arcs in such stories, of course, is the hero's struggle to communicate the threat to the community and to get them to take it seriously so that they can respond and defeat it.[7]

Some Challengers, then, have been very explicit about creating monsters that they then oppose. Dove is not the first to challenge the beauty industry—Anita Roddick in the 1980s had actually described the beauty business as "a monster selling unobtainable dreams, one that lies, cheats and exploits women."[8] And the legendary Apple "1984" spot from Chiat/Day is, in fact, as explicit a monster narrative as it is possible to be: A large monster (the dehumanized authority figure on the screen) has the community in slavish thrall, and it takes a hero in white with a single magical weapon to escape her pursuit and defeat it, thereby liberating the community. And when did Apple and Chiat/Day show this commercial? During the Super Bowl—the one time in the year when all of America sits down and watches TV together as a community. That is to say, Apple and its ad agency looked to unite the community of America against the "monster" through the media plan as much as through the spot itself.

And actually, if we look at our four classic Challenger examples from the beginning of the book—Avis, Apple, Pepsi, Virgin Atlantic—three of the four used monsters, though in different ways. Apple demonized the threat because it threatened all of us; Avis positioned itself as threatened by a Big Fish, which threat pushed it to serve us better. Virgin Atlantic ingeniously worked the two together: Overall, Virgin looked to make British Airways into, if not a monster, then the Fat Cat, and then championed "us against them."

So, if we choose to follow (or at least explore) this model of being a Challenger in our market, then having at least an enemy, and perhaps going as far as creating a monster will be an important strand of thinking for us. At the very least for the internal unity and energy of our "community" and perhaps as a source of clarity and energy for our external challenge, whether we name our enemy or leave it implicit.

IN CONCLUSION

The rich sense of possibility for us as Challengers that the application of Intelligent Naivety seems to open up will be useless unless subsequently disciplined by a fierce clarity as to where our principle challenge to the status quo will lie. It is only in very unusual cases that the opportunity will be to question every aspect of the category—more often a key part of our initial task will be to identify where we can and should be clearly different, and where we need to be the same. This imposition of this clarity may even be championed or led by another individual within the Challenger team, but it will be critical as the team as a whole moves toward working through exactly what our brand is going to stand for and against as a Challenger.[9]

The overall approach we note Challengers taking has been defined as eight "Credos"—that is to say eight principles into which Challengers put their energy, passion, and personal faith, and which collectively help define, shape, and realize their Challenger ambition. What we have been describing in this chapter, however, is not a principle so much as a key bridge between the divergent thinking of the First Credo and the clear singlemindedness of the second. And in establishing a center of gravity for the challenge we are going to make it also lays the key foundations for what our brand is going to stand for when we make it. What is going to be the foundation, in other words, of our Lighthouse Identity.

Finally, in thinking about the foundation for where we are going to stand, we note that one of the key decisions that we as a Challenger have to make is whether we will be a brand of *opposition* or a brand of *proposition*. Are we always going to have as a key part of our identity what we are opposed to? Or will we use that to transition to simply standing for something that we champion? In rare cases, this opposition is something that is inherent in one's genetic makeup; so Jimmy Lai's open pro-democracy stance in his Hong Kong newspaper, *Apple Daily*, naturally is going to rub up against the ruling Chinese Communist Party. (Newspaper brands, in fact, are generally stronger in opposition.) But more commonly, this will be a choice that we will need to make as we develop our own sense of where we are going to stand, and what we are going to stand for.

THE SECOND CREDO: BUILD A LIGHTHOUSE IDENTITY

Success means never letting the competition define you. Instead, you have to define yourself based on a point of view you care deeply about.

Tom Chappell, Tom's of Maine

The second key characteristic of Challenger brands is that they do not attempt to navigate by the consumer. Instead, they invite the consumer to navigate by them. Even if they choose to use another player in the market as a counterpoint, they are seeking to communicate clearly and insistently where they stand and why they stand there.

There is a certain school of advertising one might call "That's why" advertising. You can spot an example by the presence of those two little words in the middle. Such a television commercial might, for instance, go something like this:

We open on a person lying back on a sofa reading a business book. They are wearing a vintage Japanese T-shirt, some mid-length drawstring pants, and faintly directional hair, so we can tell they are not an old school businessperson; relaxed on the floor next to them, reading a magazine, is an attractive partner, so we know they are not sad, lonely people who have nothing better to do than read business books on the weekend.

Up to date or not, though, we can see that the toils of the week are taking their toll: As they flick through the incisive tome on their lap, we notice their eyelids begin to drift south.

The voiceover begins: "At Milo's mineral waters, we know how difficult it can be staying awake reading long business books about Challenger brands."

We see the eyelids fully close. The head starts to loll. The partner looks up, and a flicker of fond annoyance crosses their face.

The voiceover continues: *"That's why* Milo's mineral water contains *six times* the amount of caffeine of any other mineral water on the market!"

We cut to a fresh shot of the same scene. Our protagonist, fully fresh and wide awake, is reading some of the funnier passages of this obviously excellent business book to their partner, who is laughing radiantly and looking appreciatively into their eyes. This, we can all see, is the stuff that Sunday afternoons were really made for.

A tagline pops up: "Milo's Mineral Water with extra caffeine. The Joy of Six."

"That's why" advertising navigates by reference to consumers. It holds up a mirror to their lives—or what the advertiser supposes are their lives—and gives them a reason to believe the product we are selling contains something that will make their day better in some regard. It is very tempting to pursue this kind of advertising for both agency and client, because it is so hard to fault if examined logically. Together we have identified a real problem—people are tired at weekends and cannot do all the things they would like to get done; we have shown consumers that we understand how they feel about that problem (they can see that we are almost living this thing with them); and we've given them a practical solution—a clear drink with trace elements of essential minerals sourced within 160 miles of where they live, that also contains enough caffeine to make you find anything funny.

In this situation I, the brand, am acting in effect as a mirror. I see your life, and I am showing you that I see how you live.

And yet the Challengers we are looking at tend not to do any of this. They tend not to do "That's why" problem-solution advertising; in fact, in many cases they don't really talk about the consumer at all. Instead, they talk about themselves; they invite the consumer to navigate by them. They behave as what we shall call Lighthouse brands, with a Lighthouse Identity.

First, we look at the idea of lighthouses and why they might be important. Then we take the key dimensions to being a Lighthouse brand and discuss the importance of each of these in turn. Finally, we discuss the rock on which our Lighthouse brand is built.[1]

NAVIGATION, NOT COMMUNICATION

It's not that the world is more complex these days. It's that in many areas it's falling apart. It is hard to overdramatize the recent steady collapse in people's frameworks for living—the breakdown of families, the disappearance of job security, the disgrace of respected public figures and institutions, the financial embarrassment of former business icons, the displacement of basic social needs such as face-to-face time with friends and family because of the pressures of work, the personal sense of being nearly overwhelmed by the legion of pressures we cope with every day—whether those of a soccer mom, merchant banker, or magistrate. This sense of fragmentation, even collapse is fanned every night by the most consistently skeptical and graphic media commentary the Western world has yet known.

The fact that we are so close to this structural collapse ourselves sometimes makes us snow-blind to its effect. But consider one interesting symptom. The cultural critic David Marc has drawn attention to the fundamental change in the nature of popular television programming over the past 40 years.[2] Figure 6.1 shows the top six prime-time programs in the United States, by viewership, in 1960.

FIGURE 6.1   Top US Prime Time TV shows 1960–1961.

1. Gunsmoke
2. Wagon Train
3. Have Gun, Will Travel
4. Andy Griffith Show
5. Real McCoys
6. Rawhide

Source: TV Ratings Index 1960–1961

What do these shows consist of? Essentially, tales of heroism and Western grit, aspirational stories about how ordinary men and women built America and found happiness and contentment in the world they were building.

Pan forward to 2007, and look at the key shows on just one network, ABC. What does the casual observer notice about all the anchor shows, old and new alike? They are all about dysfunction: *Lost, Grey's Anatomy, Ugly Betty, Cashmere Mafia, Desperate Housewives.* One ABC executive indeed remarked at the beginning of the season that there was a "foolproof formula" in television now—base a show around four women (or men) "who have everything—except happiness." People lost in the world, perhaps, that has been built for them and with them.[3] Fueling, or fueled, by this context of uncertainty, is the striking shift that what we see happening here is a change in the nature and shape of authority in the modern world. At a time when we need role models and structures to live by, those role models and structures are less and less the authority figures of the past but, increasingly, one's peer group. The growth of social networking sites, in some cases dramatically expanding the number of active friends in our network (a number that sociologists believe for thousands of years consisted simply of 5 close friends, 15 active friends, and 150 acquaintances), of course, is both a symptom and a reinforcement of this shift. Ask yourself this: Is the social networking phenomenon simply a welcome return to connectedness after a period of apparently increasing decline in people's ability to maintain their friendships? Or is that dramatically enlarged social connectness a desire for an entirely new kind of stability, where we as nodes are suspended from 150 points of reinforcement, reassurance, and recommendation? Noting all of these shifts is not to lament the passing of a historical set of structures and values; it is an observation with practical consequences for us. People today lack certain core historical frameworks that have helped structure previous generations' lives, and now they are creating new ones of their own.

Where do brands fit into all of this? In human societies, goods have always been a form of communication—to the outside world and to oneself. Now I would go a stage further; I would suggest that brands have become a form not simply of communication but of navigation. Although it is too glib to say that brands and products increasingly provide meaning in uncertain times, it does mean that the brands that flourish today are those that have a very clear sense of who they are—that is to say, not simply a distinctive identity but a strong and self-referential identity; they stand out from the competition by their intensity and their confidence in themselves. If we were to pursue the image of the consumer adrift on uncertain waters, then we might say that the brands that flourish in this uncertain environment are those that have what we shall call a Lighthouse Identity.

That consumers find the self-confidence of such brands appealing should be no surprise. In life, people are drawn to strength and to people of character who are true to themselves. In marketing life, in using goods as communication or even navigation, people are drawn to strong brands. This strength can come from the familiarity and ubiquity of a Brand Leader as Number One; if you are a second-rank brand, it comes from an intense projection of who you are.

WHAT IS A LIGHTHOUSE IDENTITY?

A Lighthouse brand is one that has a very clear sense of where it stands, and why it stands there. This sense of self is built on rock—a product or brand truth that gives it credible ownership of this place to stand, and projected in a point of view about the way the world is, or the way the world should be, in everything that it does. And projected in every direction, inside and out. The result being that, like a lighthouse, you notice it even if you are not looking for it. Let's break down these key elements of Lighthouse brands a little more clearly.

1. *Point of view—they have a very particular take on how they see the world.* The predominant purpose of Challenger brands' every marketing action is to tell us where *they* stand. They offer an emotionally based point of view about the world. They don't attempt to tell us something about ourselves—and they certainly don't attempt to navigate themselves with reference to *us*. (This is important: The Consumer Isn't.)
2. *Intensity.* They offer an intense projection of who they are in everything they do. Weak preference will not cut it for a late entrant: Challengers need to be vivid.

3. *Salience.* They are highly intrusive; one cannot avoid noticing their activity even if not actively looking in their direction—that is, shopping their category. (Important: The Audience Isn't.) You may not be a wrestling fan, for instance, but you could absolutely tell me what WWE is all about.
4. *Built on Rock.* Their identity is built on a product or brand truth that is inarguable. This inarguable truth gives them legitimacy and credibility in the stance they are taking, a way of owning it in a very competitive world, and a compelling conviction that the stance they are taking is one that is uniquely theirs.

In the remainder of this chapter, we discuss each of these in turn, along with where the roots of identity may lie and, indeed, how one arrives at a strong identity in the first place.

A Point of View All Their Own

Challengers do not seem to plot their path by the rest of the world; they are confident enough to invite the world to navigate by them.

Let's go back to that statement at the beginning of the chapter by Tom Chappell, owner of Tom's of Maine. He is not saying, "Ignore the competition, and pay no attention to your consumer." What he is saying, though, is while it will be important to understand both these things very well, you should not let the competition define you, and you should not confuse understanding your consumer with knowing what your point of view is, the view that will represent your unique place and role in their world.

So, Challengers have a very clear sense, first and foremost, of who they are, not just in terms of their own external image, but in terms of their own internal identity. This is often because they have a founder at the center, many of whose personal beliefs they reflect and amplify. Richard Branson is offering his own personal culture within Virgin: the smiling revolutionary, the entrepreneur in a fluffy jumper, the debunker of the establishment. The sexiness of Dov Charney's American Apparel image is in a different way a projection of his own personal culture: Known to conduct interviews in his underwear, he also takes all the photographs in his intentionally controversial ad campaign himself. In these kinds of cases, everything else in the company flows from this sense of personal culture—behavior, image, communication.

But other Challenger brands we are considering have a less obvious (or nonexistent) founder: Dove, for example, Lexus (at launch, certainly), Wii, New Zealand, Diesel, Scion, and Camper are all brands that also in their own way evince an enormous self-confidence, a sense of who they are, without any permission from or reference to the world around them. They all seem to share shoe designer Kenneth Cole's publicly stated belief that "What you stand for is more important than what you stand in."[4] Whether they express themselves most effectively through design or communication, their reference point is themselves—no comparative or "That's why" advertising here. The delineation between themselves and those around them is bold and clear: The differences in identity that mark out these Challengers are not the subtle differences that emerge from weeks of discussion within the marketing/agency team over nuances of this or that word used to describe the brand's personality. They are differences that are immediately observable; they are highly defined, in or out of their category context: a jeans company with its own philosophy of living (Diesel), a social networking site that sees itself as a movement (Facebook), a sports brand where all the athletes have their own philosophy of life (WWE), a country that celebrates that it is 100 percent itself (New Zealand).

Indeed, some iconic Challengers (like Apple) have achieved such a highly defined state of identity that they have become in effect their own countries, with their own languages—they don't have help desks, they have Genius Bars; they give you protective coverings for their beautiful machines in the form of knitted socks; they have 'On' lights that pulse like a heartbeat.

And at the heart of each of these Lighthouse brands is a strong opinion. A very particular point of view about the way the world should be, what counts and does not count in it. They take a position based on a deep-seated belief. (This is as true of Challengers as people as it is as Challengers as brands, of course.)

So Target's CEO, Bob Ulrich, believes that just because you don't have money doesn't mean you don't have taste. Dieter Mateschitz of Red Bull holds that his brand is not simply an energizing liquid in a can, but a philosophy: "We believe in individualism, we hate conformism, we believe in a civil courage. We believe you have the responsibility to make up your own opinion."[5] Linus Torvalds of Linux believes that "software is like sex—it's better when it's free."[6] Twitter believes that "every moment has a caption."[7] Top-Flite is a golf ball brand that believes you should always shoot for the pin. Camper, the Spanish shoe brand born in the amiably slow-moving island of Majorca, believes we should all "Walk, not Run"—it hates the increasing velocity of the world; it hates Nike and McDonald's, as twin peddlers of contemporary speed; it believes in slowly forged friendships, and the slow, rich pace of island life. The emergent Google's "Don't be evil"—which did not come from the founders, but from a company meeting in 2000 to determine the company's values—was in large part a rejection of the (then) competition's practice of mixing paid-for advertising with search results without being transparent about it.

Let us look at one example in a little more detail—the Mini case. Facing a U.S. launch, Mini created a richly developed belief about a new driving culture, and what it believed a driving culture should be like, that was at direct odds with the natural trajectory of the prevailing category culture. The US driving culture that the Mini was launching into was one, as we have already seen, in which, on one very critical dimension, it could not win: This was a culture at whose heart the key principle was "bigger is better." And it had always been like this—from the days of fin-tailed Cadillacs with "same-day steering" right up to a more modern love affair with light trucks and SUVs. And Mini was one brand that could not win in a "bigger is better" car culture.

So the Mini team (no single owner-founder here) looked at this current driving culture and asked themselves: Even if we could be part of the predominant American car culture, would we *want* to? Look at it—a culture of people flipping fingers at each other, of road rage, of selfish parking. A world of "eat lunch or be lunch." So they looked to come up with and champion a new kind of car culture that they could believe in, and one in which they could thrive. A different kind of driving culture: one where people volunteered jumper cables, stopped intimidating each other, paid strangers' tolls, and kept their hands off the horn. And then, to really make it ownable, the team pushed the thought further: They said to themselves that they needed a new piece of language to describe this new kind of automotive culture: something other than

FIGURE 6.2   Mini: "Let's Sip, Not Guzzle."

driving. So they took up *motoring* and the rallying cry "Let's Motor." And around this thought they built the idea of a whole alternative driving culture into which the wonderfully diminutive car could fit. And one in which it could, and did, succeed. (See Figure 6.2.)

So, Challengers have a clear point of view, rooted in a unique belief or perspective on the world, and sometimes translated into a whole culture all their own. And let us note that this is across all Challengers, across all kinds of categories. If we are tempted to think this applies only to premium goods, let's look at JetBlue. Think this is more about hardware and services? Tell that to Stonyfield Farms.

Some Challengers famously go beyond championing a point of view, into being brands with an overt mission or cause. Tourism New Zealand genuinely believes that New Zealand represents something important for the world. Kashi, the cereal company (now owned by Kellogg's), describes itself as "Seven Whole Grains on a Mission," and in its website it challenges you to make big and small changes in the direction of a healthier life. Dove talks about itself very deliberately as being an "agent of change." Mozilla, the creator of the open source web browser Firefox, and Challenger to Microsoft's Internet Explorer, wants to get the world to see the benefits of openness, because it believes that openness will benefit the industry as a whole.[8] They not only have a point of view about the way the world should be, these Challengers: They are going to intercede in the world and actually make it that way. In the words of Theodor Herzl: "If we will it, it is not a dream." And they will it.

Before we move on, let's look, by contrast, at a second-rank brand that has failed to establish its own identity, either to itself or its consumers, and the effect this failure has had on its success. Reebok is a second-rank brand that has continually failed to define who it really believes itself to be, and thus has always posed a weak challenge to Nike's dominance of the footwear market. Instead of accepting that Nike has appropriated the high ground of athletic performance (and has more claim to it anyway, given the origins of the Nike brand in college sports versus Reebok's origins in aerobics fashion) and uncovering another, genuinely differentiating place for itself to live, Reebok has spent years as a weak Nike wannabe. It is a brand that lacks an identity, lacks self-belief in who it is or can be, and it shows. Born from a group of traders, it has no true north; consequently, it has failed to make any ground on the leader.

Emotion and Intensity

The purpose of a strong identity is to invite and create a more intense relationship between Challenger and user, however the latter is defined. A Challenger brand does not break through in a mature category by being more convenient or trustworthy (though both these might be important basics for it to deliver on); it succeeds because it offers the consumer an emotional reward and/or relationship that the Establishment brand cannot match. While key aspects of the product mix may satisfy certain rational needs, then, Challengers do not tend to succeed through the satisfaction of those rational needs alone (there are rarely many rational needs left in any given mature category, anyway); instead, through a Lighthouse Identity they invite a realignment of the consumer's emotions.

The Challenger brand has to possess a stronger, emotionally based relationship with the consumer than the Brand Leader does—for whatever reason. Being equally as strong is not enough. Indeed, I suggest there is a graduating scale of positive affiliation with a brand that looks something like this (let us leave aside negative equity for the moment):

- *Indifference.* A decaying brand is treated with indifference. It becomes a commodity or dies.
- *Reassurance.* A well-established Brand Leader that has failed to renew itself offers reassurance. This is valuable for a while in new categories the consumer is afraid of, like technology or art, but it is inadequate in categories wherein a consumer is more confident, like gourmet food.
- *Weak preference* is vulnerable to competitive pricing or other aggressive retaliatory tactics. It may be sufficient in high-volume, low-interest categories like fast food but will probably be insufficient for a Challenger that needs to build momentum or change buying behavior in spite of distributional disadvantages.
- *Enthusiastic preference* should be the benchmark to which a Challenger aspires. In a very few categories, this is what the Brand Leader already enjoys—Lexus, for example, in the import luxury car market.
- *Identity* is where the preference is such for the user to identify itself with what the brand offers. Apple, in the area of computers rather than iPods, has enjoyed the same emotional identification. The apparently innocent statement "I'm a Mac user" masks a host of other related beliefs in the user's own creativity, perspective on the world, and originality of thought.
- *Enhanced self* is where the brand finds itself not simply so in tune with what users want to be or to do that it builds identification, but where it actually confers something on consumers they didn't realize they wanted but makes them feel, once they experience it, more than they were. Experience brands such as the Schrager hotels at their peak, or digital brands which facilitate a fuller expression of who I am (Facebook) or which facilitate creativity (Threadless), or both (flickr). Much of the velocity of a new generation of digital brands occurs precisely because they deliver this benefit of enhanced self.

We can see, then, that as far as a brand is concerned, in all practical respects the opposite of love is not hate; it's indifference. Indifference is certainly dangerous to a Challenger, but so is weak preference. Enthusiastic preference is the least a Challenger should be aiming for.

In order to achieve this degree of preference, we have to have and project a very clear sense of who we are and what makes you different. Sympathy and solutions, characterized by "That's why" advertising, offer the consumer a mirror, but not an identity. They may build short-term sales on problem solving, but they will not create a strong enough affiliation to the brand to build medium-term momentum. Nicolas Hayek of Swatch put it eloquently: "Emotional products are about a message—a strong exciting, distinct, authentic message that tells people who you are and why you do what you do. There are many elements that make up the Swatch message. High quality. Low cost. Provocative. Joy of life. But the most important element of the Swatch message is the hardest for others to copy. Ultimately, we are not just offering watches. We are offering our own personal culture."

Salience

The final characteristic of a Lighthouse is that it intrudes on one's consciousness: One notices it even if one is not actively looking for it. So, while you may not be a leggings wearer, you could tell me what American Apparel stands for. You may never fly JetBlue, but you have a fair idea of what kind of experience it represents. You might never choose to drink Mountain Dew, but you know why and when you would. You may never have visited New Zealand, but you know it is 100 percent pure, and why that might draw you to it.

This salient understanding has partly to do with the identity itself and partly with the way the Challenger expresses that identity through its marketing communications and behavior. The whole issue of salience and how Challenger brands achieve it are covered in more depth in Chapters 6, 7 and 10; simply note at this point that its importance to a Challenger is rooted, not in the motherhoods of good business practice, but in two specific issues discussed in Chapter 2: The Category Isn't and The Consumer Isn't.

Lighthouses are built on rock. We want firm foundations for our point of view that we can credibly own, rather than having it be a piece of puffery. And we need that rock partly also to found a fierce belief in it ourselves, to ourselves, to our customers and business partners, and to our consumers. One fuels the other: If a clear identity gives differentiation externally, it also gives self-belief internally—as long as it is founded on rock.

Built on Rock

Product obsession is primary.

Jim Jannard, Oakley

There are, broadly speaking, two kinds of rock available to us: a *brand (or company) truth* and/or a *product truth*.

In the case of the brand or company truth, this often lies either in the circumstances and reasons for the original creation of the brand or in building from one of the brand's unique (though sometimes forgotten) equities. If we look at MAC cosmetics, for example, its identity—which is about a very public embracing of diversity in people—is founded on its origins, born as it was from the Toronto drag scene. The identity of Altoids, conversely, was rooted in an equity that had been physically stamped on its unique tin for 200 years—"The Original Celebrated Curiously Strong Peppermints." It is hard to argue with that: It's right there on the metal for everyone to see.

The other key kind of rock on which to build is obviously a product truth—some dimension of product performance. Knowing that our brand is different—better than the Establishment brand we are taking on in some key dimension—affects not simply our own performance and attitude, but the relationship with our customers. Brand Leaders operate a "just enough" strategy. Just enough mushrooms in the sauce, just enough thoughtfulness in the ergonomics of the bottle, just enough quality control in the product sourcing, just enough courtesy at the check-in desk—and only one packet of peanuts per passenger per flight. There is a story about Henry Ford that dramatizes the "just enough" philosophy nicely: Ford used to send his people out to scour the scrap heaps of America looking for old Ford engines. Dragging them back to Detroit, they would look for the parts that hadn't worn out and then downgrade the specifications to save money.

Yet while "just enough" is at some level simply good commercial sense for a Brand Leader, it creates an opportunity for the Challenger to create product enthusiasm, not just product satisfaction. Robin Wight has observed that brands that enjoy an iconic status in consumers' minds are not so much engineered (in the broadest sense of the word) as overengineered: They offer not just product performance but product overperformance—that is, they honor the brand promise by offering the consumer in their product dramatically superior performance on some dimension chosen by the Challenger. Absurdly generous quantities of chocolate chunks amid the ice cream, a product that is sourced only from three islands in the Honduras, a free chauffeur-driven limousine to take you to the check-in desk in the first place. Wight believes such brands have their own design standard, one that is based not in research telling them the nature of their consumer's wants and needs, but their own, almost obsessive sense of how the product should perform, how it should be able to be experienced. A Land Rover, he will tell you, has a design standard that requires it to be able to drive 4,000 miles continually off-road without requiring anything except more gasoline. It is actually hard to find 4,000 miles of off-road driving these days south of the Arctic Circle, but that is the design standard of the people building Land Rovers. (And, in some almost osmotic way, even if Land Rover purchasers are never specifically told this, they understand the machine's extraordinary capabilities.)

Many of the Challengers we are discussing reflect Wight's concept of overperformance—indeed, they parade it. They are more deliberately extreme than the Brand Leader not simply in the emotion and intensity of the way they talk about themselves, but also in the product performance they offer. When driving a car, for instance, the occasions in which one needs to be able to balance three tiers of champagne glasses on one's hood as the engine approaches 6,000 rpm are relatively rare, but Lexus's launch advertising offered you the ability to do that. Patagonia, to take another example, also has its own design standards for functional practicality. While its fashionability leads it to being referred to fondly by some of its adherents as "Pradagonia" or "Patagucci," its founder, Yvon Chouinard, has a very different kind of design standard in mind when he says: "You should be able to wash travel clothes in a sink or a cooking pot, then hang them out to dry in a hut and still look decent for the plane ride home." Able to be washed beautifully in a cooking pot? How many other brands have that as a design requirement?[9]

Does overperformance mean premium, or quality? Not necessarily. Mountain Dew has a very clear Lighthouse Identity, which is about "Pushing the Limits." And the product rock it is based on is not product quality but a product quality, or rather two of them: the fact that it is almost luminous in color and that it has a healthy dose of caffeine and sugar in each can. And it builds an identity that is firmly and unequivocally rooted in that. Or it may be that overperformance in a certain kind of reliability is important, if the Challenger is one in the field of knowledge, for instance: the thousands of volunteer contributors to Wikipedia correct acts of "vandalism" (i.e., malicious re-editing) in *just 5 minutes*, on average. (Even Southwest Airlines, in its own way, overperforms—it overperforms on enthusiasm and friendliness. It may not be to everyone's taste, but it is very engaging to those who like it.)

Overperformance, then, has many benefits for a Challenger. It is not simply an extreme point of difference that justifies the emotional position the Challenger adopts. It is not simply to create fanatics and apostles in the user base (and therefore mythology, as discussed in Chapter 11), although all these are important. Its other value is to create supreme self-belief and conviction within the company, and this is something that can be detected by those outside the company. Overperformance shows the company really cares about the product, which in turn means it is committed to delivering on the brand promise. And it gives the company the confidence to be a Lighthouse.[10]

A LIGHTHOUSE IDENTITY, NOT A LIGHTHOUSE IMAGE

This very clear sense of identity encompasses not simply what the brand is, but also what business it is really in—because it is a Lighthouse *Identity*, rather than a Lighthouse *Image*. Were it the latter, our sense of self would simply impact the communications strategy. But as a Lighthouse Identity, it impacts in reality *every* aspect of our business. And as such, in fact, is a good test of how clear and directional our belief system and point of view is.

Look at method, for instance. In its 18-page *People against Dirty* booklet, bound into women's magazines, the brand laid out how it saw the relationship between you and your home (Figure 6.3): "We believe a home is more than just a box," method told us, "it is a kind of second skin." So if this is our belief, how would it impact the way we thought about our business? We'd pay a lot of attention to the product nature, and how it acted on our skin, not just our bathtub. We'd want to signal

FIGURE 6.3   method text.

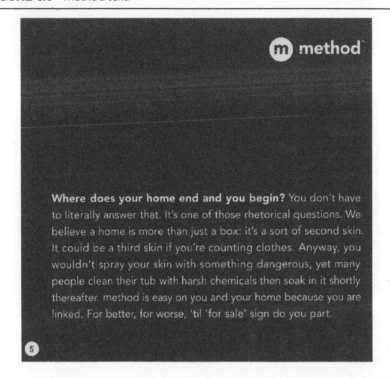

> **Where does your home end and you begin?** You don't have to literally answer that. It's one of those rhetorical questions. We believe a home is more than just a box: it's a sort of second skin. It could be a third skin if you're counting clothes. Anyway, you wouldn't spray your skin with something dangerous, yet many people clean their tub with harsh chemicals then soak in it shortly thereafter. method is easy on you and your home because you are linked. For better, for worse, 'til 'for sale' sign do you part.

this very clearly in the way you described our product promise. It would move us into a different kind of brand neighborhood: "skin care," with big implications for the quality and aesthetic of the pack, for the kind of price you would look to charge. For the kind of emotional promise you would be making, and the kind of relationship and loyalty you would be looking to generate.

If, like Toyota's Scion, you stand for and champion self-expression at the core of your Lighthouse Identity, then this will of course drive the kind of advertising and grassroots marketing you do. But it will also drive your business model—personalization will genuinely drive every aspect of the brand experience and interaction you create, whether it is a customer shopping for and personalizing their vehicle online prior to purchase, or when that customer goes into a dealership to customize their car, or whether that personalization takes place through Scion accessories or through aftermarket accessories offered by the dealer. It will drive the way you nurture and help sustain the communities of interest around the brand that you have launched, from hundreds of live events every year, to engaging the more than 150 Scion owners clubs that spring up (entirely independently), to the creation of Scion City in Second Life, where owners can go for further virtual education and inspiration about how to personalize their car.

This is a Lighthouse Identity, not a Lighthouse image.

THE SOURCES OF IDENTITY

Seeing individual Challenger founders talk of their own personal culture, it is apparent that an individual drives an identity and its cultural manifestations with a clarity and a vigor that an idea or a group finds it hard to match.

But what do the rest of us do about this, attempting as we are to transform ourselves into Challengers? Not many of us have a "strong personal culture"—or at least one that is instantly apparent to the casual acquaintance. But an organization can have one, indeed must have one, and that in turn can create our own personal culture within the organization. What, then, is the source of a highly defined identity, a point of view, for an aspiring Challenger if there is no founder or central visionary?

First, we should recognize that there *is* an answer, because we have a pool of Challengers we are talking about that are *not* born just from a founder or founders. There is a tendency in larger companies to write off Challenger behavior as the province of companies with an owner-driver or two, who set the culture and embrace risk and PR (Red Bull, innocent, etc.) in a way that a more risk-averse, publicly quoted company (with all the concomitant joys of a matrix reporting structure and corporate PR police) will not.* Yet as we have already noted, many of the Challenger brands we talk about here are not brands whose launch or relaunch is being driven by an owner-founder. So let us not allow ourselves to slip into the comfortable belief that this would all be wonderful when we start our own company, but will have to wait till then.

---

* The application of Challenger behavior in the latter is more comprehensively discussed in my second book on Challengers, *The Pirate Inside*.)

Broadly speaking, if there is no founder or strong CEO within the organization, or if the Lighthouse team members do not have a strong personal sense of what they want to put right about the category, there are a number of possible sources from which a strong central identity can emerge. Chapter 5 looked at the rich inspiration for this that can come from real clarity over the challenge we are laying down to the market—let us also consider here the reinterpreted past and the relationship with hard-core users.

THE REINTERPRETED PAST

Leslie Butterfield has observed that the role of brand planning on a mature brand is not to add value, but to *extract* value—that is, to find and amplify a part of the brand's history and essence whose relevance and potential power has been lost sight of. In his first weeks back at Apple in 1997, Steve Jobs made a speech to the resellers in which he talked about what Apple stood for. It was not about making boxes that helped people do their jobs, he said, though it did that well. The brand, the company, was fundamentally about a *belief*—a belief that people with passion could change the world for the better. And, he said, Apple had always been about that—the launch of the Mac and the 1984 execution being shining examples of this. And, he went on, while he recognized that the world had changed enormously (the competition, the pricing, the technology, the retailing landscape), beliefs and values should not change; instead they should be reinterpreted for a new world.

Part of our key task, if we work on a relatively long-established brand, is to properly understand our past: why we began, what we believed when we began or when we were at our strongest, what our equities were then, and amongst whom their strength lay, and why. By understanding and reinterpreting their past for a new world, we see a number of Challengers rekindle their Lighthouse flame. For instance, while we have in the past tended to think of Kodak as a Market Leader, as it has turned the corner into the digital world it has had to learn to be a Challenger again. We discuss in some detail in Chapter 9 how Kodak reinvigorated its camera business, and how a key part of determining its future direction came from going back—going back to George Eastman's vision for Kodak: mass market technology that made it easy for women, moms in particular, to capture and share memories easily. And in really understanding the past, also looking at what it would mean to reinterpret that to a new world.

New Zealand has drawn on its heritage in a slightly different way. Every country should clearly be concerned about sustainability and nature, but in New Zealand (and therefore for Tourism New Zealand) there is a particular truth on which its unique perspective on sustainability is based: the Maori culture of *kaitiakitanga*. A very difficult concept to put into English. Kaitiakitanga essentially stands for the guardianship of the world's natural resources and the life forces they contain, including preserving the land for future generations and, in doing so, practicing true sustainability in everything you do. (It can be argued that the Maori in New Zealand were, in a very real sense, the first environmentalists.)

Or look at Dove. While we as marketing observers feel that this is a dramatic new point of view and voice for the brand, those responsible for actually creating it are very clear that in reality it is significantly rooted in a perspective that the brand has long held. The primary communication for the brand for years had been very simple endorsement advertising featuring a real woman, talking honestly to camera. And this understanding helped give foundations and confidence to the legitimacy of "Real Beauty" as a unique and ownable place to stand for Dove moving forward, albeit one that was indeed dramatically reinterpreted.

So, we need to surface a deep understanding of the brand's past, its beginnings even. Past equities, why it was started, its initial intent and reason for being. Why it was successful when it was successful, and what that would mean today. Look for inherent truths that, while we may not be able to simply reexpress for a new world, may yet provide a fertile source for a long-term, ownable place to stand.

THE RELATIONSHIP WITH HARD-CORE USERS

In many cases, our brand will have developed a very clear identity among a small group of hard-core users or early adopters: This identity has arisen almost despite active marketing, because these users have found or projected something onto the brand from the context in which they have come to know it. Such was the case with Burger King. For years Burger King had done essentially just the same kind of marketing as McDonald's—the same kind of consumer segmentation, the same kind of meal extensions—but on a quarter of the budget, thus, in effect, just feeding the demand for the Market Leader. And the result had been seven straight years of decline. Then Burger King repitched the business, and with a new advertising agency (CPB) looked to redefine what it should stand for.

The brand team looked at the core 18- to 24-year-old target and decided to go hard after what it called its "superfan," that group of just under 20 percent of users who account for around 50 percent of visits. The company recognized that this group of heavy users didn't *want* healthy—which was the focus of much of the industry conversation at the time. (Think back to Intelligent Naivety and the upstream question: "Just because the world and the Market Leader is rushing into healthier eating options, does that really mean we should, too?") This group wanted something else from a burger. So the brand team identified three underleveraged equities—the King, the Whopper, and the idea of "Have It Your Way"—and combined these in a fresh strategic approach that would give Burger King a way to credibly and ownably break through again to the superfan.

First, they gave "Have It Your Way" a fresh new meaning. What had been previously a way of saying "You don't have to have the pickles if you don't want to" was flipped into a positive: "Indulge all you like"— and Burger King delivered concretely on this by adding a triple-decker to the menu, for instance, and chicken fries. The creative team then branded it unequivocally Burger King by re-creating a figure of "The King," whose face was based on the cap to the helium container the brand had in the past used to inflate balloons for children's birthday parties, which the agency had found on eBay. Critically, the team then extended the concept of "Have It Your Way" from the brand's attitude toward food to its attitude toward life as well. For the mostly blue-collar 18- to 24-year-old target market at the beginning of their working lives, there were not many places in their life that were encouraging them to "have it their own way." But Burger King would be one of them. At the time of this writing, Burger King has enjoyed 26 consecutive quarters of growth, reversing seven straight years of decline.

Hard core here does not simply reflect frequency of visits, of course—it can reflect a different kind of intensity of relationship. Unilever's fabric conditioner brand, Snuggle, in decline and dwarfed in advertising spend by the Market Leader in most of its key geographies, initiated a project to look at how to compete as a Challenger again. Quantitative research showed no real difference between Snuggle's users and those of the Market Leader. But in the qualitative research, the team observed that the Snuggle users were a little more tactile, a little more likely to wear primary colors in the way they dressed, and a little more likely to do things like bake (at home, for school parties, etc.). They seemed, in other words, to be people who were more sensorially motivated, more inclined to make choices by the degree to which those choices gratified their senses. The team called this group "Sensory lovers," and looked at what it would mean to build an identity that would appeal very strongly to them, even if this meant losing another segment of the potential target in doing so.

First they quantified and made sure they understood this group—often looking laterally in their questioning to get a sense of how big a group this kind of person represented (did they buy scented candles, for instance?). Then they developed a Lighthouse Identity around a brand that championed sensory pleasure in clothes, and started developing new products against this identity: products with more intense scents and more richly evocative packaging. The market research team fundamentally rethought the way they developed and tested their products. And the names they gave to their innovation launches projected the sensory intent of this Lighthouse Identity. Building an identity around this very particular group has been critical to Snuggle's success. Stemming its own global share decline, the brand is not simply now growing in a declining market, but has been able at the same time to significantly increase price and profitability, and therefore the abililty to further invest in delivering this identity.

A Lighthouse Isn't Built in a Day

So let's take stock of where we are.

Chapter 5 showed the importance of both clarity on the nature of one's challenge and the initial value of having a clear sense of what one was going to rub up against in the category or in popular culture to get a grip on the public's imagination. We saw how this sense of what one was *opposed* to helped also define what one actually *stood for*—it was in effect the catalyst for becoming clear on the culture and point of view one wanted to challenge instead. In this chapter we have discussed how this point of view is often the projection of a deeper belief system or culture, and the need for that to be founded on a brand or product truth that gives it credibility and ownability, to ourselves and our consumers. As sources for that potential identity, besides the opportunities explored in the previous chapter, we have also examined the potential in the relationship with committed users, and a fresh understanding of our own successful past. And we recognize that the product rock itself, as with Mountain Dew, may not just be a reason to believe, but an inspiration for the larger identity.

Yet reviewing some of these Challengers and the strong identities that they have created can often create in the reader a combination of both inspiration and inadequacy—the sense that while that intense sense of self is indeed what we would like to create, we are some way short of that at the moment. And it is critical to recognize that, if one leaves the artificial world of the retrofitted case history, this sense of identity was rarely fully in place right from conception (or reconception). While some Challengers, like Virgin Atlantic and American Apparel, come out of their corners with the identity more or less complete in their minds from the first bell (though in the case of American Apparel, it was the second time around for Dov Charney, his previous venture having folded a few years earlier), for others the emergence and exact nature of their identity hasn't always been evident straightaway, even to themselves. When Cirque du Soleil, for example, first left its Canadian base and crossed the border into an unambiguously English-speaking audience (the Niagara Falls area), performers carefully changed their name back to something more conventional, translating it into "Circus of the Sun." They were concerned that a U.S. audience might find a French name too outré. The name change proved a disaster: The management was inundated throughout the season with requests for refunds from disappointed customers who had thought from the (translated) name they were paying to see a conventional circus, complete with lion tamers and elephants. Cirque du Soleil learned from this that part of its identity lay in playing up its differences with conventional circuses rather than playing them down, both inside and outside the Big Top. Far from changing its name when it travels, Cirque du Soleil now dramatizes the sense of difference between itself and what the audience is used to seeing. Now every show is completely different in mood and style—not simply from any other circus the audience is familiar with, but even with previous Cirque du Soleil shows that played two years ago.

So we see that the crystallization of where the troupe's center of gravity was, in terms of their identity, was something that became apparent a few years into their journey. And of course, in the previous chapter we looked at a whole group of Challengers who started from a sense of what they rejected and hated (e.g., the "Anti-Banana")—whether about the category or the Market Leader—and then from this clarity about what they were *not* came the clarity about what they actually *were* and what they stood for in their own right. To paraphrase Tom Chappell, they used the competition initially to define themselves to themselves, and from there came to identify the point of view they cared deeply about.

All these stories demonstrate that it isn't necessary for the final identity, that clear point of view, to spring fully formed at birth from the marketing team's temples. But the drive for an identity as a foundation for all other activity does have to be a credo—something one believes in and actively moves toward. Although the identity wasn't always clear for some of these Challengers at the outset, it is something they, unlike Reebok, have sought and moved toward—seeking differentiation from those around them. It has been well observed that once you have the identity established, every other aspect of the brand's communication and behavior should flow out if it. Image, for instance, is often discussed as something that can be invented or reinvented at will. In reality, consumers' noses have evolved: They can smell a fraud (and will now blog about the smell). An image rooted in identity is the difference between reality and marketing posture. This is not to say that the image cannot evolve or offer radically new ways of thinking about the brand, but that it has always to be rooted in the brand's identity rather than being something created or marketed as a discrete entity in itself. Indeed, with Challengers, everything has to flow out of the identity: image, behavior, product innovation—and not least, the internal culture. And this is the reason that founders can be so critical to a Challenger's success—not simply as icons or as focal points for publicity, but because they root the belief system, as well as providing a source for it and continual propagation of it.

Everything Projects

We noted earlier that the impact of a Lighthouse Identity extends far beyond communications.

But clearly it does also impact communications: We said as a Lighthouse we are going to project very consistently and insistently in everything we do. And as we look to do that, let's not think that we are going to simply look for that expression to come in the form of punchy ads or supercharged viral marketing. Both of these would and will be wonderful, but we may perhaps not have the money for either, and certainly we will not want to *rely* on either. We are instead going to look at everything we have as a potential medium.

And, what a number of the iconic Challengers have shown us over the past 10 years is that we all have far more media that we think we do: We just may not be seeing them as media at the moment. Our understanding of packaging, for instance, and how we use it, has undergone a sea change over the past decade. Over here, we see method observing that in a high-visibility location like your bathroom or by your kitchen sink, the packaging is in effect a part of the product, and so the structural aesthetic of the packaging can be a key part of projecting what you stand for, even in a cleaning liquid. Over there, we see VitaminWater using continually changing body copy on its packaging, both to counterbalance with warmth and approachability the *science* of its product delivery and also to build a one-to-one relationship with each user, one bottle at a time.

Our ability and willingness to lean into using media in this way would be enhanced if we all used the frame that innocent does. In the UK, innocent is famous for its informal chattiness (being used strategically, as we noticed earlier, to help make a healthy drink a *want* rather than an *ought*), from the embossing on the bottom of the bottles, to the constantly changing package copy, to the delivery vans in the guise of cows or fields, to the customized displays on its fridges (all grass and daisies). All of these are called "House Media" by innocent—not packaging or vans or fridges, but House Media—materials and objects which you have to produce anyway and which therefore ambitious Challengers could and should be using as media to project what they stand for. One hears a lot of talk these days about brands needing to be media-neutral; this is surely nonsense, at least for a Challenger. What Challengers need to be is media-*positive*—that is, frame the way the organization is seeing everything at its disposal such that everything is a potential medium for projecting what it stands for, what makes it special. Its Lighthouse Identity.

And for a Challenger that is a service brand? Denny Clements, the General Manager of Lexus until his retirement in 2004, expressed it in a slightly different way. He remarked that when he first moved to Lexus from Toyota, where he had been Sales Director, his first question to his new team was, "When's the sales event?" He was initially shocked to find that Lexus did not hold sales events, until he began to take in the real implications of how Lexus was looking to use the quality of the dealer and owner experience to create an entirely new dimension in the luxury car market. "It took me a little while to realize," he said, "that *every customer interaction* was our sales event." They looked to embody a whole new attitude toward customer service at every touch point.

Tourism New Zealand doesn't have packaging in the formal sense, but it still projects who it is and what makes it unique in everything it does. One sees it in the little things—while two of us are interviewing the CEO in Paris, for instance, his phone goes off. The ringtone is nothing we have heard before; "What is it?" we ask. "It's a tui," he says, "a New Zealand bird." One sees it in the way the company punches above its weight in high-profile events. In Valencia, at the opening ceremonies for the America's Cup, all the countries taking part participated by sailing past the watching press, officials, and spectators in their boats, all of which were unremarkable except for the flags of their countries—except for New Zealand. Tourism New Zealand had flown in a Maori war canoe, called a *waka*, that the tattooed crew paddled while singing a Maori song—until they reached the point right in front of the press box, where they put down their oars, stood up, and performed a *haka* (a ceremonial dance of the kind performed by the All Blacks Rugby team before each international). Tourism New Zealand's sense of proactively embodying who it is extends into business relationships, too. We worked on a project with the global Tourism New Zealand team for three days in a Los Angeles hotel (perched on the hard shoulder of the 405 Freeway—about as great a contrast to the essence of New Zealand as it is possible to get); as the workshop closed, the CEO stood and said that, by way of thanks to us all, they would like to close the meeting in a New Zealand way. He led his group in an a cappella Maori song to the three

Americans and Brits sitting, astonished, in chairs 10 feet away; it was one of the most moving experiences of our business lives. These behaviors are not, the Tourism New Zealand team is clear, simply a series of symbols of New Zealand; they are about always looking for a way to offer, at some level, an entire experience of the country, to give people a sense of why New Zealand and what it stands for has an importance to the world. Lighthouse brands are, as we said, inherently media-positive and channel-neutral.

So we can see that when we talk about a brand's identity here, we are not talking about it in the sense of a color range, logo, and other kinds of visual representation that can be visually policed. We are talking instead about its projected *meaning, point of view, or voice*. For example, innocent says that its consistency of identity lies in its *tone*.

New Media Does Not Necessarily Mean Digital Media

One last story: It is a Saturday afternoon, and you are going to buy a pair of jeans. You try a new street, a new shop, pick up three or four pairs you like the look of, and head to the changing rooms. As you pull on the second pair, you become aware that the label at the back is not lying quite as snugly as it might. You put your hand round to adjust it, and realize why: It is about six times as long as a normal label. You try the jeans on, admire yourself in the mirror, and then have a look at this curiously extended label. It is, it seems, a little more than a label. It is a letter, if you like, to you from the brand that makes the jeans, howies (see Figure 6.4). You take the jeans off and read it.

It talks about why pure cotton isn't as pure as you think it is. It talks about how much pesticide the world sprays on cotton, and all the reasons why that is no good for anyone. It talks of pesticide residue in the cotton you wear, and reminds you how nicotine patches work—by releasing chemicals into your body through contact with the skin. It tells you these jeans are made of organic cotton, and that they will cost a little more, but that you'll see why it's best for all sides. You find it unanswerable, compelling. You decide to buy the jeans.

We talk a lot about new media, and we do indeed need to create new media to project what we stand for. But in doing this, let's not confuse new media with digital media. This is a new medium, and a very

FIGURE 6.4 howies' long label.

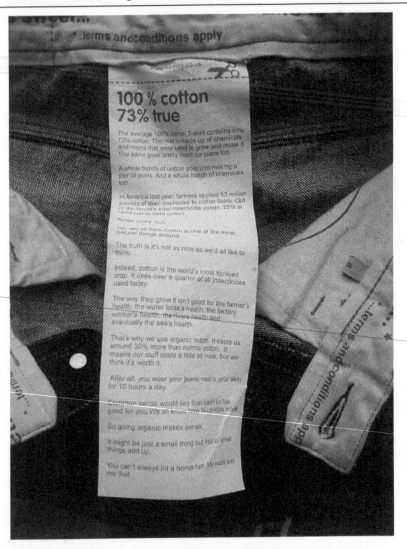

powerful new medium for this particular Challenger, but it has nothing to do with emerging technology. Digital can and will be an important part of what we do, but let's not lose sight of the possibilities of the old in search of the new.

Everything can be a medium, if we choose to see it that way.

CONCLUDING THOUGHTS

At the center of the Lighthouse Identity is a belief-driven point of view about the world. And a point of view that we see evidenced in what brands *do* as well as say. The past decade, by contrast, has also seen a lot of paper tigers—brands aspiring to be Challengers ("Here's what we believe! Go to our web site and read our manifesto!") without any real manifestation in differentiating behavior. But a belief system, if genuinely evidenced in such a way, does indeed create a trust in Lighthouse brands among consumers, a kind of shorthand for them in a world of confusing choices and fragmented meaning. Antonio Lucio, the Global CMO of Visa, argues in fact that Lighthouse brands have become in effect the new gatekeepers—that the trust engendered by the identification of the consumer with what the brand stands for allows it to potentially extend its authority beyond its immediate product field. He points to Oprah Winfrey as one of the most powerful Lighthouse brands of our time—such is the trust in what she represents that mothers will listen to her advice on raising children, even though she has no children of her own.

As the world changes to one of conversation rather than broadcast, we will come to see that Challengers will find different ways to manifest this projection, but they will always take that viewpoint and belief into any interaction and dialogue they have. For instance, the innocent brand has embraced a dialogue with its consumers right from the beginning, but within that dialogue you always know exactly what the brand stands for and what it is committed to.

Because they are based in this point of view, or belief system, Lighthouse Identities do not, at their core, change a great deal over time. They may be faced with new kinds of market dynamics to respond to and new opportunities to meet—they may even be at the center of huge relaunches of the business—but at their heart they remain the same. It is their *implications* that change. One sees Challengers deliberately reinventing themselves regularly—whether that means every decade (Patagonia's Yvon Chouinard says, "Every ten years we have to blow this place up,"[9] and it is now aiming to have a product range that is 50 percent watersports) or every six months (Diesel)—but you know that the core values of Patagonia and Diesel, their Lighthouse Identities, will continue to shine through in their next iteration.

Finally, if we begin to put the first two Credos together to create the first steps of a Challenger process or strategic approach, we suddenly find ourselves with an apparent contradiction: How are we to resolve the tension between the need for knowledge about who you are as a brand or company (building a Lighthouse Identity) and the need for an intelligent innocence regarding the confines and opportunities of the category (breaking with your immediate past)? Both need to exist and be vital within the company in order for the Challenger to flourish—the latter so that we can see the opportunities for growth, and the former so that we can realize and own them—but how? Through process or personnel, we will need to find ways of creating intelligent collisions between knowledge of the brand and inexperience of the category. It is from these collisions that a continual and renewed momentum will come—without them, we will lose our freshness and become stale.

And it is the question of momentum that lies at the heart of the next chapter.

Videolinks for this Chapter:

www.eatbigfishfood.com/etbf/lighthouseidentity

7

THE THIRD CREDO: TAKE THOUGHT LEADERSHIP OF THE CATEGORY

One way of looking at speech is to say that it is a constant strate-gem to cover nakedness.

Sir Harold Pinter[1]

We tend to talk about Brand Leadership as if it were only true of one brand in each category—the largest. In fact, there are two kinds of Brand Leader in each category. One is the Market Leader, the biggest player, the brand everyone lives with—and, chances are, the brand they probably grew up with.

But there is also another type of Brand Leader: the Thought Leader, the brand in the category that everyone talks about. While not the biggest, it is the brand that is getting the most attention. It's the one that is seen to be picking up momentum, entering the popular culture. At one distant point in its life, the existing Market Leader was this brand. But with very few exceptions, once the Brand Leader reaches the top, it stops making waves.[2]

Most of the brands we are looking at effectively made the decision that if they weren't the first of these, they needed to be the other: If they couldn't be the Market Leader, they needed to be the one every-one talked about. The one that was seen to be dynamic, the one with a sensed momentum.

They aimed to achieve Thought Leadership not just through product innovation or advertising strategy, but through *behavior*: by surprising the consumer in selectively breaking not all, but one or two of the conventions of the category they were entering or reentering so late.

BEHAVIOR THAT BREAKS THE CONVENTIONS OF THE CATEGORY

Marketeers surround themselves with rules or conventions that govern the marketing of their product within the category: You have to have some relationship with dentists if you are in toothpaste, for instance; or if in airlines, a livery that impresses. If you are in financial services, you need a serious brand name, unless you are an online bank, when you need to sound funky. Consumers have, it seems, expectations that you have to deliver on to play in the category: If people go to a circus, for instance, they expect elephants, and tamers who put their head into a lion's mouth, and performers on horseback, and clowns with big trousers and flappy shoes who run around and squirt water in each other's faces. If people are going to buy a luxury car, they expect a prestigious marque. And so on.

But the point about these conventions is that they often have little to do anymore with understanding what the consumer really wants, or rather *might want*: They have been invented by marketeers (and the Market Leader) for reasons now forgotten and so, by default, become the status quo. In turn, some secondary brands in each category have eked out a comfortable but unspectacular living by playing to the existing conventions established by the Brand Leader; and this repetition by the Establishment brands has in turn shaped consumers' expectations of how that particular product should be seen and how products of that sort are marketed. The research the established players commission from time to time often confirms the validity of these conventions, because the questioner is too close to the category to ask questions in a way that doesn't presuppose the same old answers, and the consumer has never really seen what else might be on offer.

But a Challenger enters (or reenters) a market late, almost by definition. And in entering late into a market, you have to differentiate yourself more strongly: You have to offer the consumer a powerful reason to choose you.

Finding that strong reason is not easy: While there will be times a genuine product innovation precedes the creation of a brand (such as Dyson, or the blog aggregation tool that became Bloglines), more often now the concept for the brand precedes the notion of the shape and nature of the product.

Category conventions offer a natural point of leverage to create this differentiation: The Challenger has to find a genuinely innovative insight into what the consumer really wants—and then play to that by taking one or two of those conventions and deliberately breaking them in the way it markets itself. This offers short-term leverage as the Challenger enters the market. It also offers an act of drama if that break is highlighted through publicity or advertising. (This is one of the core philosophies behind the martial art of Aikido, where you use your opponent's strength to your advantage.) The length of time the convention has stood and the degree to which the consumer assumes it is just the way the category operates adds to the drama of the convention being genuinely upset. And that is an *act* of drama—I like Pinter's invitation to think of brand *talk* as simply a way of covering up that the brand has nothing really more to offer us than just talk. What we are looking at here, then, for the most part are *acts* of Thought Leadership—a bridge between strategy and action in that they represent things that Challenger brands *do* in order to create a sense that they are the brands setting or resetting the agenda in the marketplace.

It is important to stress that this kind of convention breaking is not just about making a splash to gain attention. While one is certainly looking to be noticed, the short-term aim is also to use that break with convention in order to communicate with impact one's identity and positioning, and further the deepened consumer relationship that will come from that. Longer term, the goal is to reframe the category territory, in particular the consumer's selection criteria, to territory the Challenger has defined itself, and therefore to their own longer-term advantage. Changing the rules in the Challenger's favor.

Let's look at the kinds of conventions that surround any category. They are, essentially:

- *Conventions of Representation.* How you portray yourself.
- *Conventions of Medium.* Where consumers come across you.

- *Conventions of Product Performance.* What your product actually does.
- *Conventions of (product and service) Experience.* What you offer beyond talk or technical performance.
- *Conventions of Neighborhood and Network.* The company you keep, the company that makes you strong.
- *Conventions of Relationship.* Breaking the plane.

As the following examples show, breaks in convention are rarely created through whim or even desire; more often they are forced on Challengers because of limitations in their own resources—typically those of advertising budget, distribution base, or just the time the trade will grant them to build up critical mass before making a decision about their future. Yet the forced change precipitates the very behavior that intrigues and seduces the consumer—as well as changing the rules for everyone else.

Conventions of Representation

Conventions of Representation are those that surround how and where you portray yourself and your identity. These embrace advertising (yogurt advertising always shows a close-up of a spoon going into a mouth), packaging (mineral water is always in clear bottles), logo, those representative figures and codes that categories seem to adopt whole-sale (the celebrity muse in cosmetics/perfume advertising, for instance), and name. (Advertising conventions in and of themselves are not discussed in any detail in this chapter; the reader interested in pursuing the breaking of advertising conventions will find the subject admirably and comprehensively discussed in another volume in this Adweek series, Jean-Marie Dru's *Disruption*.)

The change in conventions of naming has been enormous over the past 20 years, no doubt because the proliferation of new launches has demanded it. We have had banks called egg, drinks called Code Red and 50 Cent, cosmetic brands called Urban Decay, messenger bags called Cheesy Disco and Sticky Date (from Crumpler), and limited edition cars available only in one paint color (Envy Green, from Scion). Each of these has explicitly sought to take a convention of the category (soft drinks must positively romance the new flavor, cosmetics make you look more alluring) and inverted that convention with an irreverent name the brand chose for itself. Each was operating in hugely cluttered marketplaces; each needed a high degree of differentiation to break through; but in this situation, each of them, by breaking convention, signals not just its desire to be different, but also both its identity and its intent to get us to look at the category and the possibilities of the category in a fresh way.

And if we want to be Thought Leaders, we need to consciously *look* for that opportunity in things we are doing already. Heston Blumenthal, the Michelin starred chef, previously only really known among the high-end restaurant fooderati, entered popular consciousness with an appetizer he created and put on his restaurant menu called Snail Porridge. It was immediately seized upon, discussed (and sometimes even eaten) by most of the British newspapers, and Blumenthal positioned alongside this coverage as someone changing the way we think about good food—a Thought Leader in fine cuisine. Snail Porridge was not intended to be either the template for every dish he made or his most popularly ordered item; it was instead one signature product he would consciously offer among his range, one that was intended to position him as the chef leading the agenda in cooking. He had no advertising budget (he had only one restaurant), so he needed to use one of his products, and his name for it, to create that perceived momentum for him.

Examining more closely what Blumenthal did here is instructive for those of us looking to create Thought Leadership ourselves. First, he deliberately created a name that would attract attention because it broke the conventions of representation—in this case, what you would call a dish on a menu in a high-end restaurant. He remarked afterward: "I could have called the porridge 'a fricassee of snails with oat risotto.' No one would have batted an eyelid." But Blumenthal didn't; he deliberately called his dish *snail porridge*. And in calling it this, he broke the convention of representation by choosing a *breakfast* nomenclature for an *evening* dish, attaching it to an unusual ingredient. Oh, and the breakfast nomenclature was for a down-to-earth, humble dish (porridge), which was being served in one of the most expensive restaurants in the United Kingdom. Whereas "fricassee of snails with oat risotto"—using evening language, with a dash of French thrown in, as you would expect a premium restaurant to talk about its food—would, as he himself says, have observed all the conventions of the category, thus ensuring that *exactly the same product* would remain largely unnoticed. The other Blumenthal dish people talk about is his egg and bacon ice cream, which is essentially the same idea: a down-to-earth, savory breakfast item, served up as the key flavor in a dessert for a luxurious dinner.[3]

Thought Leadership is, of course, no substitute for quality: It would be easy to pass off this kind of thing as pretentious frippery if the food weren't also extraordinarily good—as noted in April 2006 when a panel of international experts voted Blumenthal's restaurant, The Fat Duck, the second best in the world. And Blumenthal has now developed a broader reputation as a man with his own unique point of view on cooking, which he calls molecular gastronomy.

Thought Leadership, then, is not just about the wholesale flaunting of convention as an end in itself. If I start a band and call it "Get Cape, Wear Cape, Fly," I am to some degree creating a little publicity for myself because the name is unconventional, but it is not Thought Leadership as such, because there is no deeper intent behind it to challenge the way we think about the possibilities of the music category, nor is there the projection of a deeper identity or purpose. It is simply an eccentric name. Compare this with Dove's *Pro Age* skin care range, conversely, whose Thought Leadership comes from the direct inversion of every convention the category has traditionally represented—antiage, antiwrinkle, anticellulite—that is, being *against* everything that age brings. For a brand to invert that convention and lean into a product that helps, in effect, celebrate the beauty of age, and *then* to call it something that challenges the conventions of representation in the category, is to create an act of Thought Leadership in the category. It is anchored in a deliberate intent, born from its unique Lighthouse Identity.

For other Challengers, walking away from the conventions of the types of *icons* that typify a category has been a more defining part of the brand identity than the name. So the convention in the cosmetics category is to choose a "face" for the brand, almost invariably someone who is young, Caucasian, and female, and often without a great deal of personality of her own (the easier to write on it your own brand values). Yet in launching its signature Viva Glam range, MAC cosmetics certainly chose a muse, but one who robustly defied this convention. Instead of a young, bland, Caucasian female, MAC chose a highly characterful, male African American drag artist: RuPaul. This was not through a desire to be the cosmetic equivalent of a shock jock, but because MAC needed to be the Thought Leader in order to break through, and this choice in fact spoke to its Lighthouse Identity about inclusiveness, and indeed its original roots in providing makeup for the Toronto drag scene. The faces subsequently used by MAC for Viva Glam included Sir Elton John, who is not technically female, either, and k.d. lang, who uses neither makeup nor capitals.

The opportunity to selectively and intelligently break conventions of representation extends further into the key codes and cues that have become the landmarks of the category and that helps consumers navigate it. New World wines are a case in point: Of course, they targeted a different kind of drinker at a different price point (initially, at least), and of course the product was a good one—startlingly good, particularly to the Old World wine producers. But this new generation of winemakers also famously changed the way the category talked about itself. Instead of the arcane complexities of the *terroir* the wine came from and the reputation of the shipper, the New World winemakers changed the way one navigated the category by emphasizing instead the kind of grape used: shiraz, chardonnay, cabernet. This change of convention was continued into the way the brands selling those wines represented themselves as brands: names such as Dead Arm, Two Hands Bad Impersonator, and Le Cigare Volant reflecting very different ways of talking about yourself from "Chateau Ladidah 1999." And the visual iconography that then accompanies those kinds of brand names is, of course, very different to the familiar images of chateaux and vines that continue to populate the wine labels of France. The Old World, depositioned and a long way from Thought Leadership, has suffered: Around 84,000 commercial growers in France alone are thought to have left the business between 1994 and 2003.

Conventions of Medium

Conventions of medium concern the way the brand is delivered, both physically and emotionally. They encompass distribution (music, for instance, is always sold through music stores, whether brick or online), message delivery (discount stores advertise in downmarket periodicals), and physical packaging structure.

People expect individual categories to express themselves in particular kinds of media, so the dilemma a Challenger faces is this: Do we play in the same media in order to be seen as a legitimate contender in the category and accept a low share of voice because of the presence of other players there? Or do we leave the beaten path and derive a possible (but perhaps uncertain and short-lived) advantage by appearing in a context the consumer does not associate with the category we are attempting to enter (or reenter)?

Often, the decision is forced on a Challenger; it cannot afford the convention—it cannot afford three flights of television advertising every six months, for instance, rotating five spots at a time. As we have already observed, however, the breakthrough comes not in simply realizing that we have to play in a medium where we can be more visible, but in realizing that there is, by the same token, an opportunity to use the unconventional nature of that new medium to our own advantage.

method's use of structural packaging as a key part of its brand offer obviously came from its sense of the opportunity in home care, yet at the same time it didn't have money to advertise—the brand would have to speak for itself from the shelf. And so, method didn't just choose to make the bottle look a *little* nicer; the company deliberately chose a famous designer, Karim Rashid, to introduce an *entirely new level* of design aesthetic in home care (Thought Leadership is as much to do with degree as direction).

Moving farther east, T-box is a Turkish clothing brand launched in 2003 that has used highly unusual packaging and distribution to create a brand with a lot of momentum—but built around very simple pieces, even basic clothing. White T-shirts are sold in highly compressed cubes a couple of inches across; hats come in packaging that looks like wrapped candy. Boxers, flip-flops, beach towels, and blouses have followed, in packaging that looks like ice cream or lollipops. T-box's distribution is equally unusual: Its 1,500 purchase points range from vending machines (where the change is prepacked into the T-shirt) to luxury stores to a range of spontaneous purchase locations, from gas stations to malls, but the brand also pushes into one-off retail outlets, like sailboats, that sell T-box products to vacationers out on the water. Where

T-box has actual retail space, it can be tiny, and takes the form of metallic walls onto which the highly compressed T-box packages are stuck like so many fridge magnets. "Convention of medium" then, does not refer solely to the medium of communication. Interpreted in the broader sense of "where you are," it can also encompass product location: where the consumer finds you, and unusual forms of dispense. These ideas will flow naturally from the fresh perspective on the category you are looking to bring: If you see Juicy Tubes lipstick as "candy for your lips," it will be a relatively short step to launch them displayed on giant candy sticks.[4]

Thought Leadership in packaging and distribution fuels T-box's reputation as a cool brand, even though it is selling everyday, low-ticket items.

To take a different kind of packaging, consider Puma and the way it has packaged its sports stars. Puma has chosen, as a sports brand with a much smaller presence and marketing armory than the bigger players, to put a strong fashion and lifestyle element into the brand's offer. This fashion element extends into its involvement in sport, and so when Puma "packages" its players, it looks for Thought Leadership. For the 2004 African Cup of Nations, Puma proposed all-in-one green-and-red body suits (subsequently banned) for one of the favorites, the flamboyantly talented Cameroon team. If you missed this, then what you will have noticed (because the world's press did) was the Puma costume of Serena Williams in the 2002 U.S. Open. The conventions of tennis clothing are fairly straightforward: white clothing, relatively loose to allow freedom of movement, and the player themselves in these clothes positioned primarily as sports stars. Puma, however, outfitted Williams in a black, body-hugging catsuit made of Lycra (though it could have passed for rubber). The dominatrix went on to win the tournament, and Puma rode how it broke the conventions of tennis attire to further build its reputation as a Thought Leader in its category.

So we see that breaking these conventions can be an integral, permanent, and primary part of how you achieve your desired momentum (T-box) or simply a smaller-scale idea that is one part of your bigger ongoing ambition to be the Thought Leader in the category. These acts can be integral to the core presentation of the brand, or at the edges. So Veuve Clicquot keeps its champagne bottle shape and graphics always the same, but is continuously introducing new kinds of playfully theatrical outer packaging, such as an enormous paint can, always in the brand's signature yellow. Lush has begun to pack its mail-order products not in conventional filler but in popcorn. Why? Being 60 percent lighter than shredded paper, Lush saves 10 percent on shipping costs, and popcorn offers a sensual dimension to something as previously unremarkable as packaging filler—a sensual pleasure that is entirely in keeping with what its customers know and love about Lush. Guests for fashion shows by John Galliano, the British designer who is currently creative director of Dior, have received their invitations in forms as unusual as a red-satin ballet shoe, a school report for Miss Suzy Sphinx, a poster advertising an amateur boxing competition, a bullet in sand. Through the unexpected medium of his invitations, Galliano creates standout in a crowded season and heightens anticipation among a generally blasé press audience for the creative content of his shows.

And, of course, in terms of one's message, *context* can and should be as critical as the nature of the message itself—so when one comes across Target, a discount store, advertising not just in inexpensive downmarket weeklies but in the upmarket *New York Times Magazine*, the impact is even greater. And we can see, through the Target example, that one of the primary reasons for changing the conventions of the medium in particular is to create a *fresh level of engagement* with your message. It is not simply our familiarity with the kinds of messages that blunts their impact; it is that we are always seeing within the category the same kinds of messages *in all the same kinds of places*. Usually, we look as Challengers to changing the message to create breakthrough; as often, it can be about giving the same kind of message in an entirely different kind of medium or context. (Though this may not stay different for very long—by the time the fourth car company has set up a showroom in Second Life, the opportunity for Thought Leadership has long passed. To maintain momentum, we need to continually revisit and refresh.)

Let's conclude this section by looking at an example of how to break through by changing the convention of the medium in a far, far tougher communications arena than most of us have to face: that of teaching math to teens in a school classroom. Within education, there is increasing prominence given to teachers who are using fresh thinking to engage pupils in subjects historically thought to be dull. In the United

States, one of the most striking examples of this has been a math teacher who was held up by a national newspaper as the Thought Leader in her field because she is changing the convention of the writing medium in her classes: She is teaching her pupils polynomial equations (what some students might be forgiven for regarding as potentially rather dry and uninvolving subject matter) using shaving foam. She has found that getting them to write a polynomial equation in a writing material that is inherently fun, messy, and three-dimensional—a substance that, when used for writing, you cannot help but engage with—helps them pay attention to, engage with, and remember the subject. We might be tempted to think this is an interesting but irrelevant bit of color in this chapter, but there is an argument to be made that it is in fact the most relevant and important example of all: that if you remember just one example, this should be it. Because to some degree, if we are in the business of being Challengers, then we are all also in the education or reeducation business. We all have to "educate" consumers (or stimulate them to reeducate themselves) to think that there is a whole new criterion for choice in the market other than the ones the Market Leader has been teaching them for years. And perhaps we all need to make our reeducation as engagingly three-dimensional—and even as messy—as this teacher is making math. In doing so, we make ourselves not simply understood, but we become Thought Leaders in *the way* we made ourselves understood.

Conventions of Product Performance

These are conventions of pure performance: what your product does, over and above what it is expected to do (rather than the experience it wraps around it). Recently, we have seen the advent of hybrid technology cars give Thought Leadership to Toyota with both its Prius model and its luxury hybrids. The performance was vividly dramatized with the Prius itself on the central screen that also housed the satellite navigation system—press a button and you could watch the flow of power to the car switch between the gasoline and electric motors, brilliantly dramatizing for driver and passenger alike the invisible, barely understood feature and its benefits. For the early Prius driver, it was in many ways this dramatization of the product performance, on top of the performance itself, that gave a sense that the Prius brand was ahead of the pack.

Bang & Olufsen has for years had a relatively small but premium share of the audiovisual electronics market. One of its great strengths has been its ability to create an almost visceral desire for its products, partly through the beauty of their design, but partly through extraordinary functionality—functionality that goes beyond anything we would expect in the piece of equipment we are considering.

Sometimes this has to do with standards. So, on the BeoSound 9000, that wonderful-looking CD player Bang & Olufsen sells (even in an iPod world) with six CDs displayed in a line, two particular engineering standards stand out. The first is that when each disc stops playing, even if you have programmed the machine to shuffle between the CDs track by track, it will always stop spinning with the disc in exactly the same position as it was when it started. That is to say that if you line up your six discs so the image on each disc is "the right way up," each will always return there when not in motion. Why? Because the visual impact of six discs being visually aligned in the way you want and originally intended is as important to Bang & Olufsen as the audio impact. The second striking engineering standard is that the design brief for the engineers was that the moving laser unit had to take no longer to go from one CD to another CD, find the right track, and start playing it, than it would have taken simply to have gone onto the next track on the same CD (which, on average, is two seconds). To achieve this between the two outermost CDs, the laser unit needs to be able to move at a speed faster than a Ferrari to the new CD in order to locate and play the next track without the listener noticing any difference. And it is the comparison with the Ferrari that they will make to you when you demo the product, and that you go on to tell your friends when you buy it.

However, sometimes the ability of their extraordinary engineering to create Thought Leadership surprises even Bang & Olufsen. The BeoLab 5 speakers (shown in Figure 7.1, on either side of the BeoSound 9000) are designed to "measure" your room according to size and object placement, and to calibrate the appropriate level of bass, mid, and treble they should be producing accordingly to give you the optimum listening experience. To activate this, the owner presses a button on the individual speaker, and a sonic probe emerges from the speaker before,

FIGURE 7.1 Bang & Olufsen's BeoLab 5 speakers with BeoSound 9000.

batlike, emitting three different levels of sounds from which it makes its measurement and readjusts its outputs for you. In developing the motor for this sonic probe, the B&O engineers looked at how often people would significantly change rooms or move to a new house so that they knew what kind of life to engineer into the motor that moved the probe in and out. Would it be 12 times? Surely no more than 20? They set to work accordingly.

But within months of the new speaker being launched, Bang & Olufsen's customer support staff reported that customers were claiming that their probes were no longer working. How could this be, the company asked itself? Surely these customers weren't redesigning their living rooms every two weeks? No, they weren't—something else was happening altogether. When you bought a new pair of BeoLab 5 speakers, you became very keen to show them off to your friends. You would ask them to come for a drink or dinner, and they would be struck by the exquisite design and the wonderful sound. Then you, the proud owner, would show them something a little more. Look, you would say, here's the most amazing thing: It actually has a little thingamajig that measures the size of the room. Watch. And you would press the button, the probe would come out, make its intriguing sonic probing noises, and retreat into itself again. Holy cow, your friend would say. Impressive, isn't it? You would casually agree, giving it a proud little pat. And once you had shown it to 30 or 40 friends individually over a six-month period, the motor would give up, and you would, rather baffled, ring up your local Bang & Olufsen dealer.

So it is a potent thing, Thought Leadership. Make sure you are pre-pared for the consequences of it.

Conventions of Product and Service Experience

Conventions of product experience have to do with the experience sur-rounding the product or service rather than the actual performance of the product itself. At a simple level, the original sound of a Ping putter was one way a Challenger built experiential difference in a familiar cate-gory. At a more sophisticated level, the range of applications through which one could engage with one's network on Facebook is one of the elements of the user experience that gave it such social velocity and Thought Leadership. And if I tell you that Eurostar (the train service con-necting London, Paris and Brussels) has a new station, St. Pancras, that offers not just a champagne bar, but the longest champagne bar in Europe, that makes you stop, think, and perhaps even talk. A train sta-tion? But aren't train stations always such functional, in-and-out places? And champagne bars are places normally associated with an entirely dif-ferent level of experience than the mundanity of normal train travel. Which is, of course, exactly the point for Eurostar, in its desire to be the Thought Leader in European travel.

So it may be that one pushes for Thought Leadership by changing the convention of the *experience* one wraps around the product. This indeed has been the driver behind the extraordinary revival of cider in the UK alcoholic drinks market. As a traditional, apple-based alcoholic drink, cider was for years the cheapest and most palatable way for British teenagers to get drunk—and, at the other end of the UK citizen's life-span, it was a relatively cheap way to stay drunk once luck and society had abandoned you to the streets. Between these two inevitable life stages was the everyday marketing challenge—how to position cider as a credible mainstream alternative to beer. It would be hard to quantify the marketing and creative brainpower and money expended between 1970 and 2005 trying to pimp the cider market and its constituent brands to young, mainstream beer drinkers without ever really changing the image of the drink or the size of the market.

And then came Magners, which launched in the United Kingdom as a premium packaged cider (the first in a new segment for the category), accompanied by a glossy bottle and some unremarkable advertising that talked about naturalness, apple blossoms, and conviviality. So far, so unexciting. What really captured the consumer's imagination, though, was that as a central part of this mix, Magners introduced an entirely new way to drink cider—in a pint glass, full of ice, with the liquid poured from the bottle through the ice to chill it through. This introduction of a new experiential element added three important components that cider had been missing: First, it chilled the liquid, making the taste both more accessible and more in line with the trend in lagers to be served "extra cold"; second, it created an entirely new way to drink a "session pint," with enormous bar visibility; third, filling the pint beer glass with ice meant that the pourer always had some left in the bottle afterward, which then remained by the pint, branding this experience to those around the drinker. This change in the convention of the drinking experience gave Magners enormous momentum and appeal among a much broader group of young beer drinkers who had never taken cider seriously before. The brand went on to become the best-selling packaged long alcoholic drink in bars and pubs, outselling all premium packaged beers, and in its two key markets went on to become one of the top 10 drinks, even including draught beers. Its success has grown the category 10 percent, while beer as a whole is down. (Its key challenge now is how to retain share in a category that has copied this innovative experience wholesale.)

This fundamental change in the user experience is more profoundly seen in Nintendo's Wii. Always sedentary, gaming was becoming longer, more involving, more complex, more time-consuming, more expensive. In Chapters 9 and 10, we discuss the nature of the sacrifice and overcommitment represented by Wii, but let's note here how it highlighted the change it championed in the conventional user experience (from static, solo, and silently immersed to noisy, social physicality) through the events it publicized, the kinds of people it brought in (grannies and moms representing the enthusiast gamers of the brand)—and even a new word: *exergaming*, meaning "gaming that helps you exercise." What exergaming represented had been an ambition of game developers for years, but games that historically needed specialized equipment to play them had only been seriously adopted by (for some reason) competitive professional cyclists. But now, with Wii, people of all ages were suddenly on their feet "playing tennis," even to the point where people were starting to promote weight-loss programs using a regular regime of Wii gaming. And Wii Fit shortly followed.

We do not have to reengineer our entire product experience, however. Sometimes it is the conventions of the preparation ritual or the elements that accompany the experience that lend themselves to being redefined. In the world of spirits, for instance, Hendrick's bills itself as "a most unusual gin." Launched in the United States in 2000 (and in the United Kingdom three years later), it aims to challenge, not the Old World gins of Gordon's and Beefeater, but the new premium brands such as Bombay Sapphire and Tanqueray No. Ten. There are many ways to make a cocktail with gin, but the standard gin and tonic is an experience that has been made up of the same four ingredients for over a hundred years: gin, tonic, ice, and a slice of lemon. But Hendrick's, having already given its product a different taste through an infusion of rose petals and cucumber, wanted to create a unique experience even within this apparently finite confine—change the experience and change the ritual. So they substituted the slice of lemon with a visibly different kind of slice—one of cucumber: vegetable for fruit, green for yellow, gentle refreshment for bite and zest. Is this a shift Hendrick's has tried to build the whole brand positioning around? No. But is it something that creates conversation among consumers of premium gin, who are always looking not simply for fresh brands, but fresh thinking and fresh experience around those brands? Yes. It is a small, but highly distinctive and ownable piece of Thought Leadership in the world of gin. A little momentum behind the new Challenger.

In a service business we see exactly the same options open to us: either a fundamental reengineering of the category's service offer, which will bring us Thought Leadership, or the deliberate creation of individual service "products" within our overall service experience specifically designed (a service equivalent of snail porridge, if you like) to break with the conventions of expected experience and position us as the brand that, in big or small ways, is the brand to watch in the category. For the first of these we see Lexus, for instance, which became the Thought Leader in the U.S. luxury car market by offering a superb car, certainly, but which fundamentally broke through in the United States by deliberately changing the conventions of the ownership experience. For the second, let's look at Virgin Mobile in Australia. Fourth in its market, the brand was launched in 2000, with a Lighthouse Identity centering on an attitude—being free-spirited. Around this core thought, the brand deliberately built Thought Leadership by offering a series of services that, while not always intended to be income generators themselves, were designed to continually position Virgin Mobile as the brand in the market that really understood how its free-spirited users both used and abused their phones. "Dialing Under the Influence," for example, was a service introduced in response to a survey the brand had done of its unmarried users, which showed that if you went out with your friends on a Friday or Saturday night and got a little overrefreshed, you were twice as likely to call your ex-partner as you were your current partner—and that, if you did, no good would come of it. The new service, DUI, allowed you to bar outgoing calls to designated numbers on your phone between the hours of 11 p.m. and 6 a.m. to save you from yourself when, well, you weren't quite yourself, so to speak. How many people used the service? A relatively limited number. How many discussed it with their friends—("Who would you bar?")—in the pub on a Friday night? Rather more. How many felt that this was a phone company that understood how they really used and abused a phone? A much greater number. This has been one of a stream of services designed to generate Thought Leadership. So the brand went on to launch its SOS service, whereby if you find yourself on a bad date, you can dial 767 (SOS), hang up, and within minutes Virgin Mobile will return your call with an excuse to leave (even talking you through what to say). And, from the insight that people have all sorts of good intentions to remember people's birthdays and other key events, but just forget, the company launched a service whereby you can prepare text messages to send at the later, relevant date. Each of these services is based on an insight about how Virgin Mobile's free-spirited users live and communicate, for better or worse, but each breaks with the generic phone services and offers we have come to expect from the telecommunications giants. Why? Because the Market Leaders are offering services that make us as humans more productive, often based on "what our technology can do"; Virgin Mobile, on the other hand, is very pointedly offering services based on the kinds of human frailty that make life worth living.

And herein lies the bigger point for us. We all think that becoming a service brand is going to require real estate and large amounts of customer service people. It isn't. What the Virgin Mobile example illustrates is that you can create a series of small-scale, relatively small take-up services that still have enormous value, because the insight they display in the way they break the conventions captures the imagination of a much broader group of users and potential users, and positions them as the Thought Leaders in the category.

Finally, if we look at Challenger country brands, we can see Dubai's momentum in the world's imagination coming through in exactly such acts of Thought Leadership. Yes, Dubai's engineers are building what will be (for a while) the world's tallest building, the Burj Dubai, but this is not what sticks in our mind about the city. The two things the person in the street knows Dubai for are buildings and properties that break the conventions of representation and experience. The Burj Al Arab, built in the shape of a billowing sail (a nod to Dubai's trading past) positions itself as the first seven-star hotel—two more than the five stars we thought had been the very peak of hotel quality. (Hmm, interesting—what is our equivalent of the industry standard five-star rating, and what is our equivalent of creating a new scale two stars above it?) And the Palm Jumeirah is a series of artificial islands in the shape of a palm tree, offering an entirely new experience around beachside holiday homes. Effectively doubling Dubai's coastline, it has been followed by The World, a series of artificial islands imitating a map of the world, four kilometers offshore.

Why is this kind of behavior important for a Challenger? Eurostar's Greg Nugent talks about Thought Leadership being not so much a way of simply generating publicity as "a shortcut to the future," a perceptual bridge to where you would like to be positioned within the category in the future. In the case of Eurostar, the champagne bar we sat in a few pages ago signals a desired perceptual transition that Eurostar is making, from being "as good as flying" to "the future of European travel." In the case of Dubai, Sheik Mohamed bin Rashid al-Maktoum wants to increase the run of double-digit growth in his small country until its GDP hits $108 billion (projected in 2015). Yes, much of this will come from tourism; but, as important, 25 percent of the Fortune 500 global companies have decided to locate their regional headquarters in Dubai. There is for Dubai a considerable financial advantage in being the Thought Leader.

Increasingly, then, Challengers compete and succeed by being in the experience business: the anticipation and the delivery of an experience that breaks the category convention.

Conventions of Neighborhood and Network

The fifth convention we can break is that of neighborhoods and networks—who we partner with to create our unique offer. This partner can be another brand, another organization, a different network, or our user community itself.

This type of Thought Leadership is a little different from our other potential sources, because very often these kinds of new relationships are obviously formed for different and more fundamental reasons than the desire to create perceived momentum. Usually the primary role of the strategic alliance or community is something much more profound than this—an essential leverage, authority, distribution, or source of content creation for the better realization of the brand's potential or our core purpose. Thus we see Mayor Bloomberg of New York teaming up with other mayors to commit to Kyoto targets even though the Bush administration would not. Or Heston Blumenthal (he of the snail porridge), launching a project with the Royal Society of Chemistry to set up a new subject in schools called Kitchen Chemistry, in which children will, among other things, learn how to use liquid nitrogen to make ice cream. Panasonic's embracing of Leica lenses represented for the former, as a Challenger in cameras, an intriguingly unexpected juxtaposition of the most respected brand in old-fashioned (i.e., pre-digital) camera optics married to a huge electronics company; in a very real sense, it was the startling nature of this marriage that caught our attention—one then delivered in the quality of the images. MoveOn.org's ability to raise money from a grassroots network rather than Big Business in the 2000 elections helped put nine new people (four senators and five house members) into power in Washington. And we are all familiar with the brands that have grown their footprints, communities, and offers through user-generated content.

Now MoveOn.org, Bloomberg, and Blumenthal are not interested in doing what they do primarily to be Thought Leaders. They want to influence thoughts and actions, and they are doing it this way because they have found a new model to create sufficient muscle and mass to exert leverage on issues and politicians. Yet the *effect* of this is to make each of them a Thought Leader, even if the primary intent was something more fundamental. As the power of the community becomes more mainstream, the *fact* of this kind of community strength, of course, will become unremarkable. Instead, the unique ways the community forms and shares, and the social objects it attaches itself to, will be the elements that distinguish it.

Conventions of Relationship

On the business-conference speaking circuit, one of the differences one often notices between A-list speakers (the ones who cost $50,000 to hire for an hour) and B-list speakers (the ones who cost somewhat less than that) is the degree to which the former "break the plane." *Breaking the plane* in this particular sense has nothing to do any incidental damage to aviation equipment, but rather their preparedness to move through the invisible, yet still very real, barrier at the front of the stage between the audience and the performer. Convention says that the performer stays on one side of this invisible plane and the audience stays on the other. A-list list speakers don't observe this rule, though. They like to physically mingle, to interact; they ask questions, poke and prod their audience. Someone falling asleep? Turn the lights on them. Someone getting cocky? Call 'em out.

Breaking the plane in this context creates a different kind of energy in the room, if the speaker does it well. It creates in equal measure intimacy (we are in effect being treated as a group of individuals, and a dialogue is being created rather than a mass communication) and a simultaneous discomfort ("I hope to God they don't pick on me in front of everyone else"). It demands more involvement; it creates more connection with person and message; it fosters memorability. Worth every cent.*

"Breaking the plane" is a common way Challengers have created Thought Leadership by breaking the convention of relationship in a range of different fields. In the field of music, it is easy now to dismiss Iggy Pop as an aging curio, but you have to remember the profound effect he had early in his career, not just on the nature of the music business (the arrival of The Stooges just after Woodstock was arguably a first death knell for Sixties flower power and the music that accompanied it), but also on the nature of how rock front men performed. He was the first white singer to deliberately and provocatively break the plane, to get down in among the crowd while performing—and effectively invent crowd surfing at the same time in order to get back on stage again. While crowds now expect and welcome this from their rock gods, it was hugely polarizing at the time—some in his early audiences felt very uncomfortable, and others were enormously excited to find themselves suddenly in the same space as such a charismatic and physically dynamic performer. It was one of the elements that gave Stooges concerts an entirely different energy from other performers at the time.

These kinds of barriers, these invisible planes, with their different kinds of physical expression and visibility, have historically existed between all kinds of brands and their consumers. And one of the ways Challengers seek to create Thought Leadership is to productively break them. Banks and the banking culture is an obvious example—which is why we can see a Challenger bank, for instance, breaking the plane by having a terminal for accessing a customer's information that requires the customer to come around to the *same side* as the service agent removing the "plane"/barrier between them, and thereby a working relationship of closeness and equality. In fact, in a more metaphysical sense, the increasing visibility and celebration of the people involved in the creation of brands, which is starting to become visible even in packaged goods, is the beginning of a different kind of plane being broken, one where the consumer is being invited to become a part of the community that the brand represents, rather than merely a buyer of something the brand is selling, which leaves them standing on the opposite side of the transactional table. We do not have to go

---

* The perceptive reader will perhaps detect a certain enviousness at this point.

as far as Threadless.com, where all the T-shirts sold are designed by their consumers. We can simply look at the communities a Scion or an innocent creates to see the power of this kind of Thought Leadership.

Finally, breaking the plane, and the kind of participation it invites, is clearly a two-way affair—just as the performer can move into the crowd, so members of the crowd may be invited up on the stage, to contribute ideas to the future of the brand and the company behind it.

And sometimes, if the brand performer either entrances or outrages them, the dynamic power of a new world of blogging and social networks means they will, in effect, simply storm that stage anyway.

SOME MISCONCEPTIONS ABOUT CONVENTION BREAKING

Breaking convention has become a hot topic. But it is not wholesale rule breaking that the Challenger should aspire to. Rather, the Challenger needs to understand which conventions of representation, medium, or experience *to break* and which *to observe*.

Lexus, for example, changed some of the conventions of product experience but deliberately decided to keep other conventions of representation. The changes were forced on the company; it found in its development research that the five key attributes wanted by American luxury buyers were prestige, safety, resale value, performance, and styling, in that order. But Lexus could not compete on prestige or resale value immediately, so it focused on the last of these—performance and styling. By breaking the conventions of the product experience, Lexus redefined luxury. The resulting product, at the resulting price point, redefined what a luxury car should be.

But the Lexus launch team didn't throw out every convention in the process of redefining luxury. There was, for instance, a fierce debate within the team about whether to include a grille on the new car. Many on the Lexus design team preferred to leave out the grille—and indeed, the motoring press itself, expecting something more iconoclastic, expressed astonishment at some of the early shows when the grille was revealed on the new car. But the most senior members, including Kunihiro Uchida, the chief designer, mandated it.

In an interview afterward, Uchida was asked why he decided to include a grille—many journalists felt that a car without a grille would have been a more futuristic car; he replied that he was confident that a luxury car should have a grille. He realized that, in effect, a Challenger couldn't break every rule at once; his new car needed to anchor itself in certain conventions of representation in order to allow the broken conventions of product experience to be of mass interest.

A second misconception about convention breaking is that it will usually be welcomed or understood by our consumer without explanation. Yet often there is a real risk that the consumer may simply be confused by the change of convention, particularly if it is a convention that they had become comfortable with. So for instance, when Southwest Airlines was forced to offer open seating (i.e., sitting wherever you like rather than having an assigned seat), a number of passengers initially found this so unfamiliar as to be confusing and off-putting. So Southwest recognized this difficulty and helped its customers make the transition by framing it to them in a way that used as a reference point something similar that they *were* already familiar with: "It's open seating," Southwest told them, "like in church." Their customers were immediately much more comfortable with the convention change—because while unconventional in flying it was conventional in another category they participated in every Sunday morning.

A third, natural concern about convention breaking is that Thought Leadership through unconventional practice may forfeit conventionally desired attributes, notably quality ratings. Yet the reality is that the whole nature of what quality does and does not mean is shifting dynamically under our feet. Just look at how sustainability, citizen journalism, and YouTube have started to change our criteria for how we judge quality. If an organic carrot is grown 30 miles away, but is a little misshapen and muddy, is that now a low-quality carrot or a high-quality carrot? Is quality news reporting now about a smartly dressed news reporter talking at the scene an hour after the event, or does quality instead lie in rough footage from a camera phone taken by an amateur while the event was happening? (Or perhaps not by an amateur, but by a professional, but not a professional camera operator—a professional soldier, broadcasting from a video camera mounted on his helmet in Afghanistan or Iraq?) Is quality in news today, that is to say, about analyzed presentation, the meshing of the news with the viewpoint, or instead the transparently immediate record of the event? And if you look at YouTube's impact on our perception of quality entertainment, what is the definition of *quality* its product experience represents? Is there any consistency in the quality, in fact, of the most-watched items? And the answer is that there is, but it has nothing to do with the quality of the production values (the old definition of televisual quality). The consistency here is in the quality of the idea (or the *pass-on-ability*) that the clip represents. Expensive TV ads rub shoulders with poorly shot but hugely captivating films of fans crying over Britney. Entire notions of quality in terms of how a category talks are being overturned.

Finally, there is sometimes confusion between selectively breaking with certain conventions and simply being outrageous. The second of these does indeed have its followers, and there is a school of thought that argues, with some justice, that if you cannot afford a great deal of paid-for advertising, you should strive to do something provocative that gets you free coverage in media (we discuss the use of publicity further in Chapter 11). But in talking here about changing conventions of media or experience, for example, we are going far beyond discussing advertising aimed at generating publicity; we are not looking simply for attention, but the deliberate creation of sensed momentum. A brand that is resetting the agenda in the category.

THOUGHT LEADERSHIP AND BEHAVIOR

The third credo, then, is that of assuming Thought Leadership of the category. This is begun by deliberately breaking some of the conventions of the category while rooting yourself in others.

In most of the cases we have looked at, the breaking of convention was forced on the brands—usually because they lacked the money or pedigree to go the conventional route. But they turned this into an advantage by changing the relationship the consumer had come to take for granted between the product and the way it represented itself, or the product and the medium it used, or the product and the experience it offered.

The result has been to define the rules in their favor. The success of Lexus has meant all the other luxury brands in the United States had to raise their customer service experience. Virgin Atlantic's entertainment offering in economy class was the catalyst for British Airways to overhaul its own. One of the results of the Wii launch is that now the other video game manufacturers are trying to follow Nintendo into this broader demographic—the December after the Wii launch in the United Kingdom saw Xbox, for instance, doing advertorials to demonstrate how much family fun its console and games could be.

The payback for Thought Leadership may not always be as immediate or as measurable as some of our other initiatives. If we are looking to create it through limited-edition packaging, for example, the economics of the packaging payback may not make sense in absolute volume terms for the limited run it accompanies. We have to judge it instead by the broader impact it has on our sensed momentum.

Finally, we have to be aware that such leadership may not always meet with universal acceptance in the beginning. Thought Leaders are not always embraced by everyone at the same time. Stepping back a moment into the marketing of music, for instance, consider the early days of Elvis. While Elvis is now a figure at the center of U.S. music history, in reality, the early years were difficult. The man who launched Elvis, the legendary Sam Phillips, was unashamedly looking for a fusion that would break the musical conventions of the time—a white man with a black sound. The salient images of Elvis may now be of a sedate, middle-aged man playing to blue rinses in Vegas, but what Elvis unleashed in addition to the sound that Sam Phillips sought in the beginning was something very different. His stage act for "Hound Dog" was banned as being too inflammatory. Radio stations received death threats for playing his music; the Parent-Teacher Association called it "vulgar, animalistic noise," and the King a "rock and roll bum" and "a sex maniac." Police filmed his shows, and a year and a half after the release of "It's All Right, Mama," he was still being introduced on programs as "the most controversial name in rock and roll."

The success of Thought Leadership should be measured initially, then, by a more intense relationship with one's core target rather than by its immediate mass-market appeal.

Videolinks for this Chapter:

www.eatbigfishfood.com/etbf/thoughtleadership

THE FOURTH CREDO: CREATE
SYMBOLS OF RE-EVALUATION

One morning a group of television journalists are sitting around in the BBC canteen, brainstorming possible television programs they could make. And they come up with an idea: They will challenge one of their number, Nick Ross, to make the most boring subject in the world interesting, on national television. Take something people really don't care about at all and get them genuinely involved in it. Oh, they add, and one more thing, "We get to choose this boring subject that you have to make interesting." And after a little more conversation they come up with the topic of Road Safety.

Road safety in the United Kingdom—or anywhere, really—is something that the great British public (aside from the victims and their families) and in reality the great British legislators have no real interest in at all. Most ordinary people are pretty complacent about it—they already look both ways when crossing the road, and they are a bit more aware about alcohol and car keys these days—you know, doing their bit. And the authorities for their part felt at the time that they were doing enough as well: Road deaths were holding steady at around 6,000 a year, which wasn't too bad, and very much in line with other countries. All parties were in a comfortable rut; there were bigger things to worry about. Life—and death—went on.

134

So this journalist, Nick Ross, accepted the challenge. And, as he explored it further, he became genuinely and personally involved in the question of how one could reduce the number of deaths on British roads by snapping the public and the authorities out of the complacent rut they were in. Being a television journalist, he did indeed plan to put a piece of film at the very center of his response to the challenge, but he realized that if he were to really get all sides to sit up and take notice, a program on its own couldn't be the only element of his response. So he developed a three-part strategy to puncture the complacency of road users and legislators alike.

First, he decided he would need to reframe the whole concept of what was happening. He realized if people would not engage with the topic of road safety, then he would need to set the annual statistics— almost an abstract number as far as both sides had become concerned— in an entirely different context, both to get their attention and elicit a much more emotional response to something they had become too familiar with. So he reframed the 6,000 annual road deaths not as just another statistic, but as an "epidemic." That is, something that was not inevitable but that could be fought and overcome. A threat to the community (a monster, if you like) that we all needed to face up to and fight. And he called his BBC documentary about road safety "The Biggest Epidemic of Our Times."

Second, within this new frame, he recognized that he needed to make the abstract numbers more than just abstract numbers. He needed to find an idea that would bring them to life for people in an entirely fresh way—and in doing so would make them suddenly unacceptable. And he would need to do this very early on—as a communicator, he recognized that for the beginning of his program he would need something that would be instantly arresting (he was working in a category after all, that allows the most instant brand switching in the world—television). So as the opening of his documentary he took a typical British market town, Wallingford (population 6,000), and filmed the entire town lying down, as if dead. Every year, he began, a town the size of Wallingford dies on British roads. And within those first three minutes, he had us: We would indeed now sit down and lean forward into a program about the topic we had previously known as "road safety."

Third, Ross changed the language for the authorities, as well as the frame for the British people. He told the authorities they should revise their targets: Instead of 6,000, they should aim to *kill* only 4,000 people a year. The other side was incensed. "Kill?" What on earth was he suggesting? They thought of themselves, after all, as being in a job about saving lives, and here was this journalist suggesting that they were killing people. But the jolt that Ross's inversion from "saving lives" to "killing people," together with his own personal activism—he became Chairman of the National Road Safety Committee—led at last to his revised targets of 4,000 deaths a year being accepted. Tighter legislation and greater investment followed, and UK road deaths are now around 3,500 a year, half the average for the previous 50 years. UK roads are among the safest in the world and, in significant consequence, British mortality rates of people under 50 are among the lowest in the world.

WAKE UP, WORLD

Excited though we are about our brand and the genuine importance of our mission, and effervescent though we may be about the superiority of our product or service, or the benefits of our brilliant innovation, people outside in the street are for the most part very happy where they are, doing what they are doing. They are not waiting to change their minds about the brands they see in front of them, and in the majority of purchase decisions, they already have a range of brands that happily suit their needs (65 percent of women in the United States, for instance, say that once they find a brand that satisfies them they usually don't experiment with new ones). The purchase decision, in fact, is often not really a decision—it is a habit. It is easy to lose sight of this; like the old Steinberg cartoon of a New Yorker's view of the world, as marketeers we naturally distort our target's world to fit our own preoccupations. Since we spend all our time thinking of our targets' consumption and choices in, say, online grocery shopping, there is a natural tendency to be a little disappointed in listening to them tell us in focus groups that they don't really think about—or even want to think about—online grocery shopping at all. What they think about is how to get their sons and daughters to soccer practice and ballet class, or how they are going to find the money for college, or why their partner is in such a bad mood, or whether the cat needs putting down, or how to get the car cleaned before dinner with the Shattocks on Thursday night. That is where their time and energy are devoted. In terms of consumption and brand decisions, they are on autopilot.

But autopilot obviously favors the status quo, even the Brand Leader; and for that reason a Challenger cannot live in an autopilot world, and cannot flourish under the status quo. For a Challenger to achieve its objectives, therefore, it will need to look for ways to puncture the consumers' complacencies. To wake up the sleepwalkers, if you like. Some of this will obviously lie in sustained sampling and other ways of motivating behavior change. Some of it will lie in brilliant communication. But as brands in a hurry, Challengers also will look for ways to create Symbols of Re-evaluation—dramatic symbols or acts, often involving startling juxtapositions, that prompt consumers to sit up and rethink some of their assumptions about the category, the brand, and how they are thinking and behaving in relation to both. Acts that sometimes are brief interventions, then disappear, or acts that sometimes stay on as a visual symbol showing why the brand is different and what its challenge is.

Commercial value aside, it is not hard to understand the importance marketeers attach to such symbolism in brand building. At its most basic, if 70 percent of human communication is nonverbal, it is reasonable to look for the expression of one's identity to be manifested in some kind of visual form, over and above a graphic treatment of logo or name, simply in order to complete the communication relationship with one's desired consumer. Indeed, as we move to a consumer retreating from the marketing relationship and the need for a softer and softer verbal sell, striking visual imagery may remain the strongest way of rapidly advancing our brand's case without turning off the consumer.

But the inherent advantages for a Challenger brand go far beyond a visual manifestation of identity, important though that is. First, they have to do with immediacy—an instant signaling of identity. Phil Knight, of Nike, has remarked of the Air Jordan *Jumpman* icon, which came to embody the brand's attitude as it rose in the 1980s, that it saved a lot of time—you couldn't explain much in 60 seconds, but if you showed Michael Jordan, you didn't need to.

The second advantage for a Challenger would seem to be the communication of emotion. To continue with the Jumpman example, the impending dunk portrayed by the logo is what every amateur basketball player dreams of—the theatrical splay of the legs demonstrates not just achievement, but effortless, flamboyant achievement. The appeal of the image lies in it saying something about the emotions and style of the person, as well as the ability of the player. There is indeed an extraordinary compression in this. But it is the emotions the icon arouses in such a short time that make it so valuable.

Emotion and speed, of course, are two of a Challenger's key drivers; Challengers are, of necessity, brands in a hurry. It is not just that life is speeding up, that we have become a world of shortcuts and quick fixes, of skimmers and scanners, or that the postliterate generation has become expectant of rapid-fire communication and brand conversation. It is that both success and survival for Challengers depend on effecting change fast: Momentum and critical mass are all-important with both trade and consumer. And that change in turn hinges on establishing an emotionally centered appeal.

When we observe that one of the striking things about the Challengers we are considering is a sharp hunger for symbols and iconography, we are not talking icons in the mold of Tony the Tiger or the Pillsbury Doughboy. We are talking about symbols of *change*: Challengers deploy icons and symbols, like the town of Wallingford lying down, specifically to prompt reevaluation. They create surprising, striking visual devices and events designed to puncture the consumer's autopilot—and at the same time to reflect and communicate what they are.

PUNCTURING THE DOMINANT COMPLACENCY

What our target expects the world to be like is, within any one market, clearly multidimensional, containing a number of interlocking expectations and what we might call *complacencies*. I have called them complacencies because they are more than simply an attitude; they are settled consumer opinions that have become comfortably embedded in their way of thinking about the brand landscape. Some of these complacencies may be based on truth, while some are simply opinions. That high-fat products are bad for you, for example, or that whiskey is my dad's drink. That the French are chic but aloof. (Test for this year's graduate intake: Come up with a marketing strategy for a high-fat French whiskey.) That gaming is for guys, or that cigar smoking is antisocial. That Brand X is old-fashioned, or juvenile, or for girls.

Although within each market there is an interrelated collection of such complacencies and habits, one will be the most important, because it will be the central departure point for many other accompanying attitudes. Let us call this the *dominant consumer complacency*. For a brand that is late to relaunch, for instance, the dominant complacency may be the weak opinion the consumer has of its product. It may be the consumer's view of the category that is the dominant complacency to be overcome (perhaps high-fat categories like ice cream, or certain luxury categories like fur). Conversely, for a brand launching into markets that are established but successful, the dominant complacency may be how the consumer views the existing establishment player in the market (e.g., a nation's view of its own national carrier in the airline market). A Challenger cannot hope to pick all these locks at the same time; instead, it has to identify the *dominant* consumer complacency that it must change. These are the principal barriers to a Challenger achieving momentum, and they must be broken. And at the same time, the Challenger must use the breaking of them to assert who it is: It must build the Lighthouse Identity (our Second Credo).

As one might expect, a frequent strategic route for a Challenger involves surprise—attacking the dominant complacency head-on. Challengers put things together you wouldn't expect to find together—discount stores and art museums, skyscrapers and watches, glamorous models and vegetarianism—where the juxtaposition in each case demands that you reevaluate your position on one of the pair.

The Dominant Consumer Complacency: How the Consumer Sees You

For Challengers who are looking to relaunch themselves, or at least give themselves a significantly new direction, their key complacency to tackle will be how the consumer sees them. Brand image is famously hard to move, so we see Challengers looking to accelerate the initial impetus for themselves in their chosen direction by imaginatively addressing these complacencies with symbolic and surprising acts.

When Target unveiled the Michael Graves range, its first push into designer lines, it unveiled its new baby not at a store, but at the Whitney Museum in New York with 60 of the 200 pieces that would be part of the product line displayed throughout the Museum. The very fact of the designer range was clearly going to be something of a Symbol of Reevaluation for the brand (as well as a line of products successful in itself), and the company deliberately chose to highlight this by choosing a highly unusual place for a discount retailer to appear—one of the pre-eminent fine art museums in America. This combination of Graves and the venue in turn allowed Target to attract a strata of press that would not normally have been much interested in what the store was going to do next, including *Architectural Digest, Town & Country*, and *Food & Wine*. *Discount Store News* reported at the time, a little breathlessly: "The unveiling consisted of a mid-January gala at the Whitney Museum of American Art in one of New York's posher neighborhoods. . . . The 400-plus members of the press on hand tended toward the up-market . . . and members of Michael Graves's staff outnumbered Target employees."[1]

The symbolic nature of the elevated launch venue gave a huge initial impetus to press opinion (and, through them, consumers) about the launch, and the shift in perceptions caused by the introduction of the Graves line was the beginning of building a bold new image for Target.

More recently, for one of the 2008 U.S. Presidential primary debates shown live on CNN, YouTube enabled users to submit their questions to the candidates on TV. What makes us sit up and reappraise the brand here is the nature of the juxtaposition: between YouTube, on the one hand (easily dismissed as a place where nothing is of any real consequence at all—all skateboarding tortoises and *Evolution of Dance*), and the presidential election, on the other, perhaps the most consequential decision a citizen makes, outside of their choice of partner and job, and one whereby the people of America decide the future of their country and themselves. It is the presence of YouTube as a useful tool in helping make such a critical decision that creates such a startling juxtaposition, and thus a Symbol of Re-evaluation about the potential of the brand in our lives.[2]

The car business has historically designed and launched particular, highly remarkable models to prompt people to reappraise their brand. Recently, for instance, we have seen Audi use the R8, a supercar costing

$120,000, in exactly this way in the United States. The car's looks, performance, and price tag lured people into Audi dealerships who had not taken Audi seriously as a luxury car up to that point—people such as Porsche owners, for example. The value here to Audi was not just one of attention, or indeed a proof point (unlike advertising, the indisputable existence of one and a quarter tons of metal brooks no argument), though both of these are of course hugely valuable. It is that the car, when inspected, has a bigger story to tell: the legend behind Audi, the Quattro engine, the racing heritage. If one just runs an ad about racing, the people at Audi will tell you, people tune out; but give them an eye-popping supercar they want to know more about, and they will listen to whatever you want to tell them. The R8 has now an 18-month waiting list in the United States.

Very occasionally, our Symbol of Re-evaluation will want to remain unbranded, at least initially. Where the brand image we are trying to change is very poor, we may need to first surprise and disarm our consumer before revealing what the brand actually is. Top-Flite was once one of the most widely used golf balls in America, but its previous owners failed to invest in it, allowing it to become a small value line known primarily for being the hardest ball on the market, thus earning it the nickname of "Rock Flite." Calloway acquired the brand, bringing to the marketing of Top-Flite both a new determination and a new technology ("Dimple in Dimple"), and they gave a new name to the key relaunch product—the *D2*, deliberately chosen to echo military technology. The opinion of club pros would be critical to the product and brand's success, in terms of both the influence they carried in their personal recommendation to golfers and their influence over whether the brand would be stocked in the golf course shop. Top-Flite wanted to seed these balls with club pros before the consumer launch, but knew that the brand's "Rock Flite" reputation would be a barrier to this professional audience. So, in approaching the pros, the brand team gave them the balls, unbranded, with only the letters *RFID 07* stamped on them, asked them to try them out, and left them to it. When the pros started hitting 64s using these new unbranded balls, they wrote to the company and asked what the ball was, and what RFID 07 meant. "It's the new Top-Flite D2," the team told them. "And RFID 07 stands for 'Rock Flite is dead in 2007.' " The D2 has begun to restore the brand to some of its former sales success: the most successful product launch Top-Flite has had since 2001, it sold over 1.4 million units in its launch year and opened up distribution at approximately 1,000 golf course shops that had not previously carried the brand.[3]

Playing this out a little, one could argue that the Pepsi Challenge when it began in 1975 was a Symbol of Re-evaluation, whose reveal was individual by individual, initiated by the Challenger. But an even more dramatic example in the beverage category was seen a year later in the wine business, when a group of French critics and vintners collected in Paris in May 1976 to blind-taste the best French wines against a collection of American wines. The French were the only judges invited—and to their collective astonishment, American wines won in both the red and the white categories, as judged by the French themselves. A journalist from *Time* covered the story, which was swiftly passed on through the world's press. The effect of this event, known as "The Judgement of Paris," was not simply to wake up the world to New World quality; the power of the result was in a very real way more about *puncturing the myth of the establishment's supremacy.* This, after all, is where Challenger momentum really begins: once the myth of the supremacy of the Establishment brand is punctured, the ability of a Challenger to make real inroads in terms of image and trial increases considerably.

Several brands, realizing that the dominant complacency is in fact how the consumer sees them, have carefully orchestrated not one but a *sequence* of Symbols of Re-evaluation to move us from one perception to another. Consider Daniel Radcliffe, the boy actor who was cast from thousands to play the young Harry Potter and in whose delightfully mop-topped and bespectacled company we have all watched Harry Potter grow up in front of us on the big screen. Now, if you happen to be Daniel Radcliffe, this close identification with one role is both a good and bad thing. The good news is that it makes you a huge movie star and eye-wateringly wealthy; the bad news is that your face and person become in danger of being irreversibly entwined with this *and only this* one character—a character who lives in a world derived from childrens' books, who dresses only in gowns and wands, who lives in a world where puberty is about chaste kisses at parties and where sex doesn't really exist, and whose character is squeakily wholesome, even in the depths of teenage angst. But given that Harry Potter films will cease production when you are in your early twenties, you, as Daniel Radcliffe, will need to give yourself the ability to move into different roles in different genres (your equivalent of different categories, perhaps) if you want to remain a successful actor for the rest of your life. So what do you do?

Radcliffe chose a point, four films into the series of seven, to create two key Symbols of Re-evaluation to enhance how we, the film and television audience, see him. First, he appeared in an episode of the television comedy series *Extras*, a show whose central idea was to have stars sending up a version of themselves. On the show, he appeared as Daniel Radcliffe, but a Daniel Radcliffe in the grip of a very boyish puberty— obsessed with sex and, in one particularly memorable scene, accidentally flicking condoms onto the head of Dame Diana Rigg. He goes, in other words, through a very unwholesome puberty right in front of our eyes. Symbol number one. Fair enough, we think, so perhaps he doesn't have to be a kid all his life, but the question still is: Can he act? Can he do anything apart from agitate wands in childrens' movies? So the next time we see him, he is on the London stage acting in *Equus*, in which he plays a disturbed adolescent boy who, during the course of the drama, appears naked, has sex, smokes, and harms horses. (There is a little more than this to Peter Schaeffer's play, of course, but you wouldn't have known it from the initial press coverage about the "death of Harry Potter.")

None of this would have meant much, of course, if he had been no good in either of these roles, but he surprised the critics and public alike with the quality of the performance. And in two sequenced Symbols of Re-evaluation, he enabled himself to move beyond the box that success had put him into. He used two carefully managed moments to puncture the ways we were typecasting him and to prepare him, and us, for a credible transition into other kinds of roles, and a career beyond his immediate "category."

The Dominant Consumer Complacency: How the Consumer Sees the Category

What if the complacencies we need to puncture have to do with people's perceptions of who the category is and is not for? Sometimes events will naturally throw up a symbol that causes one to reappraise a category and, indeed, a brand within it. For example, the nature of the reporting on the tragedy of the Virginia Tech massacre caused most of us to reappraise both the future of journalism in general and citizen journalism in particular (as its central coverage, CNN showed video images from the camera phone of a student who captured the gunfire live, unlike the television cameras), as well as the future of Wikipedia, where coverage of the unfolding event was updated and edited in real time by the contributing community. But more usually, we will have to create our own points of reference, our own Symbols of Re-evaluation. This may focus on who the category is and is not for—the image of the typical user, if you like. PETA has consistently attempted to use visual symbolism to puncture consumer complacencies about the kind of people they represent. We might be lured by right-wing newspapers to think of animal lovers and vegetarians as either obsessive grannies or unwashed youth—until PETA reveals a number of statuesque spokeswomen such as Pamela Anderson and Alicia Silverstone, naked except for some strategically placed lettuce leaves. The organization went on to create a considerable stir in 2007 by publicly sending Al Gore a letter in which it accused him of not telling the world the real truth about climate change. This was striking, of course, because the man had become, since losing the 2000 US presidential election (or winning it, depending on your point of view), the patron saint of climate change awareness and activism, winning an Oscar for a key film on the subject and being awarded the Nobel Peace Prize for his tireless efforts in this regard. But PETA's point was that the greatest change you could make to your environmental impact would be to become a vegetarian, and Gore was neither talking about that, nor becoming a vegetarian himself.

Think that the only people who are going to be interested in a new gaming console are going to be 16-years-olds in basements? Nintendo's US PR machine brilliantly amplified a story about Chicago's Erickson Retirement Communities, whose septuagenarian residents were throwing Wii bowling and baseball tournaments.[4] Nintendo was not sharing this with us, of course, because it was trying to challenge more 70-year-olds to reconsider their attitudes to gaming—it was sharing this with us because if *even 70-year-olds* are having fun with this, then it is certainly no longer just for 16-year-olds. Perhaps even 40-somethings like me should check it out.

This startling juxtaposition a Challenger uses initially to push through complacency can clearly take the form of comparative facts, as well as people and images, but only if you are prepared to really look for those facts that will genuinely prompt appraisal. When the world's most successful TV chef, Jamie Oliver, challenged the British educational establishment to improve the quality of school meals, he needed to get the public behind him. And to do that, he first had to get them to sit up and care about something—school dinners—that most of them had eaten, and most of their children had eaten, for years without any real cause for complaint. How could he jerk us all out of our complacency and make us think that this was something we needed to sit up and pay attention to? He had a number of options. He could have given us facts about vitamin deficiencies and food groups, but we knew all that already. He could have compared the amount we spend on our children's lunches to the much greater amount spent by continental Europeans, for instance. But while being thought inferior to foreigners does indeed usually get the British blood boiling nicely, even this he felt would be insufficient. No, he was very specific, but didn't use as the other reference point anything to do with children or schooling at all. He pointed out (1) that we spent less on lunches for our schoolchildren than we did on lunches for our prisoners (i.e., less on an innocent member of the future of our society than on one guilty of past abuse of it) and (2) that we spent less on our children's dinners than we did on feeding an *army dog*.

Suddenly, he had our attention: We weren't going to be so damn complacent about what they were feeding our little darlings anymore.

The Dominant Consumer Complacency: An Established Brand Leader

Some Challengers have to juxtapose themselves with the competition to subvert the consumers' understanding of the existing order. Volkswagen in the 1960s, of course, innocently pitched itself as the lone voice of reason in U.S. automobile ownership, and with a highly idiosyncratic product in the context of the U.S. car industry, its symbol became itself. The Beetle should by rights never have been introduced in the United States. It would have failed every research group and test market, running, as it did, against everything the U.S. car market believed in at the time: fins, ostentation, swimming pools for gas tanks, backseats the size of Kentucky. And instead of hiding this, the company played to it and sold hundreds of thousands of cars. But Volkswagen's footprint in the United States was really the shrewd positioning of an accident of birth, to embody a car company hungrily zagging while the rest of the US automotive industry flatulently zigged.

More often, we will have to not simply amplify accidents of birth, but create symbols at our birth or rebirth that trigger reappraisal of the Market Leader as well as announce ourselves. Virgin is a brand whose consistent positioning now, across more or less any category it launches into, in any geography, is that of the "People's Champion." And it is the most celebrated example of a brand who, as it launches in each category, looks to create a Symbol of Re-evaluation which identifies some aspect of why the Brand Leader (or perhaps the whole category establishment) is nothing we consumers should be happy with.

Sir Richard Branson, as the face of Virgin, is always the media magnet at the heart of these events. His use of symbolism is rarely subtle, but each event has a theatrical gusto that makes it irresistible to press and consumer alike. How does Virgin Mobile launch in Australia, for instance? It begins with Branson flying into Sydney Harbor, suspended 100 feet below a helicopter. The helicopter hovers, he lands on a boat below, blows up a cage on the boat, and releases 50 people who swim to shore on Virgin Mobile branded buoyancy rings—a drama intended to symbolize freeing all Australian phone users from the restrictions and rip-offs that the dominant players are forcing on them. The event was covered on every major Australian news station that night.[5] Don't just sit there happily with your Vodafone account, says Branson with this televised piece of drama: There are good reasons you need someone to rescue you.

What we are discussing here, then, is not the clever use of accidents, but something more deliberately and strategically introduced—symbols that have been deliberately created as part of the long-term marketing or remarketing of an entire company. Or, even more dramatically, symbols that have been strategically *stolen* from the establishment player you are challenging.

Focus, a new weekly newsmagazine in Germany was very clear about its point of difference ("Facts, facts, facts": straight news for people without a lot of time to read news magazines), but was also clear about its desire to take a bite out of the Market Leader (*Der Spiegel*, founded almost 50 years earlier). So *Focus* took two key properties of the Market Leader and claimed them as its own. The first was *Der Spiegel's* color: red. *Focus* not only used red as its own color, but paraded it more boldly and dramatically than *Der Spiegel* ever had, splashing red paint and branding on a widely used commuter ferry in Hamburg, the hometown of *Der Spiegel*, and taking over the side of a whole building directly opposite the Market Leader's building, with "Good to know the facts" printed on a huge red background—which had up to then been *Der Spiegel's* background. Second, *Focus* cheekily stole Monday. Monday had always been publicized as "*Der Spiegel* day," though never trademarked as such. Now *Focus* simply claimed it as theirs: "Monday is *Focus* day." A new generation of news magazine was symbolically aiming to supplant the Market Leader in its heartland.

Focus now has the highest readership among the top decision makers of any German magazine.

THE MOON ROCKET AND ACCELERATION

What we are discussing, then, is the use of symbols that surprise in order to propel the Challenger more rapidly in its chosen direction: symbols and icons that prompt consumers to reevaluate their habitual attitudes toward the central issue, not with logic, but with emotion. And if these symbols can be infused with a sense of drama, they are used specifically for acceleration: to help the brand achieve critical consumer mass faster. It is famously said that a moon rocket uses half of its entire fuel simply to go the first mile—to obtain the critical momentum to leave the earth and reach its desired speed; after that, fuel is used mainly to change direction and to overcome particularly difficult transitions in its journey (re-entry, lunar landing, etc.). Although brands don't have convenient interludes of zero gravity to help them on their way, the analogy is sometimes used that the same is true of getting a brand off the ground—the real effort and difficulty lies in achieving that initial critical momentum: Half of one's disposable fuel should be used for that task alone, breaking free of the gravitational pull of consumer indifference.

In the case of Challengers, their proportional media, promotional, and trade budgets are comparatively low. How a Challenger divides its budget is therefore not so much the question, for the fuel at its disposal lies not so much in dollars as in ideas, ingenuity, and passion. It is this context in which the deployment of dramatically executed Symbols of Re-evaluation must be viewed; if they can create rapid momentum for the brand in the eyes of the consumer at the outset of a new marketing campaign, given in weeks rather than years, then they must be regarded not as idiosyncratic whims of fancy, but perhaps as some of the shrewdest marketing decisions ever made.

Look at Swatch's launch all those years ago in Germany, for example. Constructing a gigantic, fully working, orange Swatch 500 feet high, the company suspended it outside the tallest skyscraper in Frankfurt, which happened to be the headquarters of the Commerzbank, one of Germany's leading financial institutions. (See Figure 8.1.)

On the watch were written just three things: Swatch. Swiss. DM 60.

What at first sight appeared to be just a spectacular publicity stunt was in fact a brilliant piece of repositioning in one simple act. It announced Swatch; it broke the myth that all Swiss watches were luxury

FIGURE 8.1   Swatch launches large.

products that took themselves overly seriously (while still claiming Swiss quality as its own provenance); and it communicated a price that had never been associated with Swiss quality before. And, as Nicolas Hayek, the head of SMH, noted, it signaled immediately the essence of the Swatch brand promise: "It was a big provocation to hang a watch from a huge, grim skyscraper. And it was funny, fanciful, a joke—joy of life. Believe me, when we took it down, everyone we had wanted to reach had received our message."[6] Had Swatch simply pulled off a public relations coup in which it stopped the Frankfurt equivalent of Big Ben, it would have achieved notoriety, but not momentum.

Historical Challengers have, of course, made a great play of symbolism to capture the imagination and shape the views of the public—the latter, of course, being closely linked to propaganda once a Challenger gains power. The Russians have always understood the importance of the manufacture of icons, and this reached its height (in quantity, if not quality) in postrevolutionary Russian art. Or think of Gandhi. Simple white robe, shaven head: He understood the power of appearance and clothing long before the spin doctors started on Tony Blair. And on an entirely different level, the hanging of John Brown at Harper's Ferry in 1859 was called by Herman Melville "the meteor of the [U.S. Civil] war." This was not wisdom after the event; Longfellow had written in his diary the morning of the execution: "This day will be a great day in our history, the date of a new revolution—quite as much needed as the old one." What aroused the instant sense of it being a turning point was the symbol it represented: a white man dying for the cause of slavery.

But perhaps the most famous, and simple, historical use of an image as a Symbol of Re-evaluation is the Pulitzer Prize–winning photograph of six Marines raising the U.S. flag over Iwo Jima in February 1944. Probably one of the best-known images of the United States this century, it has come to represent a pivotal moment not simply in World War II—the U.S. defeat of the Japanese during a 36-day assault that would give the victors a base from which to neutralize the enemy's air and naval capabilities—but also in the twentieth century. The image seems, in retrospect, to symbolize America as victor in a more general sense: ascending from being merely one of the major players on the world stage, a young Challenger against the aging European powers, to becoming the unrivaled leader of the Free World. The image of struggle and courage and achievement by the ordinary American (none of the men pictured was above the rank of sergeant) was later re-created in bronze as a monument to the dead in Arlington National Cemetery. At that unveiling, President Nixon summed up its power thus:

> This statue symbolizes the hopes and dreams of America, and the real purpose of our foreign policy. We realized that to retain freedom for ourselves, we must be concerned when people in other parts of the world may lose theirs. There is no greater challenge to statesmanship than to find a way that such Sacrifices as this statue represents are not necessary in the future, and to build the kind of world in which people can be free, in which nations can be independent, and in which people can live together in peace and friendship.

Perhaps the most significant thing about the photograph, however, for all its power, was that it was not actually taken when the hill was originally captured and the flag originally raised. At that time, a smaller flag was raised on an existing steel pole by a lieutenant and three entirely different men, and the scene was photographed by a different photographer.

The first turned out to be not a bad photograph, imbuing the actual moment with a certain grim sense of accomplishment. But it has been largely forgotten by history because it possesses nothing like the power of the second image, taken three hours later, by a different photographer, when a second group of men were sent by their commanding officer to raise a *second, larger flag, on a pole they were to raise and plant themselves.*

The point is this: The act is one thing—raising the flag encouraged the Marines as much as it demoralized the defenders—but the way the act is presented takes it to a whole other level. With Symbols of Reevaluation, the image is the message as much as the act itself. And the marine commander, even in the middle of a 36-day all-out assault on the Japanese positions, realized that he needed not just *a* flag flying over Iwo Jima, but a *big* flag flying over Iwo Jima. And with the help of Joe Rosenthal, who won the Pulitzer Prize for the second photograph, he created an image of victory that will inspire and define the

U.S. Marine Corps—and indeed the ascendance of the United States—for as long as it exists.

THE DIFFERENT AUDIENCES FOR SYMBOLS OF RE-EVALUATION

Of course, in seeking to redefine people's perceptions of the category through Symbols of Re-evaluation, one can also position oneself through them as the exception to it. Barclays Bank, although a very large financial institution, determined in 2005 that it would consciously and explicitly introduce a Challenger ethos into the way it approached building a fresh relationship with the consumer, and in fact with its own staff. Coming out of a campaign called "Fluent in Finance," which had been stylish but opaque at best, Barclays was determined to be a brand that would be idea-centric: It would use a stream of ideas, some small, some big, to generate a fresh relationship with both the bank and, to some degree (in the consumer's case), banking. Barclays looked at the outset for symbols that it could harness to signal this change. One of the first such symbols to strike the brand team was something as small as a pen. Pens in bank branches are commonly chained to the counters to prevent customers from taking them away. While no doubt a very practical way of managing one's pen inventory, this also sends a curious cue to customers: The bank has the customers' money, the customers come in to talk to the bank about their own money—and yet the very first thing the bank does at the beginning of this transaction is to suggest its own customers might be thieves. In many ways, this small detail symbolized much that was wrong about the bigger relationship between banks and their customers. So Barclays' Marketing Director, Jim Hytner, and his team decided to make something as apparently small as chained pens a symbol of re-evaluation. Instead of chaining the existing pens so customers could not take them away, they thought, what if we had new pens that customers *could* take away—in fact were *encouraged* to take away? So they replaced the chained pens with boxes dispensing Biros, and printed on each Biro a different message that encouraged the customer to take it.

The pens were obviously accompanied and followed by a much more significant innovation program aimed at improving the customer experience, but they remained curiously potent symbols for the consumer, and in fact became easily understood symbols for two other audiences as well, quite apart from the Barclays customers themselves. First, they became symbols to the staff of the very down-to-earth, practical ideas that Hytner and his team were seeking (not least from the staff themselves) to introduce into the customer relationship in order to enhance the relationship and to position the bank as one that was genuinely thinking about those customers. The marketing team fueled this symbolic value within the staff by creating annual competitions among them to come up with messages for the next generation of pens. And, second, the pens, though an apparently small detail, became simple, clear symbols to senior management—not all of whom either understood or respected marketing—as a function of what the marketing team was trying to do and the effect it could have on both consumer and staff when it was done really well.

As we have observed, then, a Symbol of Re-evaluation doesn't have to be a piece of advertising or marketing; it can be as simple as a disposable pen—it is the *meaning* that is important. And we are also seeing that these Symbols of Re-evaluation have many consumers. The need to signal dramatic change to the consumer is one reason for the break, but often as vital is the need to change the thinking *within* the organization. We noted earlier that many Challenger CEOs claim to regard their employees as their most important audience; this is self-interest, not corporate pseudo-philanthropy: They believe if they can fill their own staff with a sense of what the brand needs to be, and with an utter belief in its superiority and imminent success, everything else will follow.

PROJECTS OF REEVALUATION

Eurostar is the high-speed train service that connects London, Paris, and Brussels. Owned by three governments, it is, in effect, a unionized business that has long been a well-run railway, but that operated very much in both geographic and operational silos. The marketing department was set within the commercial department, but had limited influence within it over and above its own communication activity. By 2005, however, Paris was falling in travelers' rankings of top European short-holiday destinations, and London had recently been hit by the terrorist bombings of 7/7. Eurostar was suffering as a result; its numbers were down for seven consecutive months. Then, one day in a sauna, the

Marketing Director gets an idea. Dan Brown's novel, *The Da Vinci Code*, is being made into a film. Sony, who was making the film, would be at the very early stages of finding strategic partners for it, and yet the plot obviously hinges on Paris and (to a lesser extent) London. Why couldn't Eurostar be the strategic partner for travel when it came to the film? So, the Eurostar team gets together with Sony, strikes a deal, and Eurostar runs a promotion in conjunction with the release of the movie, built around the idea of a "Quest." The partnership and promotion idea was an ambitious piece of chutzpah, in that Eurostar does not actually appear in Dan Brown's book at all—the characters all take the plane (i.e., the Big Fish that Eurostar was trying to eat, so to speak). But it was bold in two other, more important ways as well: It was the first time that the company had run the same piece of promotional activity in each country, and the high-speed run from London all the way through to Cannes to open the Cannes film festival was something that had never been done before.

The promotion was a considerable success. Eurostar was indeed the key travel partner for the blockbuster film, and it broke two world records: one for the most successful promotion in the world and the other for the longest high-speed run. And on that record high-speed run, Eurostar had some influential travelers: On the train, in addition to film stars Tom Hanks and Audrey Tautou, were four sets of film studio executives and 300 broadcast TV journalists, who then obligingly broadcast more than 13 hours of prime-time coverage of Eurostar's heavily branded (for this trip) interiors on this glamorous and record-breaking feat. Which made it in turn a considerable success in terms of results: Coming off a seven-month decline, the traffic between London and Paris then grew every month for the next two years.

One of the most important successes of the project, though, was the awakening of belief within the organization about what it was capable of. The London-Cannes run had been something the organization had initially resisted, from a number of the key departments necessary to make it work, because they were not sure it was possible. But the Marketing Director and his team pushed the company to overcome the problems raised by the individual silos and put their collective shoulders to the task to make it happen. And the success when it came was celebrated by the organization as a whole. Greg Nugent, the Marketing Director, calls this not a *Symbol* of Re-evaluation but a *Project of Re-evaluation*. He notes that an apparently small project within an organization preceding a much larger one can help that large organization to reappraise what it is capable of, perhaps before it starts on a larger, genuinely critical initiative. In this case, the success of *The Da Vinci Code* promotion taught Eurostar as a company three critical lessons about itself:

1. All countries could indeed work together in creating a successful initiative (and when they did so, the rewards were concomitantly higher).
2. That if Eurostar could push itself as an organization to do something it did not think it was capable of (such as a high-speed run to Cannes), and succeed, perhaps it should therefore stretch its ambitions about what could be possible. . . .
3. Success in such a venture hinged on the entire company being aligned, on transcending silos, and on delivering a strategic idea that benefited the consumer and itself.

Why was this a significant Project of Re-evaluation across these four dimensions? Because two years later the company and brand faced its greatest challenge—the relaunch of not simply the brand but of the entire service, from a new station in an entirely different part of London. And the success of what the company had achieved together in 2005 encouraged them to successfully stretch their ambition: to position Eurostar not simply as a faster train in a new home, but as a brand that was now positioned, in a very real sense, to be the future of European travel.

USING WHAT YOU HAVE

Anything can be a Symbol of Re-evaluation if you look for the opportunity it represents. Even something as simple as a sweater, if you know how to invest it with meaning.

Evo Morales, the president of Bolivia, was elected to his country's highest office in 2005. Claiming (controversially) to be the country's first indigenous head of state since the Conquistadors, much of his identity as President has been to challenge the old order, old practices (in 2006, he symbolically cut his own salary as president by 57 percent), and old alliances—in particular, what he regards as the forces of capitalism and the institutions of the world that support it.

And while most of the world could not tell you exactly what his arguments were, they could tell you about the way he dresses—and that he has chosen, in his initial interactions with the "old order," to dress very differently from the formal attire of that old order. In particular, he has become famous for the blue, red, and white striped sweater known in Bolivia as a *chompa*. What makes this sweater more than just a piece of clothing here is the context in which Morales wears it—among the dark suits of embassy receptions and gatherings of Heads of State. Wearing the sweater in a first visit with Juan Carlos II, the king of Spain, the conservative Spanish press challenged the Bolivian President, wondering aloud if there was anyone in Madrid who could lend Mr. Morales a dark suit. Others, though, recognized it as the symbol it was intended to be. *El Pais*, for instance, declared Morales's chompa to be a "knitted declaration against invisibility."[7] They commented that "while generations of Latin American leaders have worn the policies and the clothes of the IMF and the World Bank, Mr. Morales was showing that he was a man of the people."[8]

The key thing about a Symbol of Re-evaluation, then, is not size or expense, but that it be noticed and its meaning understood. That it stop you and make you reappraise your ingrained thoughts and feelings about the category, the brand in question, or the Market Leader you are seeking (directly or indirectly) to deposition.

Videolinks for this Chapter:

www.eatbigfishfood.com/etbf/symbolsofreevaluation

9

THE FIFTH CREDO: SACRIFICE

A great brand is going to evoke passion. You're going to love it or hate it. And I'm good with that. I'm good with people loving us. And I'm good with people hating us.

Peter van Stolk, Jones Soda[1]

In the world of clutter and information saturation that consumers are faced with, the greatest danger facing a brand is not rejection, but indifference. Rejection is easily spotted and easily remedied—you make a big change or you pull out—but indifference is a far more insidious and expensive problem. Selective listening allows marketeers to convince themselves that with a little tightening up here and there everything will be all right, and they pour in more and more money, over more and more time, for less and less return.

We have seen in the last few chapters that the solution to indifference for a Challenger lies in both a strong identity and, through this, a strong relationship with its consumer base. Inevitably, this means that success for the Challenger brand comes from considering very carefully what it is going to Sacrifice in order to create this relationship and identity.

Indeed, the ability to sacrifice and concentrate one's focus, voice, and actions more narrowly is one of the few advantages a Challenger has. Having to fight a war on two fronts weakens the ability to do either really well (Hitler's invasion of Russia in 1941 cost him the ability to hold

France three years later), and Brand Leaders have to fight on many fronts at once. Here frequently lies the opening for a Challenger in taking on a Brand Leader—but only if it is used as an opening, which is to say, only if the Challenger is prepared to make Sacrifices itself.

STRONG PREFERENCE IS OUR ONLY CURRENCY

Kodak is a company that has had to learn the hard way how to become a Challenger. A legendary market leader, Kodak was for many years featured in all the authoritative rankings of the "five greatest brands in the world." But the company found it hard to deal as quickly as it needed to with the rapid changes that overtook its market, and which required it to fundamentally change its entire business model and make the difficult decision to lay off tens of thousands of employees worldwide in the process.

But in several areas, at least, it has learned how to become the Challenger it will need to be to compete in the new world in which it now finds itself. And one such is the digital camera business.

Kodak entered the digital camera market in the late 1990s, and success here was intended to become a key plank in the company's bridge from the world of film to the world of digital. Yet Kodak didn't make the start it needed to—and in 2000, the company's CEO described its digital camera business, then sixth in the market, as "a train wreck"; the market was driven by male purchasers, and Kodak's cameras lacked the styling or distinctiveness to cut through in a very competitive category. Pierre Schaeffer, CMO of the digital consumer business, recognized that Kodak needed to create a significantly greater impact within the market than they were: It was clear that the brand needed, in his words, "rupture."

So what did Kodak have from which to build its new positioning? Well, it had a new product—a digital camera docking station that made it easy, through one button, to transfer pictures from a digital camera to a PC, which was the number one consumer issue at the time. But a product innovation on its own was not going to be enough: Kodak needed a bigger idea, a place to stand that it could wrap around this technical innovation, and indeed its entire digital camera range. A place to stand that would throw down a gauntlet to the rest of the camera category, that would make Kodak a credible Challenger in this emerging category and, in doing so, carve out a segment of the market it could genuinely own.

Schaeffer and his team went back to the past in order to find Kodak's future in cameras. They looked at the vision Kodak's founder, George Eastman, had had for his company and his target, and what they saw was that Eastman had never seen his company as a company for men—he had seen it as a company and a brand for women. Eastman's vision had been to create a product that would be used by the moms of America (and the world) to capture the narrative and memories of their family life. Because we are now so familiar with Kodak's traditional market territory, it is hard to see what a radical piece of thinking this was at the time, when men were still the purchasers—and often the primary users—of almost all leisure technology in the United States. But Eastman's had been a bold concept and a very clear vision, and it had found a ready and enthusiastic market. Perhaps this vision—or rather a fresh interpretation of this vision for what was obviously a very different world—could be the path to the digital future for Kodak, too.

So Schaeffer and his team looked at what a new generation of women wanted from cameras in the digital world, and how that differed from the wants and needs of men from a camera. And they discovered that the difference was profound. Men, it turned out, were primarily interested in the act of *taking* the photo—that is, framing the shot, getting the lighting and composition right, zooming the lens in and out. Women, conversely, weren't really as interested in the *taking* of the photo as such: They were interested in what happened *after* that—sharing the photo with friends and family, using the photo almost as a currency of bonding with their social and familial networks.

So the brand and agency team met for two days to look at how they could take these three elements—their product innovation, the understanding of Eastman's original vision, and the insight into how women used cameras and photographs in a different way from men—and create a bigger place for Kodak to stand, one that would build a path to the future and a more profitable business position of second or third in the camera market.

The concept they came up with was EasyShare—to brand, in effect, how easy it was to share the photos once you had taken them. In doing so, Kodak would put a new dimension—ease of use—into the category, specifically aimed at women (and moms in particular), and make it a dimension they could own. EasyShare could be initially supported by the product news Kodak had in its digital camera docking station, but they recognized that the brand would need to push further to find ways of bringing it to life that would genuinely stand out on a noisy shelf in a noisy market.

We should stop and note at this point that Kodak was making two kinds of key Sacrifices in embarking on this strategy. One clearly was to do with message: In focusing entirely on ease of use, the brand was giving up all kinds of other potentially important communication (technical advancement, for instance, or its expertise in photography). The second is that the brand was giving up not just half the target market—men— but the very half that conventional market wisdom pegged as the key buyers and decision makers in that market.

Yet Kodak leaned into the Sacrifices it was trying to make, and perhaps the boldest illustration of this commitment lay in their approach to the packaging. The appearance of the pack, and the way the camera presents itself on that pack, are clearly critical to the buying process within any noisy retail environment. And the convention within the category had been to put the *front* of the camera on the packaging, because most buyers were men, and men liked to see the camera from the front—partly because they wanted to see the design of the camera (and thus what the camera would look like as they presented it to the world they were going to photograph) and partly because they wanted to be able to see and judge the nature of the lens and the zoom.

But the team felt that this approach to the pack was entirely wrong for their redefined target, and what that target market really wanted. Women weren't interested, they knew, in what the camera *looked* like; they wanted to know how easy it would be to share the photos once they had taken them. So, for EasyShare cameras, the back of the camera would be more important and useful to see on the packaging—because it would feature the camera's sharing technology (and its emotional end benefit) rather than its picture-taking technology. So they decided to show the back of the camera, not the front of the camera on the new packaging.

The boldness of this move was swiftly illustrated by the reception given to the new packaging at a meeting with Circuit City, a key American retailer responsible for an important share of U.S. camera sales. The meeting was a disaster—the Kodak Sales and Marketing representatives were shown out within 10 minutes, and told by the retailer that they simply couldn't turn their back on what men wanted in camera packaging—men were the key buyers of cameras. Exposure at the annual Photo Marketing Association Trade Show shortly afterward was ambiguous: Some liked it, some were skeptical. It was not the most auspicious start.

But the team held their nerve; they continued to lean into their decision. They continued to focus all their marketing—packaging, products, and ad campaign—on women.

The April 2001 launch of Kodak EasyShare cameras proved to be the most successful digital product launch ever for Kodak, and the team subsequently went on to make the entire digital camera portfolio compatible with the new docking system. Kodak went number one in the US camera market in 2004, remaining there for the next three years and becoming one of the top-three digital camera manufacturers worldwide.

SACRIFICE AND STRONG PREFERENCE

Challengers recognize, as Kodak did here, that in order to break through, their only currency with the consumer is going to be strong preference. If they achieve simply weak preference or parity preference, all the other attributes the market leader has on its side will swing the vote in its favor: ubiquity, social acceptability, salience, convenience. And to create that strong preference, we as Challengers accept that we will need to do things that reach out and bind certain groups of people very strongly to us. And we will also accept that, in order to create those stronger relationships, these same actions or behaviors may (and probably will) leave other groups cold.

Some Challengers put it even more forcefully: The CEO of Patagonia believes that "if you're not pissing off at least 50 percent of the people, you are not trying hard enough."[2] Yet while actively seeking such polarity may indeed have a real value for some kinds of Challengers (certain kinds of youth or rebellion brands, for instance, or brands looking to use polarizing product attributes to break through in particularly cluttered marketplaces, or those Challengers with very small budgets and a real burning platform), actively looking for antagonism in this way will not be necessary for most of us. However, what we will all share is recognition that in many ways the most dangerous currency for a Challenger is not rejection, but indifference. Rejection is very easy to see and respond to ("Nobody liked that at all? Okay, let's not do that anymore."). But indifference is a much more insidious and expensive problem—a lot of brands spend a lot of time and money tweaking indifference (which is in reality what most marketing actually consists of) without it having any real effect on their brand performance. So we need strong preference. And we will accept, like Kodak, that this preference will be defined as much by what we choose to give up, to Sacrifice, as by what we choose to stand for and do.

The Sacrifices a Challenger makes do not lie in incidentals to the business, such as minor line extensions, a research budget, or the assistant public relations manager. They are instead fundamentals: distribution, messages, audiences, even issues like promotional pricing, or our deliberate lack of it (T-box, unlike the rest of the ready-to-wear category, never offers seasonal discounts). The overriding objective is to have significant impact of the right kind on your core audience, to achieve critical mass for your voice.

SACRIFICE IN TARGET: TRADING NUMBERS FOR ENGAGEMENT AND LOYALTY

Kodak's Challenger camera business traded numbers for engagement, giving up men as a primary target to allow itself to really focus on building a more powerful relationship with women. Scion, on the other hand, looked at a different kind of demographic Sacrifice when the new car brand narrowed its profile to really focus on youth, and in particular the *tuner* mind-set: young people who wanted to express themselves through personalizing and customizing their cars. Scion had leaned into this not simply in the brand positioning and experience, but also with the models themselves—while the xA was a small, urban hatchback, the xB was a boxy, small compact car. And the market rewarded the brand's preparedness to be distinctive: although a questioning media had initially anticipated that the more middle-of-the-road xA would be the better seller because the xB looked so unusual, they found to their surprise that it was in fact the more polarizing lines of the boxy xB that became iconic, and drew strong sales among Scion's young tuner demographic. Scion now has overtaken VW in having the youngest demographic in the United States, and the strong relationship it has built through a highly distinctive product and brand experience has translated into another part of its original strategic objective as a company: a high level of migration on to Toyota and Lexus once the customers' life stage and needs change, and they move on from the Scion brand itself.[3]

These kinds of simple demographic distinctions (men versus women, younger versus older) seem relatively easy to see—although this doesn't, of course, make the changes any easier to implement. In reality, though, we will more often be making distinctions not so much in demographics as in psychographics: differentiating between groups of people in terms of an attitude or propensity to a certain kind of experience, and choosing to give up those who are not right for the attitude we are going to embody or the experience we are going to offer.

Tourism New Zealand, for instance, has chosen to give up almost 90 percent of its potential target market to focus on a very particular kind of traveler. The nature of vacationing in New Zealand is that it does not reward the beach lover; while there are certainly times of the year when you can take that kind of holiday, and the beaches are good, TNZ found that when it surveyed visitors as they left New Zealand, the ones who had enjoyed it most were those who had not stayed in one place or city, but who got in a car or a camper van and went out and explored the country and what it had to offer. So TNZ decided to center all its marketing on this kind of person, whom they called "the interactive traveler," a group that consisted of only around 10 to 15 percent of the company's potential universe but a group that would actually engage with the country and enjoy the experience all the more for it. And a group who would then go back and tell others—the right kinds of others—about how it had been, and why they should go, too. (See Figure 9.1.)

Attitudinally, we can anticipate that MAC's appeal—driven by its bold use of unconventional icons such as RuPaul—is not for everyone. One can imagine that much of the conservative US Deep South, for example, would be left puzzled, if not affronted, by the use of a male drag star to champion a makeup range for women. Yet by the same token, MAC's desired cosmopolitan target will for the same reason find it bold, daring, intriguing, unmissable.

FIGURE 9.1 "100% Pure New Zealand."

While Homer Simpson is a part of everyone's culture now, whether you are 8 or 68, it is easy to forget that the content of Fox's ground-breaking programming (*The Simpsons, King of the Hill, The X-Files*, and so on) originally turned off many potential older, more conservative viewers; in return, however, it rewarded Fox not simply with clear differentiation against the more amorphous established players, but with two kinds of loyalty among the most fickle of audience segments—the 18- to 34-year-olds. The first kind of loyalty was viewership: Although fourth in overall ratings, Fox consistently enjoyed leadership at key periods of the week in the premium 18- to 34-year-old and 18- to 49-year-old audiences. This was lucrative for Fox—an audience for whom advertisers would pay a significant premium to reach.

The second kind of loyalty was loyalty *within* the individual program—that is, the quality of viewer attention while the program was actually on air. In the measure of "percent of adult viewers claiming to have watched at full attention selected nationally aired TV shows," Fox took *five out of the top seven* U.S. shows; even within the individual program, the network was creating a stronger relationship with its chosen audience. One might intuitively hypothesize, in fact, that there is a relationship between these two types of loyalty, and that one may well be a predictor of the other—that is, when attention/involvement within the individual program wanes, loyalty of repeat purchase will start to wane shortly thereafter. (This may also provide an example of how a Challenger can learn from categories other than its own. Most categories measure only one kind of loyalty. Why should attention or involvement loyalty not be a key measure of any Challenger operating in an experienced business? Why should this not be an important measure of, for instance, supermarket shopping? Or fast food?)

TRADING NUMBERS FOR IDENTITY: SACRIFICE IN REACH, FREQUENCY, AND DISTRIBUTION

We saw in Chapter 6 an example of a brand clearly stating what it stood for: how, one day, purchasers of U.S. women's magazines such as *Real Simple* found something unusual bound into their monthly read. Wrapped in plain brown paper and bearing simply the title *People against Dirty*, it turned out to be an 18-page booklet—nine pages of text, nine pages of beautifully shot images—outlining method's philosophy toward cleaning.

In a sense, this was method's Super Bowl spot. Just as the fledgling Apple could afford to show *1984* in only a single TV spot in the Super Bowl, choosing to give up a much greater (and cheaper) frequency of airtime in order to write its identity once, *loudly*, in the imagination of the American nation, so method on this occasion, again with limited funds, chose to Sacrifice frequency for impact and identity. And the identity doesn't come from simply from the words and images in the booklet, of course. It comes in significant measure from the fact that it is a booklet. The fact of a booklet bound into a magazine is not in itself unusual for readers to come across. But a book from a *cleaning products* company? In a glossy magazine? Outlining a brand philosophy and inviting us to be a part of it? We noted earlier the brand's ambition was to learn from the skin care category, where consumers buy into a philosophy or lifestyle and then into a range of products that reflect that: The booklet *People against Dirty* was method's very public launch of that mind-set change. method chose to trade reach and frequency in order to give that philosophy the room and depth it needed in order to be properly communicated.

When Diesel launched in New York, it deliberately chose to open opposite Levi's flagship store as a signal of intent and a statement of attitude. Since then, Levi's moon has waned, and Diesel's growth has given it a very different set of challenges, chief among them how to continue to grow while retaining a counterculture, Challenger image. Sacrifice has been critical to Diesel in doing this successfully. Recognizing that in order to manage this difficult balance it needs to have much greater control over how its brand is portrayed at point of purchase, the company has cut non-Diesel retail outlets from 10,000 to 5,500, sacrificing all those that either presented the brand poorly or gave it insufficient ability to influence the presentation. While Diesel has invested in its own branded stores at the same time (now up to 300), this recognition of what it needed to Sacrifice in distribution to preserve and indeed strengthen its identity has been critical to maintaining its momentum. Although ubiquity in distribution is good for establishment brands like Coca-Cola and AT&T, it is dangerous for Challenger brands looking to create a stronger affinity with a more focused target, be they self-styled fashion rebels, surfing wannabes, or weekend mountain bikers.

SACRIFICE IN MESSAGE: TRADING DEPTH FOR DEFINITION

The abyss between the quantity of different messages a company would like to communicate, and the single-minded simplicity that it takes to stand out to the consumer in communication is the one that most marketeers find hardest to bridge. There appears from our side to be so much that needs communicating on our brand's behalf: market motivators, tickets of entry, and, inevitably, at least two or three key competitive discriminators that the research recommendations will have highlighted. We feel somehow that if we could only sit each consumer down for half an hour in a room and tell them all the reasons our brand is superior, then maybe we could turn them into loyal buyers.

But there is no escape: Strong brands are necessarily simple and single-minded in their communication, even if it means sacrificing what might seem to be important secondary messages. Tourism New Zealand has been very good at this. It has focused all its messaging around just one communication idea—100 percent Pure New Zealand. There were plenty of other kinds of messages about how to present New Zealand to the rest of the world, all of which were felt to be important by the stakeholders: New Zealand's rapidly developing creative and technical expertise, for example, was something its government was particularly keen to communicate in some form. Yet the team recognized that to break through in the world travel market, where they were often dwarfed by the budgets of their bigger rivals, they would have to not simply focus their advertising on a single message, but focus their whole communications budget around this advertising. Before 2000, 80 percent of the marketing budget had been spent on promotional work in the local markets, and only 20 percent in advertising. With the new campaign, the Tourism New Zealand team, recognizing that they could not afford to dissipate all their efforts, spent 100 percent of their budget on advertising this very clear message. It remains perhaps the most focused and successful country marketing of the last 20 years, in spite of operating on a fraction of the media spend of some of its much larger competitors.

SACRIFICE IN PRODUCT RANGE AND LINE EXTENSIONS

Before starting the Hong Kong newspaper *Apple Daily*, its founder, Jimmy Lai, had set up a clothing retailer in Hong Kong called Giordano. Offering 300 lines through four stores, Giordano was doing well enough, but nothing remarkable. The new retailing brand's real growth didn't come, in fact, until he went to New York and walked into Gap. And in seeing it, Lai realized there was an opportunity to revolutionize his approach. He realized that maintaining a wide range of lines was an unnecessarily expensive way of offering choice, because of the intrinsic expense involved in producing different cuts of each kind of clothing, such as pants and shirts. But if he were to Sacrifice much of the width of the range, the savings would then enable him to offer a much greater richness of colors, for example, within the lines that were on sale. So Lai went back to Hong Kong and cut the number of different style lines his stores stocked from 300 to 50—but then produced 19 different colors in the cut of T-shirt he did offer, because extending the consumer's choice by dyeing cloth (versus the cost of cutting different patterns) is relatively cheap. Within eight years, the overhauled Giordano went from 4 stores to around 500, becoming the largest clothing retailer in Asia. Lai had changed the concept of choice in his Asian Challenger, by Sacrifice and Overcommitment, in effect—what the garment business calls "focused, deep assortment."

Now there are Challengers whose whole product and experience offer is built around an offer of simplicity in a complicated category, which represents a kind of Sacrifice in itself—the simple functionality of the Flip video camera, for instance, or the pared back offering represented by ING Direct. We saw in Chapter 4 that ING's CEO was inspired by players in other categories offering stripped-down essentials, a kind of "fast-food banking." So ING Direct has good rates, no fees, no minimum balances—but offers only one savings account and one current account. In the mortgage category, it offers five-year mortgages and seven-year mortgages, but no 30-year mortgages, because consumers refinance them so often; if you ring up ING Direct and ask for a 30-year mortgage, your contact will recommend an outside lender. Such simplicity clearly has a value in such a complex and undifferentiated market, as ING's growth testifies. And yet what we are examining in this chapter is also the bigger underlying theme about how companies at the same time choose to use their available resource. As a Challenger, we have to use our more limited resources (people, time, passion, energy, money) against the few things that will really make a difference, and this means being very clear on both who we are and what we are going to Sacrifice to promote that identity. Focus on the products, experiences, and marketing that will genuinely break through.

APPLE VERSUS YAHOO

Let's put two Challengers back-to-back to highlight the pivotal importance of Sacrifice in this regard—two very successful companies that find themselves in significantly different situations.

Apple, having brought itself to the brink of oblivion by the back end of the 1990s by losing sight of what it was (and instead reducing itself to creating ranges of unremarkable gray products), brought back a leader who believes in Sacrifice—who is said, in fact, to have cut within weeks of his return the number of projects in development from around 150 to just 3: the iMac, the iBook, and the G3 chip, projects that would really deliver a new future to Apple, and products that genuinely did "Think Different." Having turned the corner, Steve Jobs has continued to Sacrifice stringently. He observes that the concept of focus is often misinterpreted, that people think focus means saying yes to the project or commitment that it has already been decided to focus against: "But that's not what it means at all. It means saying no to the 100 other good ideas that there are. You have to pick carefully."[4]

Jobs claims in fact to be as proud of what Apple *hasn't* done, as what it *has* done; he points out that if Apple had committed to do a PDA, it wouldn't have had the resources to do the iPod, and that it is in large part what Apple has chosen to *Sacrifice* that has enabled it to do so well what it did choose to do. Apple in fact is so committed to this principle that it goes so far as to Sacrifice winners: The day it launched the Nano iPod, it stopped producing the mini, its hitherto most popular line.

Yahoo, conversely, burned brightly as a Challenger for a while, but is now floundering. Unfocused and reactive, it has become a brand that lacks any sense of what it is; it simply proliferates projects without any overarching sense of purpose or identity. This may seem a little cavalier as a commentary on a brand with 3.5 billion page views per day, a company that Microsoft's bid valued at $45 billion (a whisker larger than my own), but then the remarks are not mine: They are those of a Yahoo SVP, leaked in the celebrated "Peanut Butter Manifesto." In it, the writer identified the lack of exactly this very clarity as lying at the heart of the internal malaise facing the company. It was, he said, precisely Yahoo's failure to first understand what it was, and its lack of courage then to Sacrifice what it was not, that rendered it unable to move forward dynamically into the considerable challenges of a competitive new world.

THE STRATEGIC PURPOSE OF SACRIFICE

Hmm, Sacrifice. Isn't this just clear prioritization by any other name?

The difference between Sacrifice and prioritization is that the latter allows secondary and tertiary targets. Sacrifice means not doing these secondary and tertiary things at all.

Sacrifice's value, therefore, is not simply one of concentration of marketing forces externally; it also has an internal value similar to hard-pruning a plant: all the energy, all the dynamism in the company becomes devoted to the primary goal.

So, we can say from what we have seen in the preceding examples that Sacrifice serves three main strategic functions for a Challenger:

1. Sacrifice concentrates the internal and external expressions of identity by eliminating activities that might dilute it.
2. Sacrifice allows the creation of strong points of difference by changing the organization's mind-set from pursuing weak universal appeal to a more intense, narrower appeal (and thereby avoiding becoming the "mush in the middle").
3. Sacrifice generates critical mass for the communication of that identity and those differences by stripping away other secondary marketing activity. This is central to maximizing the Challenger's consumer presence, given its more limited marketing resources.

While the Brand Leader perceives its currency to be mass appeal and can afford the dilution of preference that creates because it is compensated for by the convenience of its ubiquity and distribution, Challengers need more extreme actions and gestures—they need to create a greater proportion of "committed" and "enthusiastic" users through real differentiation. Challenger currency is therefore not means but extremes: top-box preference scores or nothing. And this in turn means we need to create differences for ourselves that may well be sometimes polarizing (Lush's intense scents deter as many as they attract) but that also strongly attract as many as they deter; better a room divided than a room that doesn't care. And once we have delineated our identity through those points of difference, strip away every marketing activity that does not directly support that identity. For any brand, positioning is Sacrifice; for a Challenger, it is the path to growth. What it chooses not to do defines who and what it really is.

There is a story about, I think, Picasso. A visitor to his studio saw a huge block of stone sitting in the middle of the studio and asked the master what it was to be. A lion, came the reply. And how, pressed the visitor, will you make a lion out of this unhewn stone block?

It's easy, said Picasso. I simply get a chisel and chip away anything that doesn't look like a lion.

Videolink for this Chapter:

www.eatbigfishfood.com/etbf/sacrifice

10

THE SIXTH CREDO: OVERCOMMITMENT

It is impossible to be too strong at the decisive point.

Napoleon

GETTING INTO THE CLUB

January in New York. It is cold, very cold; snow fills the sidewalks. You have flown your whole family from New Zealand to America because you have created your own vodka, a super-premium vodka, and you want to get the top five nightclubs in New York to stock it—it is time your brand stretched its wings in the Northern Hemisphere a little. And you are here to go in person to those nightclubs and persuade them to stock this vodka you have created, called 42BELOW.

But the thing is, of course, that you are not the only super-premium vodka brand in town that is trying to get in to see these nightclubs—there is a lot of competition, for these are the key clubs that will, in reality, make or break you among those all-important opinion leaders. And with 100 new vodkas launching every year, even if you do get in to see those key decision makers, how many super-premium vodkas are they actually going to be prepared to stock? You know you can't buy your way in, because other vodkas, particularly the vodkas from the Big Fish, are going to have much deeper pockets than you. And you can't afford billboards. To paraphrase one of your most famous fellow countrymen: You don't have the money, so you will have to think.[1]

So you are sitting in your hotel room, thinking, and your wife comes up with this idea. Rather than just banging on the door and hoping they will see us, she says, let's do something else. We'll do something for them without being asked, before we have even really introduced ourselves. We'll set up "42BELOW Snow Patrol." When it starts snowing, two of us will show up, two Kiwis in "42BELOW Snow Patrol" jackets outside those key nightclubs, and just start shoveling away the snow for them. We won't ask for permission or anything—we'll just turn up and start doing it. And we'll be doing the bouncers a favor, because they won't have to do the shoveling, and we know they are very important gatekeepers to the clubs in many ways, and perhaps those outside guys will then talk about us to the inside guys, and so we'll already be on their good side, and they'll already know us when we go in and actually make our pitch.

It's a great idea, you all agree. Let's do it.

So you do. And in fact it works out even better than you had hoped. The bouncers do indeed love you, because you and the 42BELOW Snow Patrol keep the pavement clean for them. The people entering the club in their Gucci and Prada footwear love you because they don't get snow and slush all over their shoes. And the club owner loves you because the pavement looks fabulous outside their club. And the big plus is that the papers also love the story—the *New York Post*'s gossip columnist sees the 42BELOW Snow Patrol on their way into one of the clubs and writes it up on page 6. And the result is that by the time you approach the people inside those key nightclubs, the people who make the decisions about which vodka to stock, those critical decision makers have already heard about you, have already read about you, know their customers have already seen you, and are already predisposed to listen to you. And, frankly, they also recognize that this is a small company with good ideas about how to get noticed in a crowded marketplace—and to get the throughputs they want, they want to sell vodkas that know how to do exactly that.

GETTING THE RIGHT KIND OF DEALER

Before we reflect on why about why this kind of behavior, which we are going to call *Overcommitment*, is imperative for Challengers, and what characteristics lie at the heart of it, let us consider a rather different example, from a much larger company. We will then look at them together and note what they have in common.

You are a large Japanese car manufacturer—in fact, the second largest automotive manufacturer in the world. While hugely successful in the United States, your brand launched to, and then grew up with, the Boomer generation, and your average buyer age is growing older with them, so you have a long-term ambition to build a more successful brand presence among younger U.S. car buyers, and in particular the young trendsetters. While an important target group in themselves, they will also be key, long term, in getting a new generation of U.S. motorists into the Toyota and Lexus brands as their life stage and needs change and grow.

You have initiated a few years previously a significant project specifically to tackle this opportunity among youth, called Project Genesis, whereby you essentially looked to break with your immediate past and market three models—the Echo, the MR2, and the Celica—still under the Toyota brand, but with a significantly different overall marketing approach toward youth. While relatively successful in selling to young customers, the initiative fell short of its ambitions; although valuable in learning terms, it taught you that you were going to have to do more than bundle existing products in different ways through existing dealer channels. You were going to have to commit to it on a much more holistic level, embracing product, process, and marketing.

So you create a new brand, with two new models, specifically for this target. You create a new stand-alone model identity for it—it will not live under the parent brand. It will have a different purchase process, "Pure Price," where the price advertised by the dealer is the price consumers will pay, with no negotiation expected or given. It will of course need to be marketed in an entirely different way to this audience as well—a grassroots approach will be required to seed the brand and then create genuine participation among this elusive and mobile target. And the brand will also need to be genuinely respected and romanced by the dealers as a stand-alone, youth-orientated brand, rather than just the latest youth-skewed model from Toyota.

You determine, therefore, that you will look to create a new and unique in-dealer experience, as well as a new kind of mutually beneficial contract with those dealers who want to be part of the Scion brand. Not every Toyota dealer will need or want to sign up for Scion, but those who do will themselves need to commit to the new holistic model for this new youth brand: They will need to agree to give it a distinct brand space all its own in the dealership—a Scion space, rather than simply a bit of Toyota space. And because the identity is going to center around the championship of self-expression, the signing dealers will need to be active proponents of all the different ways you are going to offer in which consumers can personalize their Scion. These dealers will need to understand that to communicate genuine personalization, they will want to have a very different kind of conversation with their customers than they have had historically about the traditional and limited accessory market, because the level of personalization you are going to offer customers will extend to literally thousands of possible combinations. The options available to customers will embrace three different programs of your own, together with third-party accessories offered in the dealership (the first time this has been done), the dealer's own aftermarket accessorization, the choice of car specs the customers choose, and the formation of owners' clubs to share advice and education about how to personalize further. And in addition to committing to this holistic model and giving the brand its own distinctive space within the dealership, the

FIGURE 10.1 Customized Scion xB.

participating dealers will also need to commit to an educational program you will put on for them about how to talk to consumers about personalization in an entirely new and fresh way when they come into the showroom.

OVERCOMMITMENT

Different though they are in many ways, what do both of these stories have in common? They share both a common need: In order to genuinely succeed, the brand in each case will have to break through barriers that the team behind it can already anticipate. And both brands, although very different in size, share a common way of thinking about the solution: Let's think about those barriers and actively remove them before they occur. In other words, let's not simply commit to make this happen, let's overcommit.

In the case of 42BELOW, the Challenger had to get into the right bars to break into the New York super-premium vodka market. These key bars in turn influenced the stocking policy of the second and third tiers of bars, and the crowd who came to party at that small key group of nightclubs were themselves the opinion leaders who were also therefore the determiners of taste for the other night owls across the city as a whole. But, as we said, every other super-premium vodka obviously knew this, too—so 42BELOW looked at how it could overcome the nightclub ennui of "another day, another super-premium vodka presentation" and create not simply salient differentiation but a favorable predisposition toward 42BELOW, before the team even started presenting.

In the case of Scion, Toyota had learned from the Genesis Project that marketing alone was not going to be enough to break through against this target: The new brand would need the dealer as well as the consumer to wholly embrace and participate in a holistic new model, and they therefore had to make that holistic model genuinely a part of the reality of the dealer and customer experience. If the concept of personalization and self-expression simply became a little smoke and mirrors, they would fail. So what Toyota and its dealers did with the Scion brand was Overcommit. They anticipated all the reasons why internal intent might not translate into external behavior, and structured their business and business relationships to remove those potential barriers.

Put another way, in these two examples Scion and 42BELOW aimed two feet below the brick.

AIMING TWO FEET BELOW THE BRICK

Let us suppose you have always wanted to put your hand through a brick. You have seen it done, and it fascinates you as an achievement of flesh and will. So you seek the instruction of a karate black belt, who by chance happens to be a janitor in your building. Teach me, sensei, you say. And after making you wax a lot of cars and paint a lot of fences, he teaches you this: If you want to put your hand through a brick, you cannot succeed by aiming at the surface of the brick. To break through, you have to aim two feet the other side. Two feet below it; that is the way to ensure you will go through a surface the body will naturally flinch from.

In the same way, Challenger brands—and the people behind Challenger brands—do not succeed through commitment; they succeed through *Overcommitment*. They do not do *just enough* for success at the crucial point; instead, they Overcommit to ensure success and to overcome each identifiable pocket of inertia and resistance they will *inevitably* meet (internally and externally) in attempting to translate Challenger intention and strategy into behavior and results.

In particular, this will mean Overcommitting in delivering your chosen point of difference to your chosen target—particularly if this target is an attitudinal one (look at Facebook's opening up of application development to third-party developers to allow a constant stream of new ideas continue to make their brand of social interaction fun, for instance). But Overcommitment will clearly also be required in business practice or behavior in order to realize some of the ideas that will be necessary to prompt reevaluation or to enable Thought Leadership. Sometimes this will be Overcommitment in terms of a particular action that will be definitive in creating appraisal or reappraisal.

Take the example of Swatch we looked at earlier—the hanging of a 500-foot watch on the Commerzbank in Frankfurt. For Swatch, it was one thing to come up with the idea and quite another to make it happen. How lucky, we might be tempted to think, that the President of the

Commerzbank allowed Swatch to carry out such a bold concept. Consider instead, we mentally add, the inertia and resistance that would probably have lain within our own company when an idea like that was first suggested. And consider, if we are honest, our own personal reaction had someone within our organization suggested something similar for our brand in our next key market. Would it have been to begin enthusiastically working out how it would need to be done? Or would it have been to admire it as an entertaining idea, while mentally writing it off as something that would never reach fulfillment within our culture?

It is to overcome such hidden mental inertia, as much as overt resistance, that we need as a Challenger to aim two feet below the brick. In the case of Swatch, Overcommitment meant that luck had very little to do with the success of the outcome. Germany was potentially the largest European market for the new Swiss watch industry; so they had to make it succeed. Prior to meeting the bank, then, the Swatch team anticipated the barriers that the key decision maker—the President of the Commerzbank—would put up, and answered them *before* even the initial approach was made. They approached the local civic authorities and sought and received written permission for the project, so that later, when they actually met the President of the Commerzbank, and his first reaction proved to be something like, "You're crazy; in the first place, the authorities would never let us do it," they could reply that such a permit had in fact already been issued. When later the President expressed worry about the effect it would have on customers' opinions of the bank, Swatch showed him a survey of those very customers suggesting that they liked the bank showing its human face through a gesture such as this. By Overcommitting, by anticipating the barriers to success and overcoming them before they were raised, Swatch succeeded at the crucial point.

Sometimes this Overcommitment will not be about one action, but about setting up a structure that ensures that your key point of difference will always be consistently delivered. We saw earlier Scion really thinking through the necessary relationship with the dealer to ensure this. JetBlue is another example: in resolving to "restore the humanity to air travel," it famously made one of its key decisions of sacrificing meals for passengers, and instead spending that money on things that would actually make a difference to the quality of the flight for their passengers, such as multichannel seat-back live TV. As JetBlue's success grew, other airlines looked to emulate the concept: JetBlue's response was to actually buy the company that provided the seat-back entertainment so that no one else in its category could offer it, to make sure its key point of difference would always be delivered. In the same way, we can see a blog with great momentum, Gawker (perhaps most famous for posting the controversial video of Tom Cruise speaking to his fellow Scientologists), actually owning its own servers, so that no outside party can pressure the server owner to remove content it doesn't approve of. For Gawker, controversy means footfall, and you don't want anyone to be able to prevent you from the benefits of that footfall.

Sometimes the Overcommitment will lie in the decisions you make about staffing. To succeed in its ambition of making it easier for the British people to do something a little healthier for themselves by drinking an entirely natural smoothie every day, innocent had to something that had not really been done before: to make the man and woman in the street really engage warmly with a healthy product. And innocent realized that one critical way of doing this was to create an entirely new kind of relationship between the person and the packaging—and, through the packaging, also the brand. The packaging copy was warm, quirky, and chatty, from the way it talked about the brand to the way it spoke about the ingredients, and in order to genuinely create the sense of a brand that was talking to you and with you, innocent would do something that no brand in the United Kingdom had ever done before: Not only would it have up to eight versions of each piece of body copy in the market at any one time for each of its four initial smoothie mixes, but it would change all of them every three months. The pack conversation, if you like, would be as fresh as the contents. And, if the innocent purchasers wanted even more interaction with the company, they could call the company on the "banana phone" and/or sign up for a weekly e-mail.

The banana phone was in effect a call to the company, and the company as a whole would be responsible for answering it—and still does. But creating good copy that would be constantly renewed could have been the kind of intention that only lasted six months before the real world kicked in. So innocent Overcommitted. Even though the company consisted of only four people at the time, they hired a friend from college, Dan, whose job it would be to write the packaging copy and the e-mail newsletter. While a big financial commitment for a fledgling company and its owners—they knew that the quality of the one-to-one, engaged relationship they would build with each of their consumers would be second only to the quality of the product in determining the success of the brand. So they Overcommitted to it. And while their first weekly e-mail went out to 11 people, it now goes out to 120,000.

innocent is now the fastest-growing food and drink company in the UK. As the company has expanded to other geographies in continental Europe, this structure, of including a carefully chosen native writer as part of that initial small group, has carried over as well. They are still Overcommitting at this decisive point.

WHAT ARE OUR DECISIVE POINTS GOING TO BE?

Like a political party, Challengers are also in a sense fighting an election battle; they are campaigning for change, and a change of vote. In that campaign, the balance between success and failure in any endeavor is much narrower than one might imagine, because the consumer's decision-making process is much more precarious than one might imagine. How a particular salesperson speaks to a customer, convincing a key trade buyer of the quality of distribution needed, or the extent of the news coverage gained at launch—any of these may make the difference between preserving or reversing the status quo in the market. To slightly paraphrase one of our Challengers, every consumer interaction is a potential sales event. One reason why ING Direct, for example, while it has Sacrificed product range, has in its own way Overcommitted on customer service for a stripped-down banking service: If you call its U.S. toll-free number, you get through to a real person, and one in the same country as you. How very refreshing.

The first task in Overcommitment, then, is to identify the decisive points on which the Challenger must succeed. Clausewitz famously commented: "The general must throw his forces at the crucial point where, if he succeeds—even if he fails at all other points—victory will be his." In this, the Pareto effect (the so-called 80:20 rule) governs action as much as targeting; if we had to point to the one or two things we have done that have made most of the difference to our business's success—or even to our own personal success—over the past year, we would not have much difficulty singling them out. What we more often fail to do, however, is to *anticipate* in advance the decisive one or two points of difference on which real differentiation and trial will depend so that we can Overcommit to them.

If, as a Challenger, you are focusing on a few bold sweeps of the brush to paint your marketing picture, rather than a flurry of incremental activities—then it is relatively easy to anticipate and plan for the one or two key points, and the pockets of likely resistance that are hidden behind them. Launching into a world full of photo-sharing sites, for instance, and wanting to use its own particular sense of community as a key differentiator, flickr emphasized making new users feel welcome. So right from the beginning, it ensured there would be a member of the flickr team moderating the flickr forum 24/7, just to make new people feel part of the community. flickr made sure it welcomed each of the first 10,000 members personally, giving them tips, support, encouragement—thus overcommitting to creating the initial community that would then grow itself.

Of course, when the stakes are self-evidently this high or the company is small, motivation runs deep and overcommitment comes naturally. Swatch had the motivation: On the success of the brand's launch hung the success of the Swiss watch industry, and Germany was an enormous and vital market. If, like Cirque du Soleil opening its first show in Los Angeles, you find you have invested so much of your capital in the opening night that you don't have enough money to buy the gas to get the trucks back to Montreal if the show fails, you have a wonderful incentive for everyone in the company to make it work. There is a saying in Norway: The hungriest wolves hunt best.

This is a critically important point for us, precisely because most of us are not in this situation. We're not that small, and we still have half a tank of gas in the truck. And maybe that's part of the problem. As would-be Challengers, we have to build our hunger into the objectives we set for ourselves and the ways we anticipate and overcome resistance inside and outside the organization.

AIMING TWO FEET BELOW THE BRICK: DEFINITION OF OBJECTIVES

We said Challenger is a state of mind. It goes without saying, then, that the leader of a Challenger organization has to first develop that determination to succeed him- or herself. Personal Overcommitment sets the tone for those immediately around you, and high stakes readily develop personal Overcommitment at the top.

Such personal Overcommitment is characteristic of the great Challengers in history, even quite late in their success. Consider Alexander the Great, for example—a Macedonian younger than 20 years old who defeated the largest army in the Eastern world (the Persians) as a prelude to creating an empire encompassing all of what is now Turkey, Syria, Egypt, Iraq, Iran, and northern India. By 325 BC, with the defeat of the Persians behind him, Alexander and his Macedonians had already conquered Greece and extended his conquests to the Punjab, largely on foot. But some of his troops had been fighting for 10 years, and loyalty began to waver—while much of the army wanted to turn back, Alexander wanted to go on. The crux came when they laid siege to the hill fort of Multan. The defiant Indians inside repelled attack after attack by his increasingly disheartened Macedonians, until Alexander sensed that more than the battle hung on the result of the next attack.

He gambled. Taking a small core of his elite troops, the Companions, he personally led a charge with scaling ladders against the wall of the fort. The attack was largely repulsed, except for Alexander and three Companions, who found themselves standing alone on the parapet, with the rest of the Greek troops running back to their own lines. His Companions shouted to Alexander to jump down the outside of the walls—they would cover him until he was in the safety of his own lines; instead, he did the opposite. To the horror of the watching Greeks, he leapt *inside* the walls of the Indian fort into the middle of the enemy and out of sight of his own army.

The three Companions on top of the wall jumped down alongside him and put their backs against the wall in a ring around Alexander, attempting to hold off the defenders. Meanwhile alarm ran along the Greek attackers outside, confronted with the imminent death of their leader. Desperate, they launched themselves at the walls to rescue Alexander. While some leapt from the shoulders of their fellow soldiers to the top of the wall, others broke the ladders apart and hammered the splintered rungs as footholds into the clay walls.

This time desperation carried them to success. By the time they reached Alexander, two of the three protecting him were dead, and he was wounded, but the fort was taken. Their loyalty was renewed. And Alexander wove Northwest India into his empire before turning back.

Once the business leader, then, has developed a Challenger mindset, the next stage is to drive that same state of mind within the core group around him or her. (This is the primary function of Chapter 15. For the moment, we shall note this task, but put the nature of its achievement to one side.)

But how one motivates one's staff is an altogether different issue. Motivation of staff also depends on Overcommitment, but in terms of a joint Overcommitment to a new scale of objectives. Overcommitment in goals can help create Overcommitment in implementation.

The key point to realize is this: We cannot fool the consumer by talking about good intentions. They know about mission statements and customer-satisfaction programs, and the world that they can see doesn't seem to have changed. These wonderful intentions haven't led to a universal quality of service that they can feel or enjoy or relax with. They aren't really interested in our brand's intentions; they are interested in what we are going to do for them *now*. And as a consequence of "claim inflation"—the effective devaluation of the consumers' inclination to believe marketing promises by the gaps they consistently find between promise and delivery—they frequently don't believe you're actually going to do what you say you're going to do (remember the "Missouri Mind-set"). So intention is not enough. And the only way to translate intention into behavior—if everything hangs on the outcome—is to Overcommit.

Let us throw this back at ourselves. Assuming for the sake of argument that we have some customer interaction built into our brand's success (be it with end purchaser, trade, or some other audience), let us ask ourselves the following three questions:

1. What are the ambitions of our company's mission statement when it comes to customer service?
2. How close are we to delivering on those ambitions, really?
3. And how much closer have we really come to delivering on those objectives over the past three years?

The answers for most companies (particularly after that critical third beer on a Friday night when one starts being honest about the company one works for) will probably be:

1. "To exceed our customer's expectations. To surprise and delight them."
2. "Sort of."
3. "Not really."

Certainly, if we were to then think of ourselves as consumers of the wide variety of categories across which each of us may personally browse, we could count the brands whose service we can remember exceeding our expectations on the fingers of one knee. To generate a different kind of strategy and different kind of behavior, then, our study of Challenger companies suggests that we need to radically reframe the objectives and goals we set our staff—and work through the consequences. Imagine, for instance, ourselves in a more acute Challenger situation, where success is in fact coupled very closely with survival. Or imagine that our goals for next year are suddenly doubled— both the softer goals of customer satisfaction and the harder goals of volume. Next year you are required to achieve double the return with the same amount of marketing resources and at the same price point. How do you now approach your strategy? Your customer service objectives? The translation of both of these into a new behavior?

I suggest, if taken seriously, all these will change significantly. (A prominent leader of a large multinational is said to practice a slightly different version of this exercise: When one of his teams is unable to crack the problem, he halves the resources and halves the personnel—and through this greater adversity forces breakthrough.) One is forced to abandon all thoughts of incrementalism, or building on the tactical activities from last year, and throw oneself boldly at a few critical points. Set objectives that demand Overcommitment to succeed.

AIMING TWO FEET BELOW THE BRICK: DEALING WITH RESISTANCE OUTSIDE THE ORGANIZATION

When Oakley started to move into eyewear, it had a consumer base every bit as vital to it as the trade or its employees—the athletes Oakley was trying to woo to use its product. Without the deep pockets of a Nike, it could not pay the major athletes or even minor athletes enough to wear its product unless they genuinely became fans of the new Oakley shades. Initially, this proved difficult because of the unusual appearance of the product, which had been designed to produce the best possible lens for the application, rather than aesthetics alone (they were the first lenses to follow the curving contour of the face, for example, thus minimizing light distortion). When triathlete Scott Tinley was invited into the factory to try on the new range of performance eyewear, for instance, Mike Parnell, Oakley's president, noticed a problem. Although Tinley was enthusiastic about the performance of the sunglasses, he seemed uncomfortable with the novel styling. Invited to try them, Tinley looked at the floor and shook his head from side to side, looking for possible distortion or light interference. Yes, they seem great, he said to his toes, and he took them off before looking up again, apparently reluctant even to lift his head up and look at Parnell when wearing them.

Parnell realized Tinley was embarrassed about the appearance of the new line and knew this was a critical obstacle he had to overcome—Oakley needed Tinley, if not actually to flaunt his eyewear, at least to be seen as being comfortable wearing them, emotionally as well as physically.

Instead of confronting the issue head on, Parnell encouraged Tinley to walk around the factory wearing the new glasses and see if he felt more comfortable after wearing them for a little while (most of the employees were sports enthusiasts themselves, and used to interacting with the athletes in the casual California culture of the Oakley factory floor).

After having a cup of coffee, Tinley went for a stroll. "Cool shades, Scott," said an attractive young woman in the reception area. "Really?" said the innocent Tinley, his chin lifting a little.

Two other people commented in the next corridor. And another on the company basketball court. And the girl in the test lab.

By the time he left the building, Tinley was keen to try the new glasses on his friends.

The people who had all "spontaneously" commented had, of course, been planted by Parnell. Hopeful though he was that experience would make a fan out of the triathlete, he had left nothing to chance. Parnell had aimed two feet below the brick.

AIMING TWO FEET BELOW THE BRICK: ANTICIPATION OF RESISTANCE WITHIN THE ORGANIZATION

One may be able to buy short-term success through marketing activity. Longer-term success will hinge on the everyday behavior of the company and its employees. To get Overcommitment to the delivery of a core strand of marketing strategy at the level of the consumer's experience, we have to first get Overcommitment to implementation within the organization.

There are two simple parts of approaching the achievement of this. The first is for us to focus on each of the core tasks or marketing ideas we feel success hinges on, and for each one, to identify *the three reasons it will fail*. The second part is to then brainstorm the most effective way of overcoming each of these hidden barriers before we implement the idea.

These obstacles are not usually hard to see; it is just that they are rarely anticipated specifically in this way. And, as we saw, Challengers have ideal circumstances in which to overcome them *before* attempting to implement their core marketing activity.

This may be against the more general ambition or identity for the brand. Umpqua calls itself the "World's Greatest Bank." How do we as customers know this? Less because it is written on the walls in every store (though it is) and more because every employee, even the CEO, has to say "Hello, welcome to the world's greatest bank" when answering the phone. This is less for the benefit of the customers and more to create a constant internal prompt of what is expected of them. It keeps the bar for each member of the bank staff the highest it can be: If each of them say they are representing the world's greatest bank every time they answer the phone, then they had better deliver it every time they subsequently serve that customer, or the customer will use it against them.

It can be Overcommitment against a particular key initiative. The Dove team, presenting internally within Unilever, knew that they were going to meet with a certain skepticism as to whether their "Real Beauty" strategy was going to work. Though the brand and agency team themselves were mostly women, they would be presenting their ideas essentially to men in their later 40s and 50s, very distant from the younger women who were relatively insecure about their looks and bodies, the target group that Dove was concerned with, and therefore from the strategy and campaign they would be recommending. So before they presented to this senior male group, the team discovered which of them had daughters, and then contacted the mothers of those daughters (i.e., the executives' wives). In talking to them, they asked for a picture, and what her daughter did and did not feel comfortable about with her body. The team then put together a short piece of film consisting of a series of photographs of the daughters, with simple statements about what they were uncomfortable with in their own appearance, and played this montage at the beginning of their internal presentation to this male group of decision makers. It proved an immensely powerful beginning: Many of the fathers didn't know their own daughters felt the way they did about their nose, or their freckles, or their hair—and it left them considerably more open to the strategic intent presented by the Dove team. (A fully filmed version of this internal film, obviously using other children, subsequently ended up as the Super Bowl spot for the launch of the Dove Self-Esteem Fund.)

So the key failure for any company attempting to effect a gear change in its own performance is not the ability to define its intention or to have a good idea, but the inability to translate that intention or idea into behavior—in particular, behavior that genuinely helps it stand out. The importance of the gap between intention and delivery is highlighted by a study a few years ago that suggested that only 14 percent of all churn in customer-service businesses comes through dissatisfaction with poor treatment or rudeness on the part of a company's employees.[2] Five times that number—68 percent—switch their loyalty to a different brand because of *indifference* on the part of the service company's employees. This indifference does not arise because executives at the top of those individual companies are not interested in growth or because they fail to understand the importance of customer service. Even money says 85 percent of the "indifferent" companies in the study had as part of their mission statement something about a desire to "surprise and delight our customers with the quality of our service." This indifference came because they failed to translate strategic intent into behavior.

The first Overcommitment exercise we shall call *innocent*.

innocent *vb:* To ask oneself, for each core marketing task, the three irrefutable reasons it will fail (or be diluted into mediocrity). To then brainstorm the most effective way of neutralizing or reversing each of them.

The second exercise we shall call *Jannard*, after the founder of
Oakley.

Jannard *vb:* To ask oneself the same question in three different ways:
(1) How should we ensure this activity succeeds? (2) How would we
approach ensuring that success if our career depended on it? And
finally (and this is, if you like, why it is called *Jannard*), (3) how would
we approach it if it was our business, we were down to $300 in the
bank, and our family's livelihood depended on it?

This exercise may be seen by some to be a little flippant, but it is in
fact intended to be serious—it helps resolve the lurking tautology here,
answering the question: "How can I plan for something to take more
than I think it will take? By definition, the revised plan will *be* what I think
it will take." As one moves down each level, the answer to that question
becomes apparent.

Its other real value lies in separating natural "Challenger individuals"
from natural "establishment individuals." When trying the exercise,
some do indeed, as intended, become more committed, thinking the
task through and developing more imaginative and compelling ways of
ensuring success. Others, conversely, do exactly the opposite: As the
stakes progressively increase, they become progressively more conservative until, with their family's livelihood on the line, they are acting as
conventionally as possible.

You clearly have to decide for yourself which type of person distin-
guished by this exercise is more likely to help the Challenger company
succeed.

SACRIFICE AND OVERCOMMITMENT

We saw earlier that central to Challenger marketing is ceasing to think
about marketing as "strategy" and "execution" and breaking our
actions instead into the Challenger triad of *Attitude-Strategy-Behavior*.

Challengers are not somehow unusual in that they have a monopoly on good ideas; they are unusual, however, in that they make good ideas happen. This has to do with three things:

1. Mental preparation, and therefore preparedness to follow through (the first credo)
2. A clearer sense of how the use of ideas can define identity, create leadership, and accelerate the consumer relationship (the second, third, and fourth credos)
3. Planning: anticipating resistance and inertia in implementation, and aiming two feet below the brick (the sixth credo)

In this respect, Sacrifice is the inverse of, and the enabler of, Overcommitment: In addition to Sacrifice defining one's identity, it also allows one to Overcommit. As the active clothing brand howies says, "Having the idea is the easy part."

Videolink for this Chapter:

www.eatbigfishfood.com/etbf/overcommitment

11

THE SEVENTH CREDO: USING COMMUNICATIONS AND PUBLICITY TO ENTER SOCIAL CULTURE

Young colleagues ask me: "What is the advertising budget?"
"None!" I say. The first rule is: Never shit like a bird; shit like an
elephant. You ever seen birdshit? Not unless it hits you in the fore-
head. But you don't forget elephant shit. It's dramatic.

Adrian Zecha, founder of Aman Resorts[1]

M ost marketing communication is poor. Consumers and newspapers are constantly cruising for novelty. The combination of these
two offers a huge opportunity to aspiring Challenger brands.

We saw in Chapter 1 the formidable hurdles we had to overcome in
any communicated expression of marketing—principally the problems
of clutter, audience distraction, and claim inflation. The communication
problems these posed were summed up in a slightly different context
with more color and less political correctness by a former editor of the
New York Post to a young protégé:

Lemme tell you something, kid. You gotta grab the reader by the
throat. He's on the train. It's hot. He's trying to hit on his secretary;

she's not giving him the time of day. His wife is mad at him. His kid needs braces; he doesn't have the money. The guy next to him stinks. It's crowded. You want him to read your story? You better make it interesting.[2]

And he was talking here about news, which is something most of the target audience (at the time) paid money to see; the vast majority of advertising, on the other hand, which many now pay to avoid, perversely fails even the most basic of such requirements. Try this exercise: Sit down and watch an hour and a half of commercial television this evening with a small bag of peanuts. Take as the basic premise that any good piece of communication has to be at least relevant and distinctive. Count the number of ads that fulfill this single basic premise and mark each one with a peanut on the arm of your chair. Eat the other peanuts.

It may be depressing, but at least you don't go hungry.

So, what's the point here? The point is that, as a Challenger, in very rare cases you will indeed have such an extraordinary, game-changing product that the world will beat a path to your door. For instance, while the Tata Nano may not be a better mousetrap, it is a startlingly cheaper mousetrap, and as a startlingly cheaper mousetrap, its website got 4 million hits the day it went up. But the vast majority of us will not be in that position. We won't have extraordinary news naturally oozing from every pore of our product or brand, which means that most of us will have to *create* that news ourselves. Which in turn means we need to *look for opportunity in everything we do* to create such news. Our ambition in doing this is not simply to shift the awareness needle wildly into the red for a while: it is to become a live, and ideally self-replicating, part of popular culture.

THE VALUE OF AN IDEA

We know already, of course, that the Challenger has no choice about trying to stand out; differentiation for us is a question of survival as well as profitable growth. Which means that Challengers must demand to be noticed: Achieving front-of-mind salience and actively prompting change are the watchwords. If our real share of voice is not some artificial comparison with the rest of our category, but our media budget as a proportion of a national spend of $210 billion (bearing in mind that the "Category Isn't"), for example, then Challengers need to take a bold position in everything they do. And in communications and publicity—and the amplified interactivity that can now accompany those—they need breakthrough, rather than contentment with *awareness* and *prompted satisfaction*. And as Challengers we have much less (if any) money, of course, so whereas Establishment brands can rely on weight of exposure, repetition, and ubiquity to drive home a message, for a Challenger who aspires to do more with less, *clear* communication alone is not enough—capturing the target's imagination must be the objective.

We have consistently seen the importance of attitude to a Challenger. So, while breakthrough in this area is essential, let's not see the need to use publicity and communications to enter social culture as simply another enormous mountain to climb. For on the positive side, this perspective on our marketing challenge also represents a huge opportunity for Challengers, insofar as this is *one of the very few places where the Establishment brand is at a potential disadvantage*. Trying to protect what they already have gained, and the desire to avoid alienating the broad mass market does not encourage Brand Leaders into bold advertising or publicity-generating activities. Most Brand Leaders are by definition change-averse, and this leads to a comfortable culture (within Brand Leader cultures, one gets all too often promoted to the next level for not making a mess of one's current job) and comfortable advertising. For a Challenger, then, creativity (in all forms of communication and the generation of publicity) is a business tool, to be ruthlessly sought out and deployed as a principal source of competitive advantage against Establishment brands.

In this context, something like a communication idea doesn't become just a *part* of the marketing mix. It becomes—potentially at least—a high-leverage asset. We can go further: Communication ideas and the consistent strategic pursuit of the right publicity and word of mouth can in fact be the most powerful business tool Challengers have at their disposal. And the truth of this, and the breadth of opportunity that accompanies it, has clearly dramatically increased over the past decade: E-mail culture, the emergence of social networks and other kinds of active online communities, the daily global talent contest that is YouTube—all these have created, as never before, a new level of opportunity for Challengers with very limited budgets to rapidly build awareness and interaction around their brand idea among consumers. As long as it is a brand idea anyone cares about, or can be provoked into caring about.

For instance, let's imagine you are a well-established U.S. clothing brand looking to expand into Northern Europe. You have a cult presence there as a cool brand, but seem to have hit a plateau in terms of consumer and trade interest—and the market you are in is declining 13 percent in value terms year by year. But here's the real problem: You are a brand with surfing roots that wants to sell board-riding clothing in Nordic countries, and people don't surf in Nordic countries. So as a Challenger, what do you do?

What you do is resolve to create an instant surfing culture where there currently is none, and a surfing culture all your own. You determine you will not, in effect, be about just the sport: You will represent an attitude about life, embodied in the way you portray surfboarding within this new culture. So, you produce a piece of film. It is a video taken by a camera phone of a guy surfing on one of the lakes in Copenhagen. Curious, you may say—I wasn't aware that the lakes in Denmark get that tidal. Well, they don't: The surfer has had a little help. While the boarder is paddling out into the middle of the otherwise calm water, one of his friends throws a bundle of dynamite hurriedly off the bridge that spans it. You watch, disbelieving: They can't really be going to explode dynamite in the middle of a city like Copenhagen, can they? And then, boom, there it goes, like a depth charge. The water surges up and out, and waves begin to rush toward our surfer. He turns away in preparation and starts paddling. Catching the first wave, he stands up, rides it until the wave runs out, and sinks back down again. The end frame comes up: "Quiksilver. Original Thinking."

You can't quite believe what you have just seen. Did they really just do that? How on earth did they get away with dynamiting an urban lake? You pass it on to a couple of friends: They must see this. And they pass it on it turn.

And then, a couple of days later, you read a newspaper article: OK, so it wasn't really a camera phone, it seems—they simply degraded the film to look as if it was. And they didn't really dynamite the lake, it was CGI, but they had all of us cold on that one, too. The point is, Quiksilver has now intrigued you: Surfing in Denmark is a wonderfully weird idea. And they continue to stimulate you: when you are walking down some steps to the metro a couple of days later, you see a sticker: "Good to walk, better to ride the rail," it says. "Quiksilver. Original Thinking." And you read in the newspaper that the brand has turned 10 bus stops into skate ramps. So, as a consequence, when you take the bus into town on Saturday to buy some clothes, what kind of brand are you going to consider? And what is your attitude going to be to this Challenger board-riding brand that you had never really thought about before a couple of weeks ago?[3]

The key here, of course, is that you are not the only one seeing this initial piece of film—posted on YouTube, the Quiksilver film to date has received 35 million hits. Carefully seeded in advance to create strong initial word of mouth among the hard-core surfing sites (almost all surfing websites worldwide carried it as front-page news), it also benefited from a more general buzz between friends: receiving 3.3 million hits in the Nordic countries alone (a market, as we noted before, that doesn't surf). And entering social culture in this way obviously dramatically increased the credibility, desirability, salience, and image of Quiksilver: On the back of the publicity, distribution rose 25 percent, and sales increased 20 percent in a declining market.

What is the conclusion that we draw from this? One could infer that Challengers need to be *edgy*—yet that clearly isn't always the case (look at the nascent Google, or Orange). One could be tempted to draw a conclusion about the Internet in particular—that the Internet can spread a Challenger's brand idea broadly within social culture more rapidly (and perhaps more cheaply) than any tool a Challenger has had at their disposal before, for instance. But, while this inference may be true, let's not get too fixated on the medium just yet. Let's first focus on the principle. And to keep us balanced as we lean into this principle, let's consider alongside it a very famous story about Lexus.

The story goes like this. In the first days after Lexus launched in the United States, a dealer serviced a car for a customer, but the car was returned to the customer with a problem: The morning after the customer picked up his car, he found that his recently serviced Lexus had leaked oil onto his concrete garage floor. So they phoned the dealer to complain, and the dealer came out to the customer's house. And this is where the story gets our attention. Because not only does the Lexus dealer fix the car, but instead of simply trying to clean up the little patch of oil stain the car has left on the garage floor, the dealer takes up the existing floor and lays an entirely new concrete floor, all at his own expense. The Lexus dealer, it seemed, wants everything for his customer to be perfect. That, people told you (and still do) as they finished the story, slightly incredulous, is how committed Lexus is to a great ownership experience.

So let's compare these two examples—the Quiksilver video and the Lexus story. They are very similar. One is an act and one is a filmed act, but both created enormous word of mouth, with a value way beyond the cost of the act itself. Both are rooted in a truth about the brand: Lexus did indeed take customer service to a whole new level; Quiksilver began life as a better-thought-out board short. Both spoke volumes about the attitude of their respective brands. Both created a slight sense of disbelief. Both cost something less than a conventional communications campaign (the Quiksilver campaign cost $50,000, and the Lexus story cost the price of a concrete floor—say $2,000). One was edgy, the other anything but. Yet what they both did in their own way was to permeate social culture and create a self-replicating word of mouth, and approval, about the brand.

So we all know the examples of brands that have really hit critical mass through the Internet over the last few years: Dove's *Evolution* film, Cadbury's drumming gorilla, Mentos in Coke. We see that there clearly are all kinds of fresh, constantly emerging possibilities for Challengers to spread their stories and engage their targets. And we see that this really is the Law of Increasing Returns writ large—except that this kind of beneficially increasing return is uniquely one that we as Challengers can profit from as much as—possibly more than—anyone else. But let's not get distracted at this stage by the *kinds* of media or channels available to us at this point, particularly the new kinds. After all, while there is a tendency to treat all of this as if it were something very new, the principles are very old ones: Social media and networks have been around for hundreds of years—forums where people delighted in passing on and talking about news and ideas they had picked up—they just were called bars, cafes, and pubs. So while of course, there are critical new elements and opportunities that the digital world has brought to this opportunity to engage with social cultures (visual dynamism, interactivity, flow, acce-·lerated community, and scaled momentum), let us refocus on the common principles across both the old and new world first, and then return to some of those new dimensions of difference.

RECOGNIZING THE HUMAN NEED FOR SOCIAL TRANSACTION

When we talk of consumer needs in marketing we think of (and look for) their needs as *consumers*. That is to say that implicit in all of our questioning is their potential consumption of our product. But as we have seen they are not in fact consumers: They are simply people who sometimes buy things. And this misframing of them as *consumers* means that only very rarely, therefore, do we think enough about their broader social needs: what they want, and need to be able to do and say in order to be able to interact healthily with their peer groups, in those little everyday ways that make them happy or unhappy social animals.

As an aspiring Challenger brand, then, we need to recognize not just this human need to share, but also how and why it can be stimulated, from a brand point of view, in a way that benefits both parties: the Challenger brand's need to get people to spread our word for us, and people's need to enjoy profitable human interaction. And this sharing of a brand idea or brand news usually arises because our targets have found themselves in one of five situations regarding a brand:

1. *Bragging rights, being on the pulse.* They have the sense that they have discovered something valuable, something that makes them feel, and seem to their peers, slightly ahead of the pack; they feel they are one of the first to unearth a new super-premium tequila, for instance, or a new social network application. "I heard this new band on the radio yesterday, out of Austin. You should check them out—they're going to be huge." "Have you seen this video? It's remarkable; it is made by this hilarious blogger in Japan I am really into."

2. *Product enthusiasm.* They have come across an aspect of product performance about a brand that is startlingly impressive: that a Land Rover is designed to be able to drive 4,000 miles continually off-road, for example. That Bare Escentuals, a skin care brand, was originally developed for the extremely sensitive skin of sufferers of psoriasis

and rosacea. That Avaaz.org managed to collate an online petition from 750,000 people over the Burmese government's crackdown on the "Saffron Revolution."

3. *Aspirational identification.* They have found a brand with a strong identity and ethos (perhaps through its authenticity or because it aligns itself to certain social issues, for instance), which they admire or would like to be identified with. If I discover that in a world of sweat-shops, American Apparel is sweatshop-free and in fact makes all its products in downtown Los Angeles, I have a new respect for the brand's principles: that it has made a presumably expensive but principled decision. If I discover that the board of directors of Rip Curl, an Australian surfing brand, is still required to surf every Satur-day morning, even though the age of Rip Curl's commercial director is 53, it suggests to me that here is one apparel company that has yet to sell out (perceived authenticity is fundamental to the endurance of a Challenger).

4. *News value.* They have come across a piece of marketing activity that has surprised, strongly entertained, or shocked them sufficiently to prompt conversation with their peer group. That the government is spending less on our children's school lunches than they do on pris-oners' lunches. That Jones Soda has produced a turkey-and-gravy-flavored soft drink for Thanksgiving. That Sir Richard Branson has ripped his trousers on national television jumping off the roof of a casino in Las Vegas.

5. *Creative fingerprint.* They have found or made something that is of valuable enough social currency to be passed on, the value of this clearly being enhanced by adding to it their own creative fingerprint. Recent research among teens, for example, indicates there is a high correlation between the *creation* of content and *talking about* that content. If you want them to talk about you for this kind of reason, you need to first enable content creation through your brand. But this motivation will not be confined to teens: One-third of the content on Current TV is created by the people who watch it.

A Challenger looking for aggressive growth without using advertis-ing, then, will want and need to actively fulfil one, perhaps all of these human needs. It will want to have a product that in its own way overperforms, on which it can be confident. Then although early brag-ging rights and a sense of being in the know are valuable to create a group of evangelists, the brand self-evidently cannot rely on this after launch and early growth, so it will need to build into its identity some characteristics that can generate aspirational identification, and use its marketing budget to invest in people and ideas that can consistently create news value. Finally, if it is genuinely looking to nurture a two-way relationship with its target market, one of engagement and participa-tion, it will look to create a way those people can put something of themselves into their relationship with the brand and the way they inter-act with it.

Yet in doing this, we need to recognize that some of the biggest problems that a Challenger faces in terms of breakthrough in the new world are, in one key way at least, exactly the same as the ones it faced in the old one. We might look at Quiksilver and feel that a viral film is an easy win; but the reality is that with 65,000 new postings put up on You-Tube every day, while the opportunity presented to us is indeed greater, the concomitant clutter is, if anything, much worse online than it is off.

Which is why, more than ever, we need to recognize the strategic primacy of the idea.

THE STRATEGIC PRIMACY OF THE IDEA

Acknowledging the strategic primacy of the idea does not mean that "any interesting creative idea is the right idea for the brand," nor is it an advocacy for beginning to write the idea first (whatever the medium, from advertising or design to publicity and direct mail) and retrofit the strategy afterward.

What it does mean, though, is that "capturing the imagination of the target" is a very different brief from "communicating a message to the target," and if one wishes to capture the imagination, then, in the words of Jay Chiat, "Good enough is not enough." In an ideas-dependent business, then, which is where a Challenger necessarily falls and rises, part of the definition of a good strategy is that it should be fertile ground for one or more strong ideas. It should no longer be possible to say, "We had a great strategy, but the creative people couldn't come up with any good ideas," in this new culture. Assuming you have capable creative people, that just means it was never a great strategy in the first place. The overall vision for the brand, therefore, needs to have some inherent flexibility in its articulation, and the strategic development process needs to change to allow for such flexibility. If the identified articulation of the brand strategy fails to produce ideas that can break through and seize the retreating target's imagination, we have to find another expression of the strategy. The development needs to be organic rather than linear; while not actually developed simultaneously, the strategy needs to be flexible enough to encompass the consideration of big new ideas if they are close enough to the overall direction the brand needs to take.

This will be a difficult concept for some to embrace. Surely, having arrived at the one correct strategy through analysis and research, they will argue, that strategy becomes the rigid railroad that steers the ideas. But the premise here is flawed: While there are still indeed certain types of problems for which there is only one correct strategic solution that can be divined from rigorous deductive thinking, they are increasingly rare. Most types of strategic problems in the new business world now require imagination as much as rigorous analysis, even at the strategic stage.

AN IDEA THAT RIPPLES—WHY FOLKLORE BEATS EQUITY EVERY TIME

As Challengers, then, we need to enter social conversation: We need to get everyone who comes across us to tell our story on our behalf. This will partly be because we lack the budget for paid-for media, or it may have as much to do with the nature of our ambition—as agents of change, we might set, as Dove did, a criterion of success being to "inspire debate" about our chosen issue.

Yet what the Lexus story above illustrates is that the value of such word of mouth obviously goes way beyond even these two advantages. Brands that *consistently* create such social currency begin to create a folklore or mythology around themselves. Such folklore is more than brand equity; it lives at a level above brand equity. Because, while *brand equity* may be defined as the perceptions or facts a consumer associates with the brand when probed, *mythology* may be defined as those perceptions or facts a consumer proactively communicates, *unasked*, about the brand. Thus, while brand equity is passive, personal, and residual—sitting as a collection of perceptions in an individual's mind to be triggered within that individual when the purchase process is embarked on—folklore is active, social, and self-propagating. It is like a virus of favorable equity that gets passed on among existing and potential user groups. Indeed, it is arguable that at the times of their strongest momentum, Challengers live at a level above Brand Leaders, because while Brand Leaders enjoy strong equity, Challengers enjoy a strong folklore—either at an iconic level through the brand's advertising and marketing, making it a reference point in popular culture, or through ground-level word of mouth.[4]

Some Challengers will create such ideas themselves (Quiksilver), and some will intelligently find a mutually beneficial relationship with them as they emerge. Stride chewing gum, for instance, was a new brand launched in 2006, by Cadbury Adams in North America, with the line "The Ridiculously Long Lasting Gum." Inspired by the success of Burger King's "Subservient Chicken," Stride looked for a way to either create or ride on a social phenomenon to support the advertising that communicated this positioning. Someone sent a film of a man called Matt Harding to Stride's activation company, who sent it on to the brand manager. It was a film Harding had put together of himself dancing badly (his words) in various recognizable sites and cities all over the world, and had posted on his own site for his friends. Recognizing that a man dancing nonstop all over the globe was an intriguing way of dramatizing the brand's positioning, the Stride team phoned Harding in Austin and asked to meet. He flew to the East Coast, rolled out a map of the world on the table, and told them where he was going next. They in turn explained that they would like to sponsor him to do this full-time. "And what is it you want from me?" asked Harding. Sensitive to the way brands had abused such viral ideas in the past, Stride replied that they wanted only back-of-house branding—a Stride logo in the top right corner of just two of the many scenes of dancing, an acknowledgment at the end, and a link to the Stride website. Harding agreed.

Fresh, relevant, and hugely appealing, in 2007 Harding's Stride-sponsored video had nine million views (with the outtakes video getting another two million) and appeared on the front page of Yahoo. From Stride's point of view, besides the implicit reinforcement of its brand positioning and brand salience to its target market, the video is a primary driver of hits to its own Stride website. Two years into its life, the Stride brand is worth $145 million, and growing.[5]

RIPPLES AND RISK

If you are looking to get talked about, there is of course always the possibility that you will find yourself talked about for the wrong reasons as well as the right reasons. People are not all the same: What charms me may irritate you. What my sons find hilarious, I find gross—and that's the way it should be with parents and sons. So there are inherent risks in looking for PR, and we need to pursue these ripples with our eyes wide open about the kinds of risks we may need to face up to.

The first kind of risk with any such idea is that not everyone will like it. So Burger King knew that the decision to use the fixed plastic mask for the physical manifestation of "the King" was going to be very polarizing—and while some people were amused by the King's unblinking smile, others were indeed creeped out. But the determination of agency and client was to enter social culture, so they deliberately chose an idea that would have a higher likelihood of being picked up by other commentators and amplifiers of popular culture (like Jay Leno, as it turned out). And they knew that this social salience was going to allow them as a Challenger to punch above their media weight. All of which is undoubtedly part of the reason why Burger King's advertising became three times more effective, in terms of brand recall and message recall per dollar spent, than the Market Leader's.

The second kind of risk is that some consumers may be offended— American Apparel's Dov Charney uses not just sex to advertise his products, but his *own particular brand* of sex: younger women, semiclad, provocatively posed. The combination of the young age, the nature of the poses, and the public places he and the brand frequently display these images has some people complaining. Yet here too the brand obviously knows exactly what it is doing: The website even has a section called "Provocative Ads." The company doesn't mind creating controversy—on the contrary, it is in many ways part of the ethos of the brand to agitate (during the 2007 Democratic candidate elections, it e-mailed its customer database encouraging them to vote for Obama because of his position on immigration), and its founder has described his actions and communications as representing "a salute to contemporary adult and sexual freedom."[6] But he leans into this; he accepts that in doing so there will be controversy.

The third, related, risk is that it offends people to the point where your brand activity will be rebuked or even banned by the authorities. Again, you might even strategically seek this, for the further wave of PR the ban will generate, but only if that controversy fits the image of the brand you are trying to be. Diesel, for instance, doesn't mind controversy; it is, in effect, part of what gives the brand the image it has. When Diesel is hauled up by the Advertising Standards Bureau, for example, because it has produced a magazine ad in which topless men and women have whiplash marks on their backs in the shape of a game of tic-tac-toe, you know that Diesel is not sitting in Molvena thinking, "Hmm, perhaps we went a little too far that time." Pushing the boundaries a little is part of the whole nature of that brand, and the Challenger stance it is taking.

In discussing these kinds of risks, there is a danger of wrongly conveying incorrectly the impression that all Challengers *need* to lean into controversy. However, pushing or even flouting the boundaries of taste isn't the stance that every Challenger is taking or needs to take. There is sometimes a perception that the most vibrant Challengers are all young, hip brands, doing edgy communications and PR (whatever *edgy* means). But while that may indeed have been important for certain brands like Axe to break through with young men in the United States, it does not have to be that way. The brands Kashi and innocent are not trying to be hip; method does not court controversy; Dyson isn't particularly young; and I would defy you to find a great deal of edginess in Camper. And Matt Harding's engaging gyrations sponsored by Stride are not going to offend anyone, except perhaps dance purists. But each of these brands is and will always be actively looking to create PR and brand ideas that can ripple. At time of writing, the YouTube posting with the most hits is for a guy who performs a routine called the *Evolution of Dance* onstage in one take. This is not edgy, or gross, or in any way pushing the boundaries of taste. It involves no special effects or outrageous consumer interaction. It is a very simple idea, but one that we have never seen before.

And the final kind of risk is that you have to accept that it isn't always going to work—perhaps even worse, it may very publicly not go your way. Look at Virgin's Sir Richard Branson. In 2007, at the age of 57, he takes a running jump off the side of the 407-foot-high Palm Casino Hotel in Vegas, wearing a dinner suit and black bowtie. He is here to publicize the inaugural flight from San Francisco to Las Vegas of Virgin America, a new domestic airline in the United States. He is attached in a harness to a special rappel-like system, and he has ensured a good-size crowd and some television cameras by announcing plans to scatter a few thousand dollars worth of free air tickets as he makes his 407-foot journey straight down. But he and the organizers have not reckoned on the winds. They blow him twice against the side of the building; the seat of his pants rip, and he winces in pain.[7] This is all captured live on camera, and many TV channels and papers show it, mishap and all. So potentially very embarrassing. But do we think he is dismayed? Will it deter him from doing it again? I think we all know the answer to that: He will simply wear stronger pants.

At the center of the pursuit of social salience is the key issue of *attitude* again—not just one of "What is our attitude toward intelligently taking risk?" but also one of "How do we turn it to our advantage even when it apparently goes wrong?" While publicity can go well or badly, to some degree it will always be *what you make of it:* understanding how you should look to reframe even apparently adverse publicity to at least take the sting out of it—and perhaps even turn it to your advantage. So, for example, Itsu is the London sushi chain in whose Piccadilly restaurant a former Russian spy, Alexander Litvinenko, ate before he died of radiation poisoning. Caught up in the international media furor surrounding this extraordinary event (and in any case needing to remove any lingering radioactive residue), Itsu Piccadilly closed in November 2006, not to open again till early the following year. But the management immediately noticed an interesting ripple: All their other locations were busier than usual. A little notoriety, not of their devising, had put Itsu on the map— and they leaned into it. They put up a round white sign, framed within the interior of a rifled gun barrel (an obvious visual reference to the opening credits on a James Bond movie), outside the Piccadilly store, which read:

An international espionage incident has transformed this Itsu into a world-famous meeting place. Sad and shocked, we would like to thank you for the many emails of encouragement. Our customers and staff are magnificent. We will reopen and we will flourish. Meanwhile, enjoy *Itsu's health & happiness* at Hanover Square and 313 Regent Street.

Having brilliantly reframed the danger of radioactive fallout as, in effect, "the glamorous world of James Bond," Itsu rode the momentum while it could. While it had already been planning to expand to New York (at the World Financial Center in Manhattan), it promptly moved the launch date forward to ride the publicity from the poisoning. On the first day it opened in New York, it sold out of everything in 45 minutes; shortly afterward, three more Itsu stores opened in the city.

More often, of course, it will not be an isolated event, but a more long-term structural or cultural barrier that we need to use social conversation to help overcome. In Venezuela, 7Up was up against a large, entrenched local player, Chinotto, whose brand name had become synonymous with lemonade (it was used as a generic term for the category). People liked 7Up, and the brand was doing well, but as a foreign brand its emotional connection with consumers was inhibited by the fact that Venezuelans didn't know how to order the drink. It didn't seem to conform to the masculine/feminine divisions of the Spanish language—should you be asking for "*Un* 7Up" or "*Una* 7Up?" (Previous advertising had simply ended with a logo, leaving the question open.) The brand turned this apparent disadvantage into an idea, producing a multimedia campaign with people quarreling over the right way to ask for a 7Up, followed by the end line, "It doesn't matter how you ask for it, as long as you ask." The campaign, and debate, entered the popular vernacular. Top-of-mind awareness rose by 40 percent in six months, and a 22 percent sales uplift followed.

In other words everything—from something as shocking and violent as a supposed assassination by polonium, to as simple an obstacle as people not knowing how to ask for your brand—is a potential opportunity for ambitious Challengers to lean into, if they are open to it and if their attitude is right, if they can reframe it to their advantage in words and, more particularly, in actions. And to consistently achieve that, we as Challengers need to create, within the individual and within the company, a culture of constantly looking for the opportunity to create a conversation in popular culture.

LOOKING FOR OPPORTUNITY

A culture of looking for opportunity often exists naturally in Challenger founders or CEOs, particularly when it is based firmly on a very clear idea of what their brand's identity is and the challenge they are laying down to the category. Take, for example, Arkadi Kuhlman, CEO of ING Direct. He is very clear about the role of his brand in taking on the establishment of banking—and in doing so representing itself as the champion of the ordinary man and woman. So, when in 2005, the banking industry lobbied hard for the introduction of a new law that would enable lenders to pursue more easily those having trouble paying their bills, Kuhlman, although in theory a member of this very industry, joined with Ted Kennedy in calling a press conference to criticize the proposal on the grounds that it would simply hit the person on the street who was having a bad run of luck.[8] It was an opportunity to publicly build the brand's identity and its unique Challenger stance within the world of banking. Or look at Dunkin' Donuts. As Starbucks closes its stores for two hours to retrain its baristas in a potential symbol of reevaluation of its own, Dunkin' opportunistically and very publicly offers every frustrated Starbucks customer 99-cent coffee at its own stores instead. It's an opportunity. Nothing viral here; just always looking for ripples.

While constantly looking for ways to lean into such opportunities to engage the consumer, and create such ripples, is not confined to a Challenger CEO or CMO, very often those leaders do need to be the catalysts of this to the organization. Geoff Ross and his team at 42BELOW continually operated like this. This is Ross describing how they responded to being out of the news spotlight for (in their view) a little too long:

> Things had been a bit quiet, and so we got together. And in the newspaper someone had read that morning that the government was putting up some of the New Zealand Navy's frigates for tender, because a couple of them were now too old, and they were going to go for scrap—and you could buy a warship for a few million dollars. So we wrote a letter to the government—which we also sent to the editor of the newspaper—saying "We're tendering for the frigate (which by total chance was called F42). We're going to anchor it, and put a nightclub on it, and also build an office for

us there. Oh, and we're going to have duty-free sales, because we'd be anchored offshore, so people can row out, and buy duty-free liquor on it." And we drew up an artist's impression, so you saw this big picture with disco lights and stuff coming out of the top of the ship from where the nightclub would be, with a picture of our office on it. And we sent that to the newspaper as well.

It was a great idea. The newspaper published it. The radio stations read the newspaper—and one piece of publicity led to another.

Now in generating this publicity for his brand what Ross *doesn't* say about the process for getting there is as instructive as what he *does* say. He doesn't say, for instance: "Things had been a bit quiet, so we shouted at our PR company, and told them to come up with five ideas or we'd fire them." The 42BELOW team themselves were constantly aware of whether they were being talked about or not. They themselves took responsibility for coming up with the idea by getting together and thinking up something that they could do immediately. Their inspiration was doing something as straightforward as reading the newspaper and looking for opportunities in it: finding a context that already existed in the national news, that they could make themselves a part of. Notice, too, that they started implementing their idea that same day. And that they Overcommitted, in the sense that they drew up and sent a vivid and highly entertaining picture: They understood what the currency of a newspaper with this kind of story was, and they didn't leave it to the newspaper to do it for themselves. Overall, then, this is not unlike the approach that we saw Eric Ryan take in terms of innovation—just as Ryan's view was that "all the innovation we could ever need is already out there—we just need to find it and apply it to our business," so Ross's sense is that "all the opportunities for news for his brand are already out there, we just need to find a way to appropriate them for our brand." This, then is the first kind of attitude toward the opportunity for publicity that we need to engender in our team. It is not to say that we cannot and will not strategically be creating such events and ripples of our own, but not every month (or every year) will yield a 500-foot plastic watch or dynamite surfer, and we need to be constantly feeding that social salience and perceived momentum.

The second, related discipline we are going to develop in our culture around looking for opportunity clearly centers not just on the *fact* of the opportunity, or indeed the quantity of the opportunities, but on the *quality* of the opportunity.

Tourism New Zealand has continued to drive Thought Leadership and a sense of being a "cool" destination by the way it has intelligently created the right kinds of publicity. What has characterized its choices has been not just the way it has seized opportunities (we saw TNZ earlier singing Maori songs from a traditional war canoe to the media and opinion leaders at the opening ceremonies of the America's Cup while every other country sailed past playing pop music), but also its commitment to maximizing the *quality* of the opportunity for publicity. So, for instance, the country's great passion is the sport of rugby, and a World Cup for the sport is held somewhere in the rugby-playing world every four years. In 2007, the Rugby World Cup was in France, and four years later it would be in New Zealand, so Tourism New Zealand looked for ways to capture media attention within the French-hosted World Cup and at the same time to begin to create a desire to travel to New Zealand for the next one. The concept was to build a vast, inflated rugby ball in a public place whose interactive technology within (all made in New Zealand) would create an extraordinary experience for those who went inside. It would create an immersive, 360-degree experience of apparently being inside a rugby ball while it is kicked all the way from France to New Zealand, which then rolls around the best of that country's scenery and culture, before being kicked back to France again. The purpose was clearly to bring the experience of New Zealand alive to a group of potential travelers by dramatizing the nature of what was being shown (extraordinary scenery)—and to do it in a way that reinforced New Zealand's burgeoning reputation as a cradle of creativity and technology.

But here's the point. The ball wasn't going to be situated just anywhere in Paris, in an inconvenient public park, miles from anywhere. Tourism New Zealand wanted to put it as close to the Eiffel Tower as possible. Why? Because Tourism New Zealand knew that the French were going to suspend a small inflatable rugby ball between the girders of the iconic symbol of Paris—and so they wanted to have a much bigger one right underneath it. And so TNZ was very clear that if it couldn't put the giant rugby ball there, it wouldn't do it at all: The quality of the opportunity would directly affect the quantity of the publicity (through the juxtaposition of the New Zealand ball with the French ball), as well as directly affecting the amount of visitors coming to participate in the interactive experience. I asked George Hickton, the CEO of Tourism New Zealand, how he succeeded in obtaining such an astonishingly prime spot. "We kept on asking," he said, "and no one said 'no.' So we just did it." (See Figure 11.1.)

BUILDING IT INTO OUR STRUCTURE

In larger Challenger organizations that place a premium on PR-based ideas, one sees this constant seeking of opportunity actually structured

FIGURE 11.1   Big ball, little ball.

into the objectives for the marketing and PR function as a whole. Ryanair, for example, is said at one point to have had a practice of looking to issue three press releases *a day*. It is no accident that this is a brand that has always thrived by being in the news—it has created a concrete objective for itself that continues to fuel the reason for this salience. So let's pause here to consider this: if we applied this objective to ourselves, how would it affect the way we structured our company? How would we actually deliver against that diktat? Well, we'd need to have more than just a PR director—we'd need to have people within our marketing department who were skilled and imaginative manufacturers of stories, and perhaps a reasonable number of those kinds of people. They would have to be quite well connected to the rest of our organization—really plugged in to customer service or the gate staff in order to capture stories about where the airline had done well, as potential germs of stories that they could then work up into something more. These storymakers would have to keep a close and beady eye on everything the competition was doing and saying, and then look for ways to reframe that to their own advantage. They would, in short, have to behave very differently from the way most of us in the marketing department behave at the moment. So if we change the objective in a very concrete sense like this, we will in turn generate very different behavior. We might not, from a brand point of view, want to take all of Ryanair's belligerent scrappiness into our own brand; but when we consider that it has for some years enjoyed being the most profitable airline in the world, part of which success has been driven by the marketing and publicity that has accompanied its fiercely competitive pricing and business model, then it is hard not to feel this is the kind of objective we might also profit from having ourselves—in direction, perhaps, if not in degree.

How does Ryanair actually deliver against such a fierce brief? In large part by publicly picking fights: fights with competitors, fights with airport authorities, fights with legislators—fights, in effect, with anyone getting in the way of its championship of cheap fares for the consumer.

Clearly a potent route for certain kinds of Challenger, if done intelligently, let's now turn to how and why Challengers pick fights in order to create publicity and conversation around their brand idea, and how they do this constructively rather than destructively.

BINARY WORLDS, AND THE ART OF BEEF

Challengers often look to succeed by making the world apparently binary. As the world of choice gets more complicated, they radically simplify it: Look, they tell us, it is very simple. There are in reality only two choices here—whether to choose *this* or *that*. You can choose that huge behemoth, or us, the little human company. You can choose that overpriced rip-off, or this fashionable bargain. You can line the pockets of that fat cat, or stick it to the man and fly with us. You can help us slay the monster, or we can all die. The choices vary, but the principle is the same.

These pairings can be complementary, in which we put them together in order to reframe the choice we represent (Pork as "the other white meat," for example). More often, though, they are opposed to each other: The easiest way to dramatize this kind of "reduction to binary" is to present a conflict between the two. We know that Sun Tzu famously remarked that a direct attack was rarely the most effective strategy for the underdog (or words to that effect). Yet, as we saw right at the beginning of the book, this in many ways has long been regarded as the classic Challenger approach. You pair yourself very publicly and explicitly with the Market Leader as a choice for the consumer, and point out some flaw in the Market Leader's offer or intentions, compared to which you perform better, and you offer something that is much more in the consumer's interest. This kind of explicit pairing alongside the Market Leader is not a route for the fainthearted—many potential Challengers flinch from directly baiting the leader for fear of a damaging counterattack, in public or in the trade, that will be unleashed. Better, they feel, to carve out some kind of coexistence, disadvantageous though it may be. So why do Challengers pursue it, and how do they do it well?

The *why* is relatively easy to answer here—there are clearly a number of critical advantages such a route can have:

- If a Challenger's key task is to radically simplify choice, and consumers have an almost bewildering range of choices available to them, getting that choice apparently down to just two options, and creating the illusion of a two-horse race, is clearly a very strong card to play.
- Breaking through habitual purchase behavior is going to be very difficult—so raising awareness that there in fact is a choice to be made

here, rather than unthinkingly continuing to do the same thing, is going to be an important initial part of prompting reconsideration.

- It allows you to redefine the criteria for choice (as Miller Lite did at its two moments of greatest success).

- Using one's opponent as an "other surface" (see Chapter 5) can help more sharply define your own virtues (not simply product benefits, as in the traditional side-by-side advertising).

- You can seek to lure competitors into a response—so that they spend their marketing dollars talking about your brand, and the issue you would like consumers to consider when making their purchasing decision.

- Finally, it can be to your advantage to raise interest in the category as a whole. Roger Enrico, the legendary CEO of PepsiCo famously remarked that the "cola wars" precipitated by Pepsi were good business for both sides because they raised overall consumer interest (and participation) in the category as a whole.

The last is in many ways the one that Challenger teams seem to find hardest to embrace. We are so used to negative politics and the self-serving war of words in that world that it makes us distrustful of the motives and benefits of such a war. Surely it just brings everybody down?

In rap, this war of words, and doing it well, is known as "the Art of Beef." Beefing—essentially, where you pick a fight with another artist in your own lyrics, sometimes over a series of songs—has been a staple part of rap for years. Artists use it to gain initial attention and traction and to promote new albums as they are about to break. Take 50 Cent. Now one of the most successful musicians in the world, in 2000 he was almost unknown outside a small core of fans. He staked his claim as a Challenger by writing and producing a track called "How to Rob," in which he offered instruction on how to mug the cream of hip-hop, from the Wu-Tang Clan to Jay-Z. Their reaction was obligingly to sing about him in their own music, trashing him back—and suddenly every rap fan knew who 50 Cent was. In 2003, his debut album became the fastest-selling solo album in American history, in any genre. And this strategy has continued to work for him. In the case of the Kanye West versus 50 Cent battle in 2007, when both released albums at the same time amid some much publicized mutual rivalry, even though most critics felt that his new album had not been 50 Cent's finest hour, he still shifted

900,000 copies of that album in a single week. As Roger Enrico says, if you do a war well, then everybody wins.

Beefing, then, is about explicit attack. And while beefing comes very much from the roots of rap, it is not confined to it. In fact, 50 Cent would have made an interesting companion at dinner for the late Chairman Mao—and they together a comfortable table for three with Sir Richard Branson. Mao believed fiercely that "the best tactic in the struggle against a prevailing enemy is an adroit elasticity and ceaseless tormenting of the opponent"—he repeatedly talked and wrote about this, particularly with reference to the Chinese resistance to the invading Japanese in the 1930s.[9] And Branson, for his part, has frequently looked to pick a fight with a larger and more established competitor, partly for the news coverage, partly to throw a spotlight on his own brand's position as "the people's champion," and partly to deposition the Market Leader in the process. There are a lot of beefers in the Challenger game (particularly in the airline business, for some reason). More recently, in the gaming wars, Nintendo's US CEO Reggie Fils Aimé has represented a new approach by Nintendo, where overtly knocking your competition has historically been frowned on. Fils Aimé has become known, in part, not simply for his innovative thinking over the launch of the Wii, but for his publicly pugnacious stance against his competitors right from the beginning.

While we may, then, want to consider how we publicly square up against the competition or the Market Leader, the comparison we choose to make doesn't actually have to be as full-frontal as this. In many ways, it is more useful as we work through our strategic approach here to go back to the earlier term we used for this idea: that of *going binary*—in effect, putting a set of brackets around just the two of you to separate you from the surrounding throng, and asking the consumer to focus just on you two. Once you have done that piece of bracketing, created your pair, then you can choose *how* you want to talk about the other player in those brackets.

When we then look at the Challengers who have done this well, in pursuit of the ensuing public conversation, the comparison of us as Challengers with the Establishment brand seems to work best when:

- It is clever and/or witty, rather than simply rude. We need to emotionally engage a broader community rather than to simply dismiss the opposition.

- It has a *positive* value about the underdog to communicate rather than merely negatively knocking the competition. It represents the championing of something worth having *instead*.
- It has substance behind it. In effect, then, it is not just a war of words: There is something real to be gained for the consumer by going with us.
- It is therefore on the consumer's side, rather than its own side: The consumer wins if we win.
- It creates conversation and resets the agenda.

When it goes far beyond, in other words, two potty mouths simply attacking each other in a public playground.

MEASUREMENT AND CONFIDENCE

We observed at the beginning of the book that while the old media model had broken down, there was no clear new media model for us to move to. And the reason for that lack of an obvious new model is not that we fail to see the Challenger brands that we admire behaving in different ways from the old model—they increasingly are, and they are very clear and public about this. (Red Bull, for example, famously spends 30 percent of its revenue on marketing, but only around 20 percent of that marketing spend on advertising; most is on experiential events such as Flugtag and the Air Race.) No, the key reason for our failing to identify a clear, new model to move toward is that, if we follow the principle about "you don't know it's working unless you can measure it," we don't quite know what we should be measuring anymore. If we can't measure it, we can't tell whether it is working. And if we can't tell whether it is working, we are perpetually caught in that difficult fork between robustly justifying it to our CEO and knowing we need to find a better way to engage with our target market.

How can we robustly compare the new kinds of media, the media of engagement, community building, viral marketing, "pass-on-ability," and "word of mouse" with the old, reassuringly quantifiable world of Ratings and Opportunities to See?

There is a very simple argument to be made here—namely, that in reality there always have been two worlds for marketers: the measurable world and the unmeasurable one. We could always at some level measure the effects of sales promotions and advertising, for example, but found it much harder even then to measure the effects of PR and word of mouth. But in that old world the amount of money we were putting through the first of these two worlds represented most of our communications budget, so we were content to let that less-measured second world ride on the coattails of the first.

Yet the reality is that most Challengers have always lived very much in the second of these two worlds, anyway—they have had to. Challengers have always had very limited advertising/communication budgets and have always had to rely on very different ways to engage with consumers, and their only real measurement in this was sales, customer feedback, consumer feedback, and news coverage. Look at innocent's viewing of its use of packaging, delivery vans, and in-store display as "House Media," and the contribution of that way of seeing the world to innocent's success. Yet that is an approach to marketing that is hard to measure in any conventional way, other than sales. But in finding our confidence to live in this second world, which may for many of us be in effect the new media model we hear so often discussed, we can perhaps root that confidence in three key ways of understanding the imperative of engaging with our target in this way.

First, there is increasing evidence that creating such word of mouth is the most significant influence on a brand's success. In Field and Binet's seminal study of 880 successful communication case histories from the IPA databank, what they called "Fame strategies" (i.e., where a brand's campaign worked through creating word of mouth/mouse for itself through its communications) were not only the most successful strategies, if one analyzed the econometrics, but also the ones that had the broadest range of business results.[10] (See Figure 11.2.) Word of mouth has always been valuable, but as the world's respect for authority and authority figures breaks down, reliance on peer group recommendation, and the *quality of our trust* in this as a useful piece of information, will increasingly come from here as well. Hence, of course, part of the recent considerable interest in the Net Promoter score on the one hand, and sources such as TripAdvisor on the other.

Second, although the formal metrics do not yet exist, we as Challengers obviously need to recognize that there is an entirely different value

FIGURE 11.2   Fame campaigns achieve broader business success.

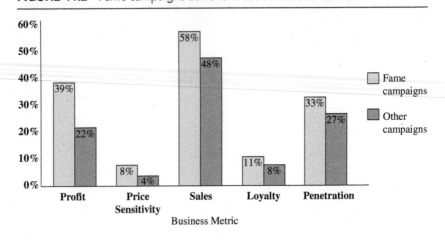

Source: Les Binet and Peter Field, *Marketing in the Era of Accountability*. Part of the IPA Datamine series.

to be attached to an audience who comes to you and engages of their own volition, compared to an audience who simply sits through what you have to say.

Rory Sutherland of Ogilvy draws an analogy to illustrate this. Imagine you are watching the Super Bowl at the Raymond Jones Stadium in Tampa (seating capacity 66,000). The stadium is packed to capacity. And imagine that instead of a rock band, the Marching Band of the 101st Airborne Division comes out at halftime and plays to the assembled crowd. And that the very next Sunday, the stadium is again full, but this time home to U2. Sutherland makes the point that if one used the way one measures audiences at the moment in media, the two musical bands would be rated just as successful as each other: Both played to 66,000 people. Yet in reality the relationship between each of these two bands and their audience is very different: U2 *drew* people to the stadium, whereas the military marching band was peripheral to what the audience really came to see. How does one assign relative value to each of these two? What greater value should one put on an audience that voluntarily comes and participates? Are they perhaps 10 times more valuable to us in terms of their desire to engage with us, with what we have to stand for, and with what we have to offer? 100 times? 1,000? While we may not know exactly the metrics, we understand Sutherland's point: We recognize which of these two kinds of engagement we will need to create in order to succeed, and the media choices we will need to make in how we communicate *with* them—rather than *to* them.

Third, we embrace the opportunity for a greater depth of involvement in *time spent with us*, as well as an involvement of openness and inclination. Look at the celebrated launch of a Challenger in shaving: the Philips Norelco Bodygroom, a new body-grooming shaver for men. While the launch included some advertising, the key launch medium was a website, shaveeverywhere.com, which featured a man in a terry-cloth robe (whom the brand team called *Innuendo Man*) humorously alluding to the benefits of shaving in all the right places through metaphors such as topiary and peaches, and an overall consumer benefit they called the "extra optical inch." In the first month alone, shaveeerywhere. com received 1 million hits (extending to 1.75 million over the first year); the average site visit in that period lasted for seven and a half minutes. And this for a media budget of less than a million dollars.

So how do you measure the success of this kind of Challenger approach? At one level, the initial response is only 1 million hits: a small reach compared to television, and nothing like the viewing figures we saw for Quiksilver at the beginning of this chapter, which spent less than a tenth as much as Philips Norelco. On the other hand, look at the *depth* of that engagement in terms of time on the site. One way to evaluate this is simply to translate the time this represents into something those of us approaching the new world from the old world (as so-called digital immigrants) can understand a little better. According to the Nielsen Media Research blog, if you have a site generating 1.5m hits, with a viewing time on average of seven and half minutes, that translates into the same as 22.5 million viewings of a 30-second TV spot. Yet while trying to translate it back into the old currencies may certainly be one way to look at it, surely the key value as a Challenger is not the translation back into the old currency, but the value of the new currency. If one million people voluntarily spend almost eight minutes of their time engaging with our brand, that has a value very much greater than its translation into viewership of advertising that they didn't actually want to see in the first place. If 47 percent of all visitors to the site then immediately pass it on to a friend, as they did, that has a value very much greater than simply chatting about it to someone they happen to see at work the following day. And in terms of word of mouse, how does one quantify its subsequent appearance on 2,000 blogs, as well as its discussion on CNBC and in the *Wall Street Journal*? The short answer is that one quantifies it in terms of results, of course: eight weeks as Amazon's number one health and personal care best seller, 70 percent share of the category after a year, and increasing Norelco's grooming business 33 percent in the process.

None of this is to say in any way that traditional advertising is dead. Field and Binet's work shows that while its reach may be diminishing, in fact all the evidence suggests that *where it works well*, TV advertising, for example, is more powerful than ever. But the point is that the new possibilities in media are making it abundantly clear that we should be setting whole new objectives for whatever we do, and that even simply talking in terms of thinking about "engagement" is too loose. Personal inclination to engage, depth of participation, the degree of give-and-take in that engagement, the value of mood and moment to that interaction, the social currency derived from being able to pass that on, the personal emotional and functional utility derived from that interaction—all these, which are so fundamental to Challenger success, are going to be increasingly pivotal measures for us. And yet we simply have no way of measuring most of them at the moment.

So the canvas open to us as Challengers is a more exciting one than ever before. On the one hand, we see some of the world's favorite brands—Google, Costco, flickr, Zara—never advertising at all, and instead illustrating the possibilities of succeeding entirely through how they Sacrifice and Overcommit in creating a highly differentiated user–store experience and value. On the other hand, we see the digital world offering us the potential of a visual dynamism, interactive flow, accelerated community, and scaled momentum in our ambition to enter social culture with communication ideas that we could never have imagined 20 years ago. And between those two alternatives, we see brands like innocent and method completely overturning our understanding of how we can use packaging structure and communication to build new kinds of relationships on our behalf. We will not be able to measure many of these new opportunities open to us in the same tidy ways we could in the past. But if we embrace the consistent Challenger principles behind why and how we use each of them, these can at least give us some guidelines to the future.

And we can't just accept that because we can't measure them now, they are unmeasurable. We will need to find our confidence and give others confidence through such measurement. We will need to fight for newer, better measures—of quality rather than just of quantity—that can give us and those around us confidence in how we create the Challengers of the future.

Videolink for this Chapter:

www.eatbigfishfood.com/etbf/Usingcandp

12

THE EIGHTH CREDO: BECOME IDEA-CENTERED, NOT CONSUMER-CENTERED

If we want things to stay as they are, they will have to change.
Giuseppe di Lampedusa, *The Leopard*

S uccess, of course, is a very dangerous thing. Successfully entering or reentering a category as a Challenger is one kind of problem; surviving that success without becoming hamstrung by complacency, overexpansion, or a new preoccupation with simply keeping the gains you have made is quite another. From the big cage rattlers (Body Shop) to smarter online services (GeoCities), the marketing battlefields of the West are strewn with wounded Challengers who started brightly but found it hard to maintain their momentum. And the process we have committed ourselves to, of defining the strategic "software program" for a successful Challenger, would therefore not be complete if we did not consider as well the question of how we address this problem *before* it occurs—that is, how Challengers sustain momentum, rather than regain it through adversity.

THE TWO KINDS OF MOMENTUM

Momentum is vital to Challengers for two reasons. *Actual* momentum is the source of the return on investment—and as such, the measure of immediate growth in sales and revenue return. *Perceived* momentum—

the sense the consumer has that this is the brand making the running in the category, that this is a brand to watch—is the basis of its future equity, the seeds, perhaps, of a future return on investment that will outstrip today's.

The reason most Challengers lose momentum is that they fail to realize that they have to change in order to remain the same. That is, they have to change not their core identity, but *the way the consumer experiences and is stimulated by that identity*. The basis for a Challenger brand's initial success in a mature category, after all, is that it develops from the beginning a different kind of *relationship* with its users than those users have with the Brand Leader. At the time fresh and different, this relationship comes from the consumers' response to being presented with a brand that in some way breaks the mold of what they were used to in the category.

But the success of one brand means the rest of the category assimilates the foundations of that success, too; one ice beer leads to another, and another, and another, until being an ice beer or an entertaining airline or a photo-sharing site is no longer enough. Ideas, like innovations, are replicated (albeit often in more diluted form) and so in turn dilute the power of the original idea to sustain the original relationship. So Challengers that rely on their original product proposition lose their freshness.

And, of course, as consumers we get easily bored; what excited us yesterday jades us today. (This is a human, rather than twentieth-century phenomenon: When the Roman poet Lucretius commented disparagingly of the Roman people that they desired *semper aliquid novi*—always something new—he was writing more than 2,000 years ago.) It is not just that we all have a low boredom threshold; it is that our comfort zone expands to include what once seemed startling and fresh. But comfort zones favor only the Brand Leader—if a Challenger fails to stay just outside that comfort zone, be just a little provocatively different, it becomes an increasingly invisible part of the distribution landscape and slowly dies through consumer indifference. The voracious consumer, hungry for *aliquid novi*, moves on to a newer, more tempting morsel in the category.

Which means that the idea or ideas on which the Challenger launched itself inevitably cannot sustain it. It needs more frequently to feed and refresh the relationship with the consumer, which means in turn that it needs to consistently produce ideas that stimulate and provoke the consumer—not once or twice, but continually. It needs to continually keep the relationship fresh: as fresh as it was when the relationship was new. We must never lose sight of the fact that the underlying driver for a Challenger is momentum—*the sense that our brand is making the running in the category.* Successful Challenger brands can therefore never afford to be static. They constantly add to themselves to keep ahead of the market in their relationship with the consumer; and the fuel for that movement is ideas.

Failure to sustain *actual* momentum leads to the temptation to grow volume instead by accepting the potentially poisoned chalices of line extension or distribution; with these may come erosion of the core equity, loss of the core users, and an erosion of the shape of the user base, leading to a relatively rapid decline. This is exactly what Diesel's Sacrifice in distribution that we noted in Chapter 8 is structured to fight.

Failure to sustain *perceived* momentum, on the other hand, can lead to the "freeze-drying" of the brand, associated in consumers' minds with being locked in to a particular time or trend in their past when they principally noticed it—and therefore by definition not a brand of the moment. The more successful the brand is, the greater this danger. The shoe brand Crocs is facing exactly this challenge: Regardless of its actual range development, for many, the hugely successful brand is associated with a particular style, and perhaps two particular summers: a very particular time and a place. The bigger such a Challenger's success, then, the bigger its evolutionary jump will need to be to prevent it from becoming flash-frozen at that point in our emotional history.

MAINTAINING MOMENTUM, PART 1: THE CONTINUAL MANUFACTURE OF IDEAS

To say that a relationship has to be fed by ideas is in no way the same as saying it has to be fed by technical innovation or product news. There are indeed obvious categories that still rely primarily on innovation to drive and renew them (3M, for instance, which historically has taken—and still has as its stated ambition to take—30 percent of its revenue from products it has introduced in the past five years); and, of course, it is a part of marketing motherhood for even non-high-tech firms to produce product news at regular intervals for big brands to perk up the advertising's effectiveness. Such news usually takes the form of minor product innovations—20 percent more lanolin, or a thicker, crunchier coating, or slightly easier home page navigation—and works well for Brand Leaders, who by and large simply have to sustain mass. Their place as the Establishment brand is easily confirmed by the updating of their product, reassuring the consumer that their functional credentials are second to none.

But when we look at Challengers, we can see that the ideas they employ are very different from product news. The difference between innovation and an idea is illustrated neatly by recent developments by flickr. For the photo-sharing site to launch a place to share video along-side photos is an innovation, but to limit that video to 90 seconds and call it a "long photograph" is an idea (and one that reflects flickr's identi-ty). In the airline business, electronic ticketing is an innovation, but a bar in the first-class cabin is an idea. For the world's number two champagne to launch a four-pack of small bottles for a group of four individuals to enjoy is an innovation, but to make that pack come in the form of an oversized paint tin is an idea. Challenger ideas do not tend to come out of the R&D department; they come out of the core marketing team, or an enthusiastic customer, or anyone who happens to be passing the founder's office—and they tend not to be product ideas but marketing ideas: very ambitious marketing ideas that will provoke and stimulate the consumer's imagination.

At the simplest level, Challengers seem to use such communication ideas over and above conventional marketing practices (advertisements, promotions, sponsorships, etc.), because in order to unseat the existing player in the category, they need to *engage the imagination and emotion* of consumers who think their needs have already been satisfied by the Brand Leader.

Veuve Clicquot is a champagne brand that has turned two or three initially interesting Thought Leadership ideas into a regular stream of imaginative introductions, some of which you can buy at your local wine store, some of which are to enhance brand visibility and image commu-nication in the restaurant trade, and some of which are very high end limited editions, designed primarily to communicate the brand's identity through PR. All of these ideas in its signature yellow color, and all with-out changing the core bottle design or label at all. So the consumer ideas over the past 10 years have included a stylish yellow cooler case with a molded inside, shaped to carry a bottle and two special glasses, the introduction (mentioned earlier) of the paint can containing four small bottles, a neoprene outer jacket to keep the champagne cool (which also acts as a buoyancy jacket if you wish to float your champagne in a stream or the pool to cool it), and a piece of outer packaging that uses cardboard engineering to open almost like an enormous yellow and black flower and turns into an ice bucket, with plastic seals to keep the ice secure. Along the way, we notice the Pucci-designed cover for the Grand Dame bottle and look for an excuse to justify purchasing it for a special occasion. But we also see—in use or in the press—the brand's trade ideas, such as the Tw'ice bucket, whose vivid yellow polycarbonate side holds the champagne, while the aluminium side twists elegantly 180 degrees (so it can either sit on top of a table or attach to the tabletop's side). And we desire, but at a little more of a distance, some of Veuve Clicquot's collaborations with high-end designers, such as the Karim Rashid Loveseat: two linked chairs with an integrated champagne cooler between them to get things going between the happy couple. Or the same designer's specially commissioned Globalight—a futuristic cooler that is also a lamp, bathing perfectly chilled rosé champagne in a soft pink aura. And of course we wish we could only find room in the kitchen for the Porsche "Vertical Limit" wine cellar—$70,000 of handmade brushed steel, with 12 individually lit drawers, each keeping one magnum of Veuve Clicquot's finest vintage at a perfectly regulated 12 degrees. In other words, this is a brand constantly using ideas not simply to develop our sense of its own premium lifestyle image, but each in its way continuing to push our sense of the possibilities of how champagne could be enjoyed—sometimes reverentially, sometimes playfully, but always *sustaining* our sense of it being a brand that is moving, that has continual momentum. And that, as I say, without changing its core bottle or identity at all.[1]

Vodka brand 42Below has been very specific about building the pursuit of continually refreshing ideas into its culture—inspired from the outset, as we saw, not by the marketing of other spirits, but by the principles of *categories that relied on constant renewal*, such as music and fashion. As a result, the company has placed great emphasis on sustaining a culture of "speed and hunger"—a "hunger to keep feeding the brand ideas, new ideas, keep it fresh."[2] And we see this strongly in fashion businesses, of course. So T-box, the Turkish clothing brand we discussed in Chapter 7, has continued to use ideas that combine functionality and creativity in order to sustain the considerable momentum and Thought Leadership it achieved at launch, precisely because it is in the business of fun fashion. Noticing qualitatively that people were starting to use the fun packs as small gifts, for example, T-box has developed ideas specifically around gifting occasions. It is customary in Turkey, for instance, to exchange gifts on New Year's Day, and T-box developed small packages of red underwear that would be fun, and talked-about, gifts for this occasion, including bulk packs for offices and friends. It has gone on to produce new signature innovations for each New Year's Day, and followed up by offering special sets of paired underwear for Valentine's Day, for example. This combination of functionality and creativity in product and packaging ideas has been accompanied by following exactly the same two principles in the constant development of highly publicized distribution ideas to prompt spontaneous purchase: street vendors selling the T-box range from bicycles, temporary tables selling T-box outside cinemas for people in the mood for a fun night out, bumboats on the water offering beach hats and T-shirts to touring boats. A constant stream of ideas delivering against T-box's ambition of "speed, fun, and fashion," constantly renewing the consumer's relationship with the brand.

But what of brands that are not in a fashion business? That may be in fact diametrically opposed to everything the fashion business is all about? Is being idea-led really important for them? We have seen earlier in the book how Umpqua, a regional bank in Oregon, Washington, and Northern California, is determined to be the "world's greatest bank"—precisely by not looking and acting like a bank. It has deliberately sought to stay fresh and relevant, not by simply defining what it stood for and then regularly renewing its advertising campaigns, but by regularly and significantly developing its offer and then expressing this in a continual flow of new ideas. In 1995, Umpqua prototyped a new kind of branch, which it had developed by deliberately looking outside the industry at other kinds of service and experience companies, such as Starbucks, Ritz-Carlton, and Gap. Wanting to pursue a retailing rather than a banking ethos, Umpqua called it a *store* rather a branch, took down the

FIGURE 12.1 Umpqua store.

screens and barriers between the customers and the staff, and introduced a much stronger service ethic inside (with each staff member getting two weeks of intensive training on this service ethic). It was at this
point that Umpqua looked at how to bring full engagement of all five
senses into the store experience—the smell of freshly made coffee,
chocolates to eat following your transaction, music, and so on. This then
became the model that it rolled out across the branch/store network,
integrating acquisitions into that model as they went. (See Figure 12.1.)

Seven years later, Umpqua pushed the model again, partly because,
in the words of the CEO, "you've got to keep going" and partly because
it wanted to ensure the brand gap it created would be maintained, even
as other institutions (e.g., Washington Mutual) were starting to find new
ways to differentiate. And the biggest shift for Umpqua here was the
way of thinking about the store's role in the community—not just how
each store looked and behaved once you were in it, but how the store
behaved in its relationship with the community around it. The completion of a new prototype store in 2003—with open seating arrangements
and projection equipment for showing everything from business presen-
tations to movie nights—enabled this community concept to take form.

The model Umpqua had in mind was to become just that: a community center rather than simply a retailer of financial products. Always implicit in its thinking, the bank now pushed this thought explicitly further: How would a community center genuinely behave? And how could Umpqua empower the people on the front line to behave in a way that exemplified and expressed this within each branch? How could it actively experiment? From this reframing, a constant stream of ideas then flowed, in significant part from the briefed and empowered local managers. Initially the ideas were simple and straightforward. Ask yourself, they said: What would a good member of the community do for valued neighbors when they came by? Well, you'd greet them at the door as they came in. When they got a bit further inside, you'd want them to feel a warm welcome, so you would change the job title of your receptionist to "Director of Smiles," which would clarify to the receptionists exactly what was expected of them in making their customers feel welcome. And if customers weren't coming in, but just out walking their dog out in the neighborhood? You would put out a dog bowl so they could stop and have a drink of water. And of course you'd want to get out beyond your own front porch, go out and interact with these neighbors of yours—but not in a big, corporate advertising kind of way. Umpqua has in fact always believed less in conventional communication and more in what it calls "handshake marketing"—ice cream vans, for example, that simply go round and hand out ice cream sandwiches in the community, like good neighbors would (and then switch to cups of hot chocolate in the winter). One year, in fact, Umpqua cut all its mass-market advertising spend and put it into handshake and street marketing such as the ice cream vans. For this Challenger handshake marketing is not a gimmick, but a fundamental lens through which Umpqua sees the way it builds its community and the strong relationship it enjoys with it.

But, and perhaps most critically, if you really wanted to put yourself at the heart of your community as a bank, you would obviously also ask yourself what you could do to turn the branch itself into a community center. And perhaps you would recognize that you have a bit of real estate that is in fact always there at the center of the community, even when it is not open as a bank. So you would open the store to offer banking services from 9 a.m. to 7 p.m. and then use it to offer some other kind of service from 7 p.m. to 9 p.m. that would benefit the community. Reach out to that cool local yoga instructor whom you know wants to attract new customers, and partner with her to offer yoga classes in the store. Host your own "stitch and bitch" session—a club for people who wanted to sew and talk in the evenings. Some of these events and services would be regular, some of them would be one-offs—so when there is a particularly heavy snowfall, and everywhere else closes, you'd put on some coffee, open your doors, and host a movie night. Or when a new residential high-rise neighborhood goes up, you'd invite locals to come in and get to know one another over a rousing round of Wii bowling.

And indeed, even within banking hours, Umpqua has created space within the bank to support other local businesses in the community, whether it is allowing informal meetings to take place on the premises, or acting as an environment for more formal gatherings of businesses from the surrounding area. They display, and even help sell, the wares of local new businesses looking to get established—one branch actually sold a rug on behalf of a local merchant. And they start seeding this sense of local entrepreneurship early; one summer, Umpqua launched a program aimed at small businesses that at the same time encouraged children to think entrepreneurially. The bank created its own lemonade stands and invited children who wanted to try their hand in a start-up business of their own to come along and apply for one; if they got it, Umpqua would give them a lemonade stand start-up kit, tips for success, and $10 in start-up capital for the lemons to get them going. A huge success in itself, the program in addition brought a dramatic increase in Umpqua's small business loans.

This impact on the community is starting to be substantive. In Umpqua's Innovation Lab in the up-and-coming new part of Portland called South Waterfront, there's a Community Wall built from six 42-inch flat-panel touch screen displays. This is the place to learn about the neighborhood, tell a story, post a comment and so on—an engaging, interactive bulletin board for the community center, if you will. At the time of my partner Mark's visit, someone had posted a question to the community about where they felt the local public transport system should go next after the street corner outside the bank (this being a new part of town, that is where the service currently ends); a number of options had been provided as possibilities. After several days of collecting answers from customers and passersby, the store had built up a pretty good sample of answers, with a clear preference emerging. The data were so good, in fact, that the transport authorities themselves got wind of it and came down to the store to learn more. When you can turn a bank into a source of real insight about the community in which it operates, then you know for sure that you have transcended "banking as usual."

Over 13 years, we see here an initial revolution followed by a second evolution. But as important in many ways as these two key points is the continual stream of smaller ideas that Umpqua has explored with its customers; with an advertising budget that is a fraction of the amount that competitors such as Bank of America and Wells Fargo spend, it is these ideas that are constantly feeding and renewing Umpqua's sensed momentum. The strategy has never changed, but the way of bringing that strategy to life is constantly evolving and being manifested through this flow. We are, says Lani Hayward, Head of Creative Strategies (like the "Director of Smiles," a deliberate title change from "Head of Marketing" to denote the different way of thinking), "constantly hunting for new ideas; we never stop."

How can we judge whether they have succeeded? Two measures to think about: One is that over 13 years Umpqua has grown from six branches with $140 million in assets to 187 stores and $8 billion in assets, and it enjoys consistently strong organic growth even after acquisitions. The other is the stream of banks from around the globe that continue to visit Umpqua to learn about its strategy. More recently, the bank has even entertained well-known retailers who want to see what they can learn from how Umpqua is succeeding—precisely, of course, because it is not acting anything like a traditional bank. And Umpqua itself adds an additional measure: Its emphasis in all of this is ROQ (return on quality) rather than simply ROI.

Key in making these ideas happen is for Umpqua to have a very clear demarcation about where the local store managers and staff are and are not empowered. There's a set process in place for things like customer contact and opening new accounts, but the local feel and culture is a vision that managers implement themselves according to the particular opportunities in their communities. This empowerment has led to occasional moments of questioning from the key management ("You're going to do *yoga* in there? What are you *thinking?*"), and not all ideas have been equally successful (the pet psychic evening, for instance, has yet to be repeated). But marketing and store management alike have been given considerable freedom to experiment.

So this continual manufacture of ideas is one of the two key ways in which a Challenger like Umpqua, outspent as it is in conventional paid-for media, seeks to constantly fuel that critical consumer perception of momentum. Ingrained in the culture, and driven from the top, we see this same restless searching within Scion, whose core team members describe themselves as "constantly striving for innovation." In their case, appealing as they are to not just a younger demographic but the more creative and expressive end of that demographic, their customers are themselves constantly reinventing their lives; so to stay not simply current but ideally one step ahead, the brand team is always looking for new ideas. Not once a quarter or once a month, but daily—"It is a constant dialogue here."[3] Although Scion is sold only in the United States, members of the Scion team are actively studying what is happening in Japan, the UK, anywhere they think they can learn or gather ideas—looking at how to take the new and fresh and make it their own, and they have a deliberately broad suite of 20-plus agencies to make sure they have a good supply of ideas from their outside partners, too. As with Umpqua, some things are constants—Scion does not change certain core aspects of its offer. But almost everything else is an opportunity for innovation—the brand has even recently launched a program to allow users to customize their own Scion crest.

A CLIMATE OF EXPERIMENTATION

The kind of constant experimentation that we saw happening at Umpqua is, of course, a key quality of the digital world. Digital brands, particularly retailers or social sites, rapidly prototype everything, from new applications to the shape and nature of their stores, every day. If it doesn't work, their consumers let them know quickly, and they change it. They are in rapid and constant experimentation, using small groups of empowered people who launch and learn. They are not necessarily obsessed with big ideas right out of the box, partly because their experience within developing digital applications and brands is that you learn from the accidents as much as what you were intending to build in the first place. Famously, the technology behind flickr was originally intended to be a feature for a web-based game, but during its development, flickr recognized that the application was more potent than the game it was intended for, and so put its money and energy behind the accident instead. And in this sense of having small groups of empowered people constantly launching fresh ideas to strengthen their emotional relationship with their consumers and maintain momentum, T-box, Umpqua, and the great digital brands are not so far apart.

There is a difference in scope, of course. In digital, you can develop and test ideas live within a day. You can get small groups of people to do large things very quickly—change your entire storefront and see what happens. These things are much harder in the bricks-and-mortar world, (cardboard packaging, for example, takes six months to redesign, print, and ship). But there is an underlying principle here that we see a lot of these Challengers in both digital and nondigital worlds sharing: To quote Russell Davies, they are "always in beta."[4] They are always experimenting.

CONSUMER-INTIMATE, BUT IDEA-LED

Key here is recognizing the difference between *understanding* your consumers and *being led by* them. While some of these companies (e.g., those moving into fashion or lifestyle areas) are very specifically focused on leading their consumers and pay a limited attention to researching them, others make a very clear distinction that they are consumer-intimate, but idea-led. Ask Scion for its three bits of advice about succeeding in launching a new brand among the creative end of the youth market, and the first will be "listen to your consumers"—but the next piece of advice will be to look to bring those same consumers ideas that are fresh and new. On the whole, the consumer cannot tell you what those ideas should be, but the understanding that you have of them will give you that visceral confidence to innovate in the right direction.

There is, of course, a changing dynamic here: In talking about our target as a whole, we shouldn't walk past a smaller group of people who can and will usefully co-create with us. This can be in one of two ways: by observing how they are already customizing or adapting (*hacking*) our products and brand for their own enhanced use and pleasure, or by actively engaging them in the act of co-creation itself.

How one effectively co-creates in this way is the subject of a book in itself, but we explore its potential values and limitations in Chapter 14 ("Areas of Necessary Impact").

ONE, TWO, MANY

One can see that the force of the Umpqua promise lay in the multiplicity and consistency of the ideas it put in front of the consumer. There was a Native American tribe that supposedly had no word for *three:* It counted "One, two, many." In the same way, the cynical and overpromised consumer, seeing one idea implemented, may feel it is a drop in the ocean; seeing two, that the brand is certainly trying but the jury is still out, and seeing three, well, three starts to become hard to argue with. So for Umpqua it was the *insistent* demonstration of the promise through successive new ideas that proved compelling.

The concept that ideas are fundamental to economic health, incidentally, is not confined to brands, or the microlevel of a particular market. The so-called New Growth Theory, largely made famous by Stanford professor Paul Romer, states that ideas are in fact what drive successful modern national economies. The value of ideas in driving an economy, for Romer, is that they are, like knowledge, abundant; they can build on each other; and they are relatively cheap to develop and reproduce.

So, while Brand Leaders have historically maintained their mass and consumer trust by the use of product news, and updating the satisfaction of rational needs, the objective for Challengers is to maintain actual and perceived momentum, and this is done through the continual deployment of ideas that feed and constantly restimulate the relationship with the target. Inherent in these ideas is their ability to provoke and surprise the target consumers, take them just beyond what they are already familiar and comfortable with. This in turn, as we will come to see, springs from our own ability to anticipate rather than simply reflect the consumer's emotional desires.

Seems simple, doesn't it? It is, after all, no different in essence from how Challengers came to be successful in the first place. But be it complacency or protectiveness, many Challengers, once they have reached a certain level of success, fail to continue feeding the relationship at the same rate as they did at their period of greatest acceleration.

I am not making the facile point that it is important to go on having good ideas. If there seems to be a natural tendency to relax when one is successful (what Claude Bonnange has called "The Warrior's Rest"), and yet the Challenger above all other kinds of brands has the need to sustain momentum—which occurs only by maintaining the freshness of the consumer relationship through provocative ideas—then the real issue here is that we need to be more *systematic* about how we build the production of those ideas into the way our company and marketing lives are structured.

MAINTAINING MOMENTUM, PART 2: PROVIDING DIFFERENT WAYS TO ACCESS THE IDENTITY/EXPERIENCE

We have seen that the currency of Challenger momentum—and therefore success—is ideas. Those Challengers that have started strongly and then are *seen* to run dry of ideas, like Yahoo (whether it is true or not), peak and start to perceptually slide. Those that consistently manufacture, and are seen to manufacture, ideas that refresh the relationship, like Umpqua, continue to grow.

But there is another kind of challenge that a Challenger faces as it grows, namely, the change in the *meaning* of the brand to the consumer. Whereas Brand Leaders offer the consumer a sense of belonging, being a part of a greater community, Challengers (at least at the outset of their lives) offer the ability to individualize, to be a part of something different, perhaps ahead of the curve. For a Challenger to sustain its own early pace and momentum is difficult, therefore, not just because consumers become bored, but because the brand loses its ability to individualize, to be a piece of communication about the consumer. Its meaning, therefore, begins to fundamentally change: How can it say something of value about the individual consumer if everyone else seems to be using it as well? And what does this success and size do to its fundamental relationship with its loyal buyer?

Successful Challengers, therefore, face a medium-term fork in the road: Does one try to preserve one's early formula for success in order to maintain one's core loyalists, or change the nature of one's appeal in order to maintain growth?

Route 1: The Peter Pan Strategy

Some Challengers attempt to be Peter Pan and sustain success by never growing up, preserving what worked for them in the early days. Quiksilver speaks of the need to keep the brand authentic—"in the water," as the company puts it: Once the committed surfers felt that their clothes were available to kids in malls in Chicago, they would stop wearing those clothes. Other fashion brands spoke of the need to keep it *discoverable*—deliberately limiting distribution. Both of these strategies, while viable, naturally put a ceiling on volume and momentum in the interests of longevity.

Route 2: The Reinvention Strategy

Diesel has a policy of reinventing itself twice a year. New lines of clothes, yes, but new marketing and new ideas to flow into the consumer relationship along with that. Of course, these follow themes that tend to run for three- to five-year periods, but the overall feeling the consumer gets from the brand in both its ethos and its clothing is that it is constantly moving forward.

Zara, however, makes the rest of the fashion business look slow. Working from a vision of "freshly baked fashion," it focuses a key part of its business model on a much more frequent turnover of its lines, rotating its entire stock every two weeks. Zara consumers have no time to become complacent, to have a look around the store and then go away and think about that little black jacket for a couple of weeks—because it simply won't be there when they get back. This rapid turnover creates, short term, a very different relationship with the brand and the local store— anticipation (the delivery date of new stock is known by Zara aficionados as "Z Day"), urgency ("If I don't buy it now it will be gone"), and frequency of visit (the average Zara shopper goes in 17 times a year, considerably more frequently than to stores with just four seasons). Because the brand doesn't advertise, the speed of renewal of the merchandise (Zara produces over 10,000 lines a year) also carries the longer-term weight of renewing the relationship with the consumer every two weeks.

Route 3: The Line Renewal Strategy

Some Challengers that do not begin with multiple access points build them in as they grow.

We might call this *line renewal*, then, rather than *line extension*. Whereas line extension offers the *same* relationship with the consumer, expressed in other product forms, line renewal attempts to offer a renewal of the relationship by offering "the same, but different." For Las Vegas, it is the new-themed hotels that restimulate interest in the city as a whole: The opening of a miniature version of the ultimate city (New York) transplanted to the middle of the desert is followed immediately by the reconstruction of the most romantic of European cities (Paris). And while this is still only half built, ground is already being broken for an Italian lakeside village (the five-star Bellagio), created, of course, in a state notoriously deficient in water. Each new-themed hotel provides a new and rich experience, which, besides being lucrative in itself, offers a new access point for the consumer's relationship with the city as a whole. The identity of Las Vegas as a fantasy entertainment destination remains the same, but consumers can choose and individualize the fantasy through which they access that brand experience. Two couples visit Las Vegas: One couple prefers Caesar's Palace, the other Paris, but both get to talk about how much they enjoy gambling there. Next time, one will stay at Caesar's, the other will go to the newly opened Venetian— one likes the fantasy to stay the same, one likes new experiences. (The additional value of new points of access into the brand is that they allow the enthusiastic consumers to be ahead of the rest of the pack. Las Vegas's constant creation of new and different ways to access the experience is akin in some ways to a fashion brand's philosophy of keeping it discoverable—even though Oakley was talking about it as a factor of distribution.) Occupancy rates in Las Vegas are at 95 percent.

One might say that the line renewal strategy is also part of Google's continued momentum. While we still know and use Google primarily for search, the new products that the company has since launched, such as Google Earth, Google Maps, and Google Images, have added whole new dimensions to our rational, emotional, and sensory pleasure in searching and exploring, using the brand's simple access and apparently universal scope.

We can see, then, that there are four elements to the line renewal strategy:

1. The continual use of ideas rather than simply communication
2. The construction of new facets or embodiments of the brand, offering fresh departure platforms for such ideas and at the same time differentiated points of access
3. The creation of fresh ways of thinking about the brand's identity at each of these new points of access
4. And, in terms of implementation, doing this systematically and consistently

Note that the core identity for each of the two brands discussed earlier doesn't change—Las Vegas consistently offers a different kind of altered state: the fantasy of glamour, of being a high roller with the potential to enjoy permanently the lifestyle whose fantasy surrounds you. Google is still all about search. This strategy of line renewal, in fact, could not work without a strongly defined core identity: Line renewal of a hollow brand, one without a Lighthouse Identity, would simply be one of product and brand diffusion.

Route 4: Developing Your Challenger Stance

The fourth way we see Challengers sustaining their relationship with the consumer and their momentum within their market is by evolving not simply their meaning as a brand, but their *stance as a Challenger*. Being in effect conscious of the different ways in which they can engage consumers with their challenge of the market, and intelligently evolving through them between life stages. I mentioned in the preface that it was a mistake to allow our thinking about Challengers to get channeled into the default Challenger position of "David versus Goliath" (or the archetypal categorization of the Challenger as *Outlaw*)—the stances open to us as Challengers are much more varied than that. Figure 12.2 shows a universe of such stances, reflecting broadly the kinds of challenges that we discussed in Chapter 5. If the Eight Credos represent the component elements of Challenger thinking and behavior, there clearly is an overarching stance that a Challenger will take in the market that structures how it uses all those elements, a stance around which it will build each piece of its unique Challenger mix. These 12 represent the most common stances taken; while there is, of course, a little overlap in some of the cases used as examples, we can recognize fairly easily how the stances differ from one another, and the different kinds of challenges that each has at its center.

So the table in Figure 12.2 shows five columns. The first on the left is the type of Challenger stance. The second from the left offers a short illustrative group of examples, followed by the central column, which gives a brief description of the key elements of the stance taken. The fourth column from the left, playing this out a little, looks specifically at what the Challenger is actively challenging. And finally, the last column on the right looks at why groups of the buying public might be attracted to this stance.

What is interesting to us in discussing how Challengers maintain momentum is not simply the initial stance taken by each Challenger brand, but how we see some of them subsequently *evolve* through different stances. So in the airline business, we can see the evolution of Value Changers into different narrative stances as they gain their confidence, develop their consumer base, and grow. Southwest moved from being in effect just a low-fare airline to talking about "Giving America the freedom to fly"—a Democratizer, in effect, opening up to Americans of all income groups the ability to use air travel. Virgin Atlantic started as a "More for Less" Value Changer, moved through an Irreverent Maverick phase (capitalizing on the existing Virgin image), and has in effect evolved to take a "People's Champion" stance (the overall positioning is that of a Robin Hood, taking from the rich and giving to the people). It is still irreverent, of course, but it has determined to take a higher-level position.

Apple has moved from being a Game Changer (with the Apple II) to being a David ("1984") to being an Irreverent Maverick (a user image that sustained Mac users even during the lean product years after Jobs was pushed out) and back to Game Changer again (iMac, iPod, iTunes, iPhone). Is it in fact a Challenger at all any more? One could argue that the iPod advertising is now simply a case of the Market Leader advertising the category generic, and owning it through the white iconography. Yet as Apple pushes beyond its core businesses, it is of course

FIGURE 12.2 Twelve Challenger stances.

Challenger Stance	Example	Brief Description	Challenging What?	Reason for Attraction
The People's Champion	Virgin Atlantic, Linux, Wikipedia, Avaaz, Daffy's	Consciously sets self up as on the side of the consumer, often specifically against the "cynical"/"fat cat market leader	Motives and Interests of the Market Leader	They are fighting for me – I win.
The Scrappy David (vs. Goliath)	Miller Lite 2005, Ryanair, Avis 1960s, Pepsi Challenge	Stick it to the King	The dominance of (and unthinking consumer preference for) the market leader	"Nobody roots for Goliath" – people like underdogs.
The Enlightened Zagger	Camper, Nextel, PETA, Fosters	The enlightened brand deliberately swimming against the prevailing cultural tide. Often takes low status/blue collar stance	A prevailing and commonly/ unthinkingly accepted aspect of contemporary culture	Engaged by the counter (often un PC) stance.
The "Real and Human" Challenger	Southwest, Ben and Jerry's, Sam Adams, innocent	A "real" people brand in a faceless category. Sometimes real people (founders, but not necessarily just founders) are visible behind the brand. Often accompanied by the perception of "small" in stature	The joyless impersonality of the market leader or category	"Thank god for some real people who get what I am about – and who really care about what they are doing."
The Missionary	Dove, JetBlue, Al Gore 2.0	A challenger fired up with a view about the world it has to share. Often looking to "put the category right" in some way	The belief system underpinning the category to date	Identification with beliefs about category (and way category fits into world).
The Democratiser	IKEA, Target, Zara, Digg, YouTube, Current TV	A brand that is taking something previously exclusive (stylish, luxurious, hi tech or "controlled" by a particular profession), and making it much more broadly available to the masses	Elitism, the idea that something should be available only to the privileged, wealthy, or expert	They enable me to enjoy living and participating in the world in a way I thought was only for the few.

	Examples			
The Irreverent Maverick	Red Bull, MAC, Mountain Dew, Crumpler	Countercultural attitude in a box	The complacency and narrowmindedness of the status quo and those who keep to it	Identification with the attitude.
The Visionary	method, Whole Foods, Zipcar	Sets out higher vision that transcends category nature	The mundanity of the way the category thinks about its nature and role	Identification with vision.
The Game Changer	Wii, Lush, Lexus	A brand and product with an entirely new perspective on the possibilities of a category, which invites the consumer to participate in the category in a whole new way	The fundamental drivers and codes of the category to date. Not the beliefs or values – more the dimensions of the consumer experience it has played up and played down	Engaged by fresh perspective on a familiar market. "Wow, I'd never thought of the category like that before."
The Killer App (Product or Experience)	Napster, Skype, Joost	A product or service (without much branding attached to it) that is so revolutionary, it becomes de facto a Challenger brand	The way consumers think about product in the category	This changes everything. That product is so good at what it does, brand loyalty has just become irrelevant.
The Next Generation	Pepsi Next Generation, Silk soymilk ("The New Milk"), Eurostar (the future of European travel)	That was then and this is now	The relevance of the market leader (or perhaps every player in the market) to the modern world, or current generation	New times call for new brands, and I as a person am part of the new times.
More for less/The Same for much less	"Two Buck Chuck," 50% of insurance companies, Motel 6, Easyjet, early private label	A challenger offering a proposition rooted in *significantly* superior value for money	The current value equation	You can't argue with the price.

challenging both the incumbents in its new categories and many of the design and usage drivers and codes of those categories at the same time.[5]

So why is it that Challengers move between these different stances? In part it is about the desire to refresh the way one presents oneself to the consumer—stopping ourselves from becoming just another part of the brand landscape, once the consumer has become familiar with our stance and the expression of that stance. In part it is about discovering new and fresh sources of challenge and conflict, from which to create fresh interest in our story, and our ambition within the category in the imagination of the consumer. And there may also be a more significant kind of evolution here—one might even argue that some of these stances represent *higher-order positions* that Challengers naturally evolve into.

But underpinning all of these stances, and transitions between them, is perhaps the key requirement for a Challenger, *namely, to never be seen to win*. As a Challenger succeeds in achieving one goal, or over-coming (really or apparently) one struggle, it evolves its narrative, and public ambition, and moves on to the next. Being a Challenger is, after all, in essence about a state of mind, not a state of market.[*]

ALCHEMY AND ETERNAL LIFE

Establishment brands and establishment-minded players you talk to are eager to disparage Challengers. Take the long view, they say, and they point out that while Challengers might be interesting models for short-term growth, they are frequently poor examples of steady longer-term growth. And this is, of course, true. Challengers can stumble, go stale, and/or plateau after initial promise—and the spotlight thrown by that initial promise makes their weakness all the more noticeable when it comes.

I tend to give two answers to this. The first is that to accuse Challeng-ers of failing to sustain growth consistently is not actually the issue—all brands wax and wane: of the 500 companies that initially made the

---

[*] Those who are interested in exploring the range of challenger stances in more detail on their own brand will find a more thorough unpacking of this strand of thinking, the individual stances themselves, and their relation to archetypal theory at www .eatbigfish.com/12stances.

Fortune 500 list in 1955, only 71 are still there. No, the failure Challengers really face, it seems to me, is the failure to reinvent or re-create themselves once they start waning—that is, the failure to understand that they have to change in order to stay the same.

My second response is that we are not holding up Challengers as perfect paragons of business in every way. That we can learn some valuable lessons from their success in building rapid growth for themselves against the run of play does not mean we are required to slavishly follow their subsequent ups and downs. Or that we cannot narrow our focus in looking at the longer term. Some Challengers have put in place measures to ensure longer-term success in a way that others didn't.

And in discussing the Eighth Credo, we are, of course, on the most speculative ground. This is an extraordinarily difficult and ambitious area to consider—we are looking for the marketing equivalent of the alchemist's stone, or the secret of eternal life. But if we are prepared to venture on, we can see that maintaining momentum will require not just the observation of the marketing attitude, strategy, and behavior outlined in this chapter, but an underlying *cultural* change. It is one thing to *say* that it is essential for a Challenger to continually create ideas that seize the consumer's imagination, and it is quite another to do it: Ideas do not come along with the punctuality and obligingness of a Pop-Tart (i.e., announce you are hungry and in three minutes one pops up, hot enough to burn your mouth). Ideas are irregular, rarely arrive on demand, and, even when they do, are easily trampled on and lost.

We need, then, to reevaluate the *whole way we think about supporting the brand and structuring the organization*. We need to move, in other words, from being a consumer-led culture to an ideas-led culture.

Videolink for this Chapter:

www.eatbigfishfood.com/etbf/ideacentered

PART 3

APPLYING THE CHALLENGER PROGRAM

13

WRITING THE CHALLENGER PROGRAM: THE TWO-DAY OFF-SITE

I said at the outset of the book that, having established the nature of the Eight Credos, I would attempt to turn them into the beginnings of a process that we could apply to our own brand. I noted that, although this formalization of a Challenger approach constituted an enormous postrationalization, in the sense that none of the Challengers as *individuals* had ever formally put themselves through such a process, I was interested in structuring a stimulating and clearly understandable way for us to try to follow in the steps of their *collective* marketing intuition. This chapter, then, offers a structured series of exercises for those interested in practice, as well as theory. But first, some thoughts from reviewing the Eight Credos together.

Being a Challenger is not a series of actions in and of themselves. It is a mind-set, a way of seeing the world, which is manifested in those actions. As a mind-set, it is innate or emotionally held and committed to, hence the use of the word *Credo*, as a representation of almost religious faith. While our sense of *what* we have to Sacrifice may change, for instance, the belief that we *have* to Sacrifice cannot.

Reflecting this mind-set, the Eight Credos clearly do not operate in isolation of each other; we have already observed that they can be seen together as a sequence, a four-stage strategic marketing process (in the Preface, on page xx). In this process, decisions or actions taken in regard to one Credo are necessarily reflected or dramatized in another—the first seven Credos in particular must all center around the one or two central challenges and priorities for the brand. The practice rather than the theory of this has, I hope, been immediately apparent in the overlap in brand examples used among the chapters so far: So, for instance, the conventions of the category broken will often be used as Symbols of Re-evaluation for the brand, and if the target for this reevaluation is external, they will in turn be expressed through dramatic advertising or publicity-generating events.

Furthermore, although the Credos between them certainly have huge implications for marketing strategy, it is clear that marketing strategy is just one strand in the Challenger marketing triad:

- Attitude and preparation
- Marketing strategy
- Marketing behavior

Marketing behavior is a way of thinking about the expression of one's identity and positioning to the consumer that goes far beyond what has historically been regarded as the template of the marketeer's activity, namely, the Four Ps (*positioning*, *product*, *promotion*, and *price*). And the Attitude and Preparation has been necessary not only to open the mind, to reengender innocence, but also to drive *marketing strategy into behavior*. One of the greatest failings of the marketing company is incompletion. Lee Clow, when asked by a client how we could get breakthrough thinking from his agency, replied: "You have to want it." Incompletion usually occurs because there has been no mental preparation: Those involved do not "want it" badly enough.

So there is in fact a structural (rather than a necessarily chronological) relationship between the Eight Credos.

Not all Challengers fit all Eight Credos, of course. Not all Challengers are starting from inexperience and Intelligent Naivety, and few of the online retail Challengers, for example, have ever offered any dramatic

Symbols of Re-evaluation. This is an important counter, because the way to test a hypothesis is, after all, not to try to prove it, but to try to *disprove* it.

The response to this falls into two parts. The first is that in drawing on so many different Challengers it would be startling to see an absolute uniformity of plan: It is more likely that we would see a fit that usefully describes the majority of them, much like a piece of regression analysis maps a series of points of data to a line of commonality. Some examples will fall on either side of the overall pattern here or there, but the overall shape and nature of the common thread remains clear.

The second part of the answer is that this book is not supposed to represent an absolute formula to be imposed in blanket fashion with disregard for category, culture, or starting place. It is more usefully viewed as a cluster of activities that, taken together in a structured way, can help overcome a strategic problem or market blind spot that is inhibiting growth.

What is important is that, whatever its application, it is regarded at the very least as a cluster of related activities, rather than an à la carte menu. Because trying to become half a Challenger is like trying to become half pregnant—it creates the same amount of mess but is bound to lead to disappointing results. When Mao Zedong wrote "All reactionaries are Paper Tigers," he meant, of course, that there are some who affect to be fierce Challengers but who lack the real substance to succeed (being made of paper rather than muscle). In the same way, we cannot cherry-pick the two or three most interesting Credos, take them for a spin, and sit back to see what happens. In the first place, this sends confusing signals to the external and internal consumer (are we kicking ass and taking names, or not?) In the second, it fails to create a lasting momentum. We're either in, or we're out.

PREPARATION FOR THE OFF-SITE

We are moving from a hardware society to a software society. From a business perspective, this means we are moving from companies that succeed through physical product to companies that succeed through the consumer experience they offer. And just as it's not the size of the box that is important anymore, but what the contents of the box do for us, so it's not the number of people or even the talent of our workforce, but the way they think about the task and the behavior they adopt that will be the key discriminator in the future. And that has to start with the behavior and example of the core group at the top. The key figures in our company need to run on a Challenger program. We don't need soldiers; we need apostles.

Architects talk about "programming the building"—working out how the building needs to interact with the people who will be working in it. In the same way, since the concept of *Challenger* is not really a series of actions but an underlying way of thinking about the problem, the key will not be you or me "getting" that way of thinking, but rather programming the core group so that they get it—or rather getting that group to program themselves. Our programming them is not simply a distasteful idea, but it is an *impractical* distasteful idea. They have to program themselves; they have to turn themselves into Challengers. But we can give them a goal that makes this imperative, and a way of seeing the world that makes this possible.

So this off-site, then, is about getting a small group of key figures in the company to run a Challenger program, by getting them to program themselves. Like a piece of software, the two-day program (and the much longer strategic process of which it is only a taste) will again be improved and updated by the group in two years' time—in the spirit of the constant updating of a genuine software program, where work on the next upgrade has started even before the current one has launched.

An Agreed Consumer Starting Point

Our experience in doing this work makes it very clear that while the temptation is for a Challenger group to start with everything being open, everything in play, in reality you will need one or two fixed points to begin to have a productive and directional conversation.

The most critical of these is to have a common and shared sense of your target consumer before you start, in demographic terms at least. This should be shared before the workshop begins, and reprised with a 20-minute presentation at the beginning of the workshop.

You may as your work progresses come on to define a particular mindset or psychographic you will be targeting within this demographic in the work you do, particularly in developing your Lighthouse Identity, but you will need some kind of commonly agreed consumer foundation for the conversations you are going to have, that all the group buys into at the beginning. Otherwise, you will simply burn up half the workshop debating whom you should be talking to; while this is a conversation that needs to be had, you don't want to bring 12 people together to have it.

PREPARATION

Our Own

Then there must be Overcommitment. It may seem obvious, but we, as leaders of this initiative, cannot do an exercise like this as a "toe in the water." It has to be viewed by us and others as a watershed, a catalyst for a change in attitude.

One practical reason for wholeheartedly attacking the exercise in this way is that the people whom you will want to be part of the two days will have other important issues and conflicting priorities coming up; within a week of scheduling, there will always be one prospective member of the group who will have one excellent excuse for not being able to attend. We have to decide what we are prepared to demand in order to ensure that everybody will be there, and will be a part of the opening of the group's new thinking. What kind of example are we prepared to set that will in turn communicate our expectations of the importance of these two days to them?

There will also need to be Sacrifice. This group will need to be manageable—no more than 16 people initially, and preferably 12 to 14. Again, this will send a signal; we need to determine carefully our own personal objectives for the session. Who will be the core figures who will really make the difference—in this meeting and, by implication, thereafter? Who will be excluded, and what message will that send to them and the world? What will be the public message the fact of this group sends, and how can we make that message as beneficial as possible?

Their Preparation

They should, at the very least, read a 10-page outline of *Eating the Big Fish*, and preferably the book itself. (You can request a 10-page outline by contacting adam@eatbigfish.com.) It is important that they each have some basic knowledge of the benefits of looking at case histories outside their own categories before coming to the off-site.

An optional piece of preparation to consider in addition might be this: Imagine you have replaced your existing board of directors or VP group—replaced not the people, but their titles and job responsibilities. Instead of VP of Sales, or Marketing, or Finance, or Customer Service, choose a title that reflects some of the ideas we have been talking about, for instance:

- VP of Difference
- VP of Momentum
- VP of Offense and Defense
- VP of the Big Fish
- VP of Overlooked Equities

Give each attendee one of these new titles. Each is required to prepare and report to the group on the performance of the company over the past year with respect to each of these issues. For example, the VP of Difference would be required to pull together the five ways this product or service is genuinely different from the rest of the category or from the Market Leader. These differences will embrace current disadvantages as well as obvious advantages. Remember Avis: It was disadvantaged, so it tried harder.

The VP of the Big Fish would have the responsibility of ensuring the company has correctly identified, and is collectively focused on overcoming, the one central issue that poses the greatest challenge to a healthy and growing future for it. This report would focus on whether this was the case last year, whether there was perceived to be explicit agreement on the central challenge, the nature of the Big Fish, and whether the entire company or marketing group was putting its individual and collective energies toward meeting that challenge.

The VP of Momentum would have the responsibility of looking at the actual (sales) and perceived (consumer impression) momentum of the company over the past 5 to 10 years. What were the contributors at times of greatest acceleration or slowing at each stage?

The VP of Overlooked Equities would have the task of examining the equities the brand has created and that have been important at key points in its life, and why they might have a fresh relevance and meaning for a new world.

The VP of Offense and Defense would take Dieter Mateschitz's idea of borrowing the structure of one's marketing department from American football, and would be tasked with a point of view of what these two departments would have as their brief on this brand, and how they would be best set up to genuinely deliver on these briefs as potent offensive and defensive teams.

Of course, there are any number of different kinds of inputs you might want to have. These are simply examples; the book may have stimulated others in your mind along the way.

Why is this stage optional? Because the response to it will depend on the kind of people you invite. You may decide your group is naturally imaginative and will embrace the lateral view required by an exercise of this type. Conversely, you may feel that one of the issues you face is that your group is highly rational in their approach and not yet imaginative enough. In the latter case, you may want to withhold such an exercise until some of the effects of the off-site have set in.

Regardless, ask everyone to bring to the meeting *their sense of the Big Fish:* What is the single greatest challenge facing the brand, the company, or the business?

Collectively

During the off-site, some basic rules of this kind of exploratory thinking will need to be observed:

1. Nobody is allowed to say, "But my category is different." Instead, each has to work out what the parallel in their own category for any given example would be. The example of how one extracts the relevance from Google to a car dealership (in Chapter 3) might serve as a reminder for those prone to forget the way this is done.
2. All challenge should be positive. We all attend so many workshops these days that this could come as second nature, but apparently it doesn't. You will need to be watchful for this.
3. Strategy and ideas will travel together. We will interlink idea generation and tools to prompt bigger strategic thinking, and use one to

inspire, stimulate, or make concrete the other. This will be particularly valuable for the people in the room who are not used to conceptual thinking; for these, an idea is often going to be the way they "see" the strategic path forward for your fledgling Challenger.

4. Make sure the person with a pen capturing ideas at the front of the room or in breakouts is not an editor. That person's job (and yours) is not to write up some ideas (the ones that person thinks are "good") and not bother to write up others (the ones they think aren't). If you allow the person with the pen to behave in this way, you will find that once people have volunteered two ideas or thoughts that don't get written up, the room gets pretty quiet pretty quickly. You don't want quiet—you want noisy. Make it clear to the group that there will be separate times in the workshop to *collectively* review and edit the outputs.

Location

It will be a large room, twice the size you technically need for the number of people you have, with plenty of space to record your thinking and ideas around you. This room will be away from the office: Besides the symbolism of a new beginning, we will need focused attention.

Over the course of the two days, the purpose is not just to explore a number of different approaches to developing the company, or brand, and its business. In the spirit of the "Garage," it is to create something altogether new: a new company, a new idea for the brand, a new place to start for the future. (You may wish to leave a version of this room, translated back to the office, in existence once the workshop has ended; this would remain your garage or war room, in which the core group can meet and implement the agreements reached after the initial meeting.)

We should note, finally, that these two days are not supposed to be either a quick fix or a substitute for a much longer process of marketing and cultural change. Put formally, the objectives may be said to be these:

1. To begin to develop *innovative strategic approaches* that have the potential to radically transform a company's business
2. To create the beginning of a *new way of seeing the market and its possibilities* for the core marketing, production, and sales team of the company

3. To help generate a new, more aggressive *attitude* toward business development by and between all those present at the program

The workshop is intended, in short, to be a *beginning*, an acceleration, the first steps of the journey that a prospective Challenger needs to make: starting to get the rocket off the ground.

THE TWO DAYS

What follows are some suggested exercises for each stage. You should not try to do all of them—I have offered more rather than less, because each brand will be in a different stage of development, and one brand will need to focus on different kinds of stages from another. Certainly, there is too much to do in two days. Decide where you want the center of gravity to be in this kind of work, and structure your handful of exercises around it across the two days. The conversation and thinking that the exercises create are more important than the exercises themselves—don't be so preoccupied with getting through more exercises that you compromise on the conversation and cross fertilization. But equally, don't let the group confuse conversation with progress—keep them moving forward.

Stage One: Attitude and Preparation

At the back end of everything we plan, we will need to drive behavior—completion is a major differentiator between companies. Many companies dream, and many companies contain people who come up with potent ideas, but very few companies complete. This is because they never get the attitude right. Beginning to get the attitude right, then, is the first purpose of the Challenger Program. While this is the stage that people are most inclined to shortchange, it is probably the most important stage of all in the process.

Breaking with the Immediate Past
Premise
Everything needs to be reconsidered, every assumption put in play—including the currently valued brand and advertising equities and the rules of the category.

There is an important distinction to be made here between reconsideration and rejection; we are not necessarily rejecting at this stage, but we are vigorously questioning everything. At the beginning of the two days, we are going to break with our immediate past in order to clear our minds, to be able to see clearly the real challenges, possibilities, and assets in front of us. As the two days pass, some of the values and assets we originally sink may float to the surface again. Others will be replaced. But unless everything is put aside, genuinely, right at the beginning, we will never be able to see the possibilities that present themselves.

At the same time, you will also want to identify a small selection of *Givens*—those two or three things that are *not* up for debate. These will include the name of your company/brand, perhaps, and one or two more, such as your defined consumer demographic (the psychographic may be one of the things that emerges from this process, in conjunction with your Lighthouse Identity). Do not feel compelled to have any of these as Givens (we have often done work where there are none at all, apart from the initial sense of the consumer); but you might want one or two constants, particularly if you are building from some good strategic thinking or research that has already taken place.

Exercise: "Grove"

Fire ourselves. Leave the building and offices we have worked in. Come into our new room as an entirely new team coming in. And not just any new team—let us define our cultural set. We are practical but imaginative entrepreneurs: Branson, Bezos, those Google guys. Ambitious and in a hurry.

Imagine that we are looking at everything afresh. Instinctively, what is the first thing that each of us would do with the fresh, realistic, and ambitious eyes of our own successor?

Like the man who gave this exercise its name, we may wish to divide this into two parts. First, identify the one thing we would *stop* doing (in Grove's case, this was staying in the memory business), and then establish what is the one thing we would start doing instead (e.g., focus on microprocessors). This is the first phase of breaking with our immediate past.

The second phase is to write the five "rules of the category" on the wall in front of us. Get the group to work in small teams to come up with a compelling reason why each individual rule is no longer valid.

Third, do the same for our brand. What are the five anchor stones of our marketing strategy? These will probably comprise:

- Category definition
- Target definition
- The key brand equities
- Brand promise
- Valuable advertising equities

Again, ask the team put next to each definition at least one reason why it is no longer relevant. Write this counterpoint on the wall. Remember, at this stage everything is in play.

What Is Our Central Issue? Our Big Fish?
Premise

We get too involved in the day-to-day details, become snow-blind to the bigger issues and opportunities. Enmeshed in the logistics and the tactics of how to fight yesterday's targets, we sometimes lose sight of the central issue we have to overcome now, the Big Fish we are up against today.

Exercise: "Big Fish"

This session is about identifying the Big Fish: the challenge that will eat us if we don't eat it first. Some of the potential answers to this will already have been thrown up (at least implicitly) in the reasoning behind the group's answers during the previous exercise, but this session serves to make the articulation of this challenge more explicit and clearly defined.

(Continued)

(continued)

Ask the group to work in smaller groups to identify each of:

1. The key competitive issue
2. The key consumer issue
3. The key internal issue

And then highlight which of these three is genuinely the most important to our success.[*]

Once all three areas have then been discussed in the room, agree on the Big Fish. Write it on a central chart that dominates the room. You may find as you progress through the two days that your collective view of the Big Fish changes, but the group always needs to have a commonly agreed, primary challenge in front of them. And the nature of that challenge always needs to be a dominant and influencing presence on the consequent attitude the team is going to adopt to counter it.

---

[*] In my experience, people tend to start this process by thinking the Big Fish is one of the first two. They tend to end up recognizing the key issue is in fact an internal one.

Stage Two: Intelligent Naivety

Having identified our Big Fish, and put everything in play, it is now time to open our thinking to some of the possibilities before us. Two of them will focus on upending the conventions of the category, the other on learning from another category completely. (You won't have time to do all three, so choose two.)

Exercise: "Dyson"

Dyson had a demonstrably superior product, but also then wrapped that product in a beautiful design. Yet if you had been working in the vacuum cleaning category for years people would have told you that no one wanted or would look at a beautiful vacuum design: Vacuuming was a low-status, solitary activity. It seems they were wrong.

So . . . write down two "truths" about the way the category has perceived itself and/or presented itself up to now. Then write down why they are no longer true.

Now write down the two "truths" about the way our brand has perceived and presented itself up to now. And then write down why these are no longer true. Share and discuss the answers to both questions.

The purpose of this exercise is not to reach unanimous agreement at this stage. It is simply to open up the thinking and liberate the group by letting them see and feel that we are opening up the thinking.

But it will also usually throw out one or more big thoughts and possibilities to be played out as you go further through the process.

Exercise: "The Positive Negative"

Remember Nando's and the Stones. They deliberately tried to be the opposite of everything the Market Leader represented. Create a photographic negative, so to speak, and make that into a *positive* and clearly different place to stand.

So there are two parts to this exercise. First, take a sheet of paper and draw a line down the middle. On the left-hand side, write down the 7 to 10 key qualities of the Market Leader: its personality, its style of product or service, what it emphasizes, how it positions the product role, how it uses media, and so on. On the right-hand side, simply write down what it would mean to be the opposite (or at least very different) on each of these dimensions for us as a brand.

Bear in mind that at this stage we are still exploring where our differentiation does and could lie—and the dimensions we could push that differentiation into: This is why we are doing this exercise. Be clear with the group that at this stage we are *not* at this stage trying to write the blueprint for the brand.

Discuss it in the room. In discussing which dimensions does the energy of the room rise? Why is that?

(Continued)

(continued)

Second, take another sheet of paper, draw a line down the middle, and write down that same list of qualities and dimensions you have identified in the first part of the exercise as being the definers of the Market Leader.

Along those 7 to 10 key dimensions, now discuss where you need to be the *same* as the Market Leader, to compete directly with them, and where you need to be *different* (or significantly better). In the gaming business, for instance, there were some critical dimensions on which Nintendo had not matched the Market Leader in the past, like choice of games. In launching the Wii, Nintendo didn't want to be different in this particular dimension—it knew it had to be at least as good in order to really compete. It just wanted to match PlayStation here. The Wii's key compelling differences as a Challenger would come on other key dimensions—the experience of the gameplay, for example. Being a Challenger is not about changing everything. It lies in knowing where you need to be different, and where you need to be the same.

Exercise: "Schrager—Overlaying the Rules of Another Category onto Your Own"

This exercise is best done in breakout groups, in pairs. First, pick four other Challenger brands that the group admires and that have no immediate relationship to your own category. These might be, for instance:

Linux in the software market
JetBlue in the airline market
Umpqua in the financial services market
Scion in the car market

Approach, then, the developing and marketing of your own brand as if it were in their category. What are the ways that they broke through in their market, and what would it mean to do exactly the same kind of thing in yours? If we look at Linux, for instance, what would open up our brand to that principle of collective co-creation and, so to speak, put it at the heart of the brand? How would we build and nurture that community? Why would we champion this in our category? What would be the underlying belief or cause about why it is important, one that would unite this community for us and perhaps against the Market Leader? And so on.

Some may find it easier to think through the eyes of the founder of this other brand: How would the founders or marketing directors of these brands market our brand, treating it as if it (or some aspect of it) were the category they had come from?

Stage Three: Challenger Strategy

Building a Lighthouse Identity (Credo 2)
Premise

Fundamental to a Challenger's success is a very clear sense of who you are, and the insistent and salient communication of that identity.

Furthermore, since a Challenger has fewer resources at its disposal than the Brand Leader it is at least indirectly taking on, it needs to make sure *everything it does* is communicating that identity as strongly as possible; for a Challenger, everything communicates.

Exercise: "The Brand Vault"

This is an exercise for an existing brand, to help rediscover what it stands for. It will clearly not be necessary for a new brand.

The underlying premise here is that the identity of the company already exists—that is, there are potentially valuable components of the brand's past stored away in a metaphorical vault—and we just need to find the most relevant dimensions of those facts, equities, or ideas to the current challenge and amplify them. In this, we are attempting to extract (and reapply) value rather than add value.

Have someone either prepare a short presentation or an exhibit mounted on one of the walls of the room, which reviews:

(Continued)

(continued)
- Why did the brand begin? Why was it first launched?

- What were the three key factors in its early success (what it stood for and why that mattered to people who responded to it at the time)?

- What kinds of people did it most appeal to at the time, and why?

- What were the key moments in its innovation and communications history that at some level defined the brand? Why were they so powerful at the time? What could a re-expression of them mean now, in a new cultural and social context?

- What are the equities that have been created over time—either visual equities or equities of any other form? What are ownable brand assets to rebuild this brand from?

Identify three possible brand truths from this history that might, if re-expressed in a relevant way, be part of the rock on which to build our Lighthouse.

Exercise: "Product or Service Rock"

Take Robin Wight's famous invocation to "Interrogate the product until it confesses its strengths."

Talk to the technical people, the scientists, the engineers, the service trainers. Get the most interesting one or two of them on film.

Get them to tell you facts (what makes us different), underlying philosophies, stories that they think define the culture, and what they are most proud of.

What could be the two or three product or service truths we are building from? That are uniquely ours, in fact or philosophy? What could be the identity elements, the unique beliefs, and perspectives on the category and the world, that we could ladder up from one or more of these?

Exercise: "Defining the Challenge"

Having done some of this exploratory thinking, let us start to be clear on where is the center of our *Challenge to the category or the culture* going to lie? Which of these kinds of Challenge will it fall into?

- Challenging some fundamental dimension or driver of our category
- Challenging some aspect of the way the consumer shops for, experiences, or consumes our product
- Challenging the culture surrounding the category
- Challenging some broader aspect of contemporary culture
- Challenging some dimension or quality of the competition or Market Leader

Bearing in mind our discussion of these possible kinds of Challenge in Chapter 5, remember that you will need to have a sense of two things: (1) which of these your Challenge will lie in and (2) whether the Challenge (at least initially) is going to be *implicit* or *explicit* in the way we express it.

Exercise: "Going Binary"

This is a way of teasing out some of the outputs of the previous exercise. If you are already very clear on your challenge, you can simply move on.

In this exercise you are going to explicitly pair yourself with one other brand or one other kind of choice (e.g., a particular behavior) in the market. You are going to present the world to the consumer as one that comes down to just two choices. Do this in a couple of different ways—choices of actions, and choices of brands:

- *Actions.* You can do *this* (and such and such a consequence will happen) or you can do *that* (and a different consequence will happen).

(Continued)

(*continued*)
- *Brand choice.* You can choose *that* brand and have that kind of experience, or you can choose *our* brand and have this kind of experience.

Important: The purpose here is as much to create *clarity* about what the two choices are, as it is to see whether we would actually want to talk about this in communications. The latter is a separate conversation.

Exercise: "Two Kinds of People"

In Chapter 5 we looked at the moment when we productively juxtaposed ice cream people and yogurt people together. In this exercise we do the same within our category and our brand; it will be particularly useful for a group who are slightly intimidated by or jealous of the opposition that they face.

What are you, as a challenger brand group, most jealous of elsewhere in the category? What is the "gold standard" of the category? The brand or product you all secretly (or openly) envy?

Write a piece about two different kinds of people—the people who use your brand and the people who use this other brand or product. Show the people who use your brand to their best advantage (all the things you love about them). Show the people who use this other brand or product at their worst (their smugness and vanity, their pretensions, narrow-mindedness, and idiocies). How would you compare them to one another to make your brand and user group the one that is genuinely aspirational? (Remember our observation, for example, that one of the classic beer strategies in any market reflects a down-to-earth, blue-collar, no-nonsense, tell-it-like-it-is attitude. Could this work in your category, too?)

Create two kinds of comparison that would give us an aspirational attitude to wrap around our brand.

Exercise: "The Lighthouse Point of View"

What is our unique point of view about the world, building from some or all of the preceding exercises? What makes us different?

What is the category orthodoxy, if you like, and what is our unique take on it?

And why does this point of view really *matter*? Why would the world be the poorer without it?

Exercise: "Picasso"

Having started to identify who we are, let's now start to look at the degree to which we are and are not projecting that sense of self. This first stage is, in effect, an audit of our current *projection*.

Put on the wall every piece of marketing activity from the past two years, together with what is proposed for next year, if available.

Divide the activity into three groups:

1. Which activity strongly communicates the identity?
2. Which activity is consistent with the identity (even if it doesn't strongly promote it)?
3. Which activity is not consistent with the identity?

Discard anything that falls into categories 2 and 3 (consistency is not enough: we should be looking to find a way of projecting strongly who we are and what we stand for). How much is left up on the wall? Which are the areas and activities from those we have taken down into which we should be devoting our creativity and energy in order to communicate our Lighthouse Identity?

Exercise: "House Media"

Imagine your traditional paid-for media are denied you.

What you have at your disposal instead is all the media you are already producing, but just not seeing as media at the moment.

(Continued)

(continued)

Packs, bottle tops, boxes, internal wrapping, price tags, shelf displays, cardboard outers, delivery vehicles, door signs—anything and everything you are already making. How could you brightly project your identity and your message through these as media?

It may be of value to add impetus to this exercise through the concept of "doubling and denying": How would you use these kinds of media to *double* your awareness with your current audience if you were denied your current dominant medium?

Assuming Thought Leadership of the Category (Credo 3)

Premise

In order to achieve rapid growth, a Challenger must develop a new kind of relationship with the consumer for the category. This is done through the selective breaking of key conventions in the category, such as those of representation, medium, and experience.

There is a choice of exercises in this section, which offer practical and substantive ways of thinking about convention breaking. How many you try in the time you have set aside depends on how well they work and how much time you have available. If one proves unrewarding for your brand or in your situation, then move on.

Exercise: "Schultz"

When Starbucks began, one of the striking things that Howard Schultz succeeded in doing was turning what should have been a bad part of the experience (waiting in line for a cup of coffee) into a very good part of the experience: a moment of education (showing us how beans were roasted) and feeling of sophistication (contemplating the language of the menu choices) in an otherwise humdrum day.

In this exercise, then, identify the part of the purchase/consumption process that consumers currently *like least* and then look at how you would turn it into their favorite part of the experience. What could you add to that moment that would make it unexpectedly positive?

Some prompts to consider here might be: What could give our target a sense of discernment of reward? A sense of learning, or the pleasure of play? What would make them feel special? Individual? Flatter them? Increase their sense of self-esteem?

Exercise: "Galliano"

John Galliano used unusually evocative invitations to heighten his audience's expectations of the show they were about to experience. This exercise looks at how we might precondition our consumers *before* they experience our brand or come into contact with us.

First we need to identify the following:

- The expectations the consumer has of us.
- The gateways they pass through to interacting with us (e.g., landing at an airport or checking into a hotel if I am a car rental company).

How could we use these gateways to raise the level of expectation and favorable predisposition toward our product? (And what would we have to be sure we could deliver to ensure those expectations were met?)

Exercise: "Pinter"

Sir Harold Pinter remarked that sometimes speech is just a strategy to cover nakedness. This exercise is to push our point of view beyond speech (on pack, in the homepage, in an ad, and so on), and to actually make it impact what we *do*. It is after all the way Lighthouse brands *behave*, the actions they take over and above what messages

(Continued)

(continued)

they use, that really cement their relationship with the consumer and their place in popular culture. Think of Dove with its Self-Esteem Fund, and programs for schools.

So in this exercise you are asked to divide your media budget into two. Half is a "saying" budget, to be used in communication through media as we have always done. The other half is a "doing" budget, to be spent in activities or events that demonstrate the brand is serious about living its chosen Lighthouse Identity.

What would you spend your doing budget on, in order to really live out and exemplify your point of view?

Exercise: "Areas of Impact"

Use the map and process described in Chapter 15. Where are you going to use your Lighthouse Identity to create Thought Leadership on this map?

Push out toward the edges—think of each area as having a ten-point scale, with 0 at the center and 10 at the outer edge. What would it take to deliver a 10 on your chosen dimension, rather than simply an 8?

Distinguish in doing this exercise between acts of Thought Leadership which you would only do for a limited time, and those that might become permanent and signature parts of your experience.

Exercise: "Focus"

Remember the chutzpah of the German magazine launch.

Take two symbolic properties or icons associated with the Market Leader and steal them for yourself.

Which would they be?

And how would you do it in an engaging and highly visible way?

Creating Symbols of Re-evaluation (Credo 4)
Premise
You need to force rapid appraisal or reappraisal of your brand, generating salience and momentum.

Exercise: "Hayek"

Phase One

Agree on the key consumer complacencies that stand between the company or brand and rapid growth—or, indeed, success at all.

Of all of these, which is the dominant consumer complacency?

Phase Two

What single piece of communication about our brand would change, puncture, or reverse this complacency? (You may want to make this three communication points, as Swatch did with "Swatch. Swiss. 60DM").

In particular, suppose you could put some incarnation of your product on the tallest skyscraper in the city for two weeks:

- What product or idea would it be?
- In what form would it appear?
- What three things would you write on it?

Exercise: "Radcliffe"

We saw Daniel Radcliffe breaking down his transition from lovable magical moppet to credibly versatile adult actor into a sequence of clear and purposefully staged Symbols of Re-evaluation.

What is the journey we need to make to get to our challenger future?

What are the three steps it would break down into, and what would be the clear Symbol of Re-evaluation we would introduce in order to take the consumer with us at each stage?

Stage Three: Translating Strategy into Challenger Behavior

Sacrifice: What Are We Going to Sacrifice? (Credo 5)

Premise

One or two marketing actions are going to make 80 percent of the difference in the fortunes of the brand next year. The rest must be Sacrificed in order to make achieving these priorities possible.

The question of what those one or two things actually might be, when taken in isolation, is obviously much easier to answer in retrospect than in advance. There may, then, be value in beginning with the past: When reviewing all the marketing activities that took place last year, which were the one or two that made 80 percent of the difference? What real difference would it have made to the performance of the brand to have Sacrificed *everything* else?

Then apply that learning to this year: Does this give us an indication of how we can decide what the critical points will be again this year?

It may be useful to distinguish between goals and activities:

- On the wall, write the year's goals for the brand. If it helps, break these goals down into the marketing areas discussed in the first stage of day one (audience, distribution, media, etc.).
  Which is the least important?
  Cut it.
  The next least important?
  Cut it.
  Cut them down one by one, until we are down to two.
  Stand back. Using last year as a guide, how much have we really lost?
- Write up all the marketing activities aimed at achieving these two goals.
  Cut them down to two.
  If you could commit to only these two activities, on these two goals—but could *overcommit* on them—how successful would the brand be?

Overcommit (Credo 6)

Then, clearly, we need to ensure genuine success for the few critical areas that we have agreed Challenger success depends on.

We need to aim two feet below the brick.

Exercise: "innocent"

For each core marketing task, name three irrefutable reasons it will fail (or be diluted into mediocrity). Then brainstorm the most effective way of neutralizing or reversing each of them.

What does two feet below the brick look like, then, in overcoming that resistance?

Using Communications and Publicity to Enter Social Culture (Credo 7)

You will have business partners with you who will be developing ideas that will give you the profile and visibility you need. Here are three exercises to help clarify the mind-set you will need.

Exercise: "Stance"

Review the different kinds of challenger stances in Chapter 12. Which of these stances best informs how we will be positioning ourselves in that market? How do other challengers we admire use communications and publicity in taking that stance? How are they able through their use of this stance to accomplish much more than we seem to be at the moment? What should be the implications of that for us going forward?

Exercise: "Ross"

Remember the story of the 42BELOW team and the story they created about buying the Navy frigate.

Give every member of the group one of today's newspapers. They have 20 minutes. Each member of the group has to come up with three stories taken from that newspaper which they could use to create publicity around your Lighthouse Identity.

(Continued)

(continued)

Share the stories, and how they could be used. From a group of 12 people, you will now have 36 suggestions.

Which are the most overlapping? More important, which one or two gave the group the most energy when it was read out loud? Which one would make an arresting picture? Which could you go out and do later today?

Exercise: "Ryanair"

Ryanair is supposed to have had, at one point, a policy of issuing three press releases a day (although there is always the possibility that this was simply a story in one of its own press releases). Let us take this organizational thought very seriously, though, at this point.

How would we need to think about structuring ourselves and our behavior in order to genuinely be able to deliver three interesting press releases a day? Not to brief someone else to do it, but to be able to deliver it ourselves?

Identify three key changes you would need to make in the people, the structure, the internal relationships with the rest of the company, or any other aspect of how you currently operate.

What is to stop you from doing these tomorrow?

SUMMARY AND PLAN

The purpose of the final part of the two days is to pull out the key strands of thinking agreed on by everyone, while not yet judging irrevocably the thoughts that were thrown up or fixating prematurely on any new connecting tissue that emerged from one exercise to another.

Three questions, then, will serve as a summary at the end of the second day:

1. What is the Big Fish?
2. Who are we? What is our unique point of view and why does it matter?

3. What are the three ideas in each section that have the most opportunity to transform our business?

Note that there are no exercises during these two days for the implementation of the Eighth Credo. This process will begin at a rather later stage of the overall journey.

What Next?

Arrange a follow-up day or two to take place four weeks later. Give over a third of that time to pulling everything together: Which ideas and concepts continue to seem to be central to your future as a Challenger?

Spend a third of the time examining how well equipped you are as a company to making the journey, in terms of the following:

- Partners
- Passion
- Knowledge
- Ideas
- Titles and remits
- Culture

Spend the last third of the time preparing an initial plan for the next six months, to cover both external (consumer) marketing and the signals and briefs that will herald the beginning of adopting a Challenger mindset internally.

Then Overcommit to it.

14

THE SCOPE OF THE LIGHTHOUSE KEEPER

The Lamps shall be kept burning bright and clear every night from sunset to sunrise . . .

From *Duties of the Light-Keepers, 1847*
By-laws and Rules and Regulations of the Commissioners of
Northern Lighthouses

WHEN IS A BRAND NOT A BRAND?

It's hard, frankly, to find a Challenger who just wants to be a brand anymore. Method and Scion describe themselves as lifestyles, Red Bull is a philosophy, Dove an agent of change, Facebook a movement.

There's a reason for that. Richard Reed of innocent explains his reluctance to talk about innocent as a brand, because he feels brands are inherently contrived and artificial things, and from the bottom of his being he doesn't want innocent to be something contrived. The founder of Jones Soda makes a more general observation about the current zeitgeist: "Look at somebody like Jon Stewart. Why is he so funny and so in sync with people? Because he's real. And Coke says it's real. But saying it and being it are two different things. So if you say it, you better be it."[1] So this chapter will explore how Lighthouse Identities manifest their "realness" (i.e., their real footprint) in the way they develop their experience and relationship with the world around them. Which primary areas do they need to genuinely impact, and what is the relationship between those areas?

First, though, let's review some of the advice the marketing world is giving us as Keepers of the Lighthouse, with responsibility to turn this sense of our brand into actions and behaviors, and be clear about which pieces of that advice we are and are not going to pay attention to. We have noted throughout the book that the dynamic emergence of new kinds of technologies, and people's restlessly inventive exploration of the possibilities that are created by and within these technologies (the connections, cultures, voices, and leverage that they make possible), make the world (and therefore the world of brands) a hugely fluid and dynamic place in which to live. They make it a hard place in which simply to stay where we are, even if we wanted to, and a hugely stimulating environment in which to chart our future. And in this environment, all around us we hear regularly repeated a number of key precepts for progression, such as "dialogue not monologue," "the consumer is in control," "the imperative of transparency," and "everything is social."

Which of these, and others like them, should we really pay attention to? What does this new sociodigital economy mean for us as Lighthouse Keepers, so to speak, of our Lighthouse brands? And if the consumer is now in control, who is the keeper of the Lighthouse, anyway?

WHO IS THE LIGHTHOUSE KEEPER, ANYWAY?

Here's a very simple question. If you are the Church of Scientology, who is the "Lighthouse Keeper" so to speak? Is it the church's chief? Is it Tom Cruise, as its most famous public figure and proponent? Or is it Gawker, the website that first posted Cruise's controversial Scientology video, which within months of the posting picked up 2.5 million hits for the video, and has arguably done as much to shape the public perception of the "brand" of Scientology in those few months as years of carefully controlled communication from the church itself?

Or, if you are a cognac brand, and a rapper starts singing about you, and the song hits number one on the charts and is splashed across every music video station, causing it to be seen and heard by more people than anything you (as the brand owner) do this year, then who is the

Lighthouse Keeper? If you are a Challenger for the Democratic nomination for President in the U.S. elections, and supporters post upbeat videos—an attractive woman singing her admiration for you ("Obama Girl"), a selection from key speeches set to music ("Yes We Can")—or some primary influencers of U.S. culture (Oprah) pitch your case, who is the Lighthouse Keeper?

Not so simple a question. With reference to Obama, the *Boston Globe* answered it (in part) like this:

> Oprah Winfrey . . . is now trying to lead the public in the presidential campaign. Whether the public will listen is another, open question; if her candidate of choice, Barack Obama, prevails in the early primaries . . . he might owe as much credit to "Obama Girl." That was the YouTube video sensation that solidified his image as someone hip, handsome and new. And Obama was smart enough not to protest. Like other politicians who came to terms with the Internet this season, he learned that you can't control the snarks. You can only ride the wave.[2]

The way that many people interpret this kind of profound change is to say that now "the consumer is in control." The Obama Girl video, after all was apparently made by ordinary people who were fans of the Democrat. But of all the current mantras about modern marketing, the notion that the consumer is now "in control" is surely the most confused and dangerous.

One can understand the temptation to believe it—look at the evidence:

- While most consumers are paying no more attention to the daily bread-and-butter brands around them than they ever were (as we saw in Chapter 2), a handful of vocal consumers, however, are paying much more attention to them, and have much more potential influence, than ever before. The combination of the blogosphere and Web 2.0 gives this smaller group of consumers the ability not simply to post their opinions about your brand and company, and the actions of both, but also gives the ability to determined and vocal individuals to have a disproportionately high influence on the world's perceptions of your brands. Hilary Clinton calls this the symptom of a "hyperdemocracy"—a citizenry of state or marketplace that is informed, plugged in, and able to make their voices heard (from their desks) at a level of noise and influence never previously experienced. So, for instance, when in 2004 a single (though respected) blog posted a story that there was going to be a serious delay in two of Apple's key new launches, the iPhone and the Leopard operating system, Apple shares plummeted in value by $4 billion within half an hour. The story was in fact unfounded—Apple issued a denial, and the stock bounced back—but the unprecedented power of an individual to affect a huge business was profoundly demonstrated. It used to be said that if you were satisfied as a customer, you talked to three people; if you were dissatisfied, you talked to 10 to 20 people. Nowadays, if you are dissatisfied and can edit film, you can talk to hundreds of thousands, perhaps millions. Conversely, if you are Will.i.am and can write a song supporting your favored Democratic candidate, and edit it to incorporate one of his speeches, you can create an idea that will be seen by 18 million people. There are 70 million bloggers out there with a point of view, and who want to share that point of view.

- Should they want it, all of our consumers have more access to information on brands and products than ever before—either because they themselves can see "behind the curtain," and inside the company (Starbucks Gossip) or because they have access to user groups (e.g., Amazon reviewers, flickr posters, TripAdvisor) that have passed this way before.
- Brands are actively inviting consumers to play with them, whether creating their own scenarios in gaming, customizing their cars, or making their advertising (the Doritos Super Bowl spots, written by consumers, lifted sales of a static brand 15 percent).
- Some consumers are playing with brands within this new public sphere, whether they are invited to or not, from customizing a brand's products for entirely different uses, to shooting and posting videos that are their creative comments on those brands.
- Whole new brands and brand movements are being formed in effect by consumers themselves (in reality there is always a founder and center to them but the democratic nature of these brands means that the consumer is one or all of creator, voter, and decision maker. From

open-source software to clothing companies where all the designs are created and chosen by the community of creators themselves, to information sources, news sites, and financial services.

We need, however, to make a critical distinction between recognizing the power and ability of creative consumers to impact our brands on the one hand (bringing with it the opportunity to co-create with them), and the notion of ceding control to them on the other. Real clarity about the difference between these two things will be critical to us and the way we manage our brand.

First, consumers, the vast majority of consumers, are not busy co-creating brands, whatever you may read in the blogs. They are getting on with their lives. They may be vigilant for BS, and a few of them may be posting videos of rats in the Taco Bell restaurant in Greenwich Village or of service engineers dozing on their couches, and a much larger group may be very happy to watch those videos when they are forwarded to them, and may be doing a little benign customization now and again of their own on MySpace/Facebook/Bebo, but the vast majority of people are not trying to take control of anything in the world of brands. They have more important things to do—pay the bills, feed the kids, prepare for the meeting, worry about why the weather is changing so much.

Second, for the most part they don't actually want to take control of external things like brands. What they really want is for *brands to take control of themselves*—for brands to be real, to have some ethics, to actually do what they say, to not disappoint them. And, increasingly, they want brands to play a part in making the world a better place while they are at it.

To frame this as "the consumer is in control" is to think of it the wrong way. It is absolutely true that the consumer has an ability to influence us as never before and that we are not the only ones controlling the image of our brand these days, and that this is a future that we need to lean into. And as we said, there clearly are brands over which the consumer is very much in control, because that is the brand's nature/product (Wikipedia) or business model (Threadless). And we can also choose, like Doritos, to put the consumer at key points in control of certain aspects of what our brand does or says. But most of us are not, nor should we be, handing over control of the brand to the consumer. They don't want that, and we shouldn't want it. They want us to actually stand for something—to be a Lighthouse rather than an amoeba. This does not mean we have to be always in broadcast mode—we can and will, of course, have a two-way conversation. But having a Lighthouse Identity means we will engage in that two-way conversation always coming from a very particular perspective, one all our own.

In the same way, let us be careful of the idea one also hears bandied about that the consumer wants "complete transparency." Some consumers do, in some categories. And most consumers want brands to do the right thing, to be what they say they are—and they understandably become aggrieved if you take an ethical stance and then your CEO is found engaging in unethical activities (Whole Foods). But do they really want to know why meat is so cheap? No. Do they really want to know how much that $150 pair of sneakers costs to make? No. There are some truths they don't want to see at all. They are, after all, simply human.

So let us recognize and embrace the way the world is changing, but let us be very clear as Challengers and keepers of our individual Lighthouse brands about what that does and doesn't mean for us. In summary, it is not a conversation about who does or doesn't have control. In many ways, it is more useful to think that "we now have more kinds of communications and content partners." Some we pay, some we don't. Some we brief, some we don't. Some are strident, some playful. Some are selfish, some community-minded. But on all sides they will play, essentially one of four roles:

1. *Proposition* ("Love this!"). Target has a number of Facebook groups devoted to loving it.
2. *Opposition* ("Hate this!"). "Keep Austin Weird" is a community rallying cry, mostly seen on bumper stickers and T-shirts, resisting the increasing commercial homogenization of a proudly idiosyncratic town in southwest Texas.
3. *Play and display* ("Look at this!"). Ikea hackers is an engaging community of people who are innovating with basic IKEA products, then posting and sharing their ideas with like-minded souls (a television base turned into a tortoise tank, for example). They are not advocating that IKEA move into full-time manufacture of tortoise tanks—they are just showing others what they have done.

4. *Create/Re-create* ("Make this!" or sometimes "Put this right!").
   These center more on product-centric issues: whereas Opposition
   has to do with a macroissue or brand (people who hate Starbucks, for
   instance), this has to do with making or improving products *within* a
   brand (Dell, for example).

The more interesting and important question for us to devote our
energies to, then, is how to build our ability to feed, trigger, and respond to each of these sources of consumer energy around our brand.

So we still have to keep the Lighthouse. We are going to engage with
the consumer, but we are not going to simply give over what we stand
for to them; they don't want that, and nor should we. We are going to
recognize the ways in which communities of consumers unite around
Challengers such as ours, which stand for something in the popular
imagination, and explore ways to feed the most beneficial forms of this
kind of energetic community.

And we are also as Lighthouse Keepers going to need to have a very
clear sense of what our scope as a brand is, moving forward, in terms of
the key agendas our Lighthouse Identity will want or need to impact.

THE FOUR KEY AGENDAS

We have noted throughout the book that while Challengers have a central point of view, what matters is what they *do* that projects that point of
view: the agenda they use to pursue it.

The word *agenda* comes from the Latin word *ago*, which means "I
do" or "I make happen." If I asked you to talk about any of the Challengers we have discussed so far, you would find one of the easiest
things to talk about is something they *did*. And if we look at how
Challengers translate their point of view, we can see that they have
four different kinds of agendas, the most common areas that seem to
make up their canvas of implementation, which can be represented
on a map as shown in Figure 14.1. The map will represent in effect
both our scope and our brief: Once we have mapped the scope, we
will look at how we as Challengers need to implement across it, in
terms of our product development, our social and ethical policies,
and our experience design.

FIGURE 14.1 The Four Most Common Agendas.

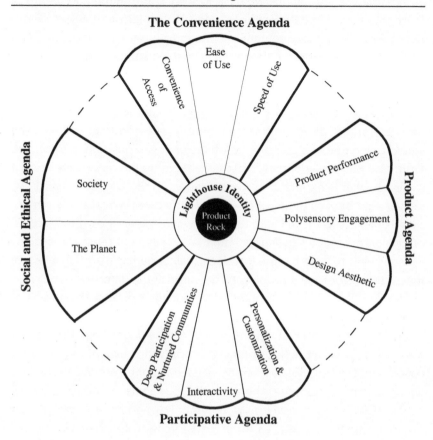

The Convenience Agenda

The Planet / Society — Social and Ethical Agenda

Product Performance / Polysensory Engagement / Design Aesthetic — Product Agenda

Participative Agenda

The desire in doing it this way is to break away from channel-based implementation schematics, which have historically been the character-istic of "360-degree implementation" plans. If we had been going to pursue that kind of model, then we would put the Lighthouse at the cen-ter and all the different kinds of communication and engagement chan-nel around the outside, to show that this would be projected in all directions and through all media.

But we know this already—we don't need a map to tell us that. This instead is a strategic map, rather than a communications map. It looks instead at the four most common *areas of necessary impact* for us as Challengers, which our Lighthouse Identity will need to influence, *each of which can be amplified and promoted through a variety of activation and media channels.* Once we have looked at the shape and nature of these four areas of strategic impact, we will then look at how we choose from them in our implementation strategy to further our understanding of where the key opportunities might lie in the creation of Thought Leadership, in how we are going to use Symbols of Re-evaluation, and where we need to Sacrifice and Overcommit.

In looking at Figure 14.1, the agendas should be considered as four separate areas, *each moving dynamically outward* (rather than each strand being one of a pair of axes whose ends are polar opposites). The further we push out along each of them, the more the way we are using it will push what is expected in the category: So the degree in which we deliver against each dimension will obviously be as critical as the dimension itself. As such, it will help us clarify *where we are going to manifest our differences as a Challenger*—that is, on which of these dimensions we are going to be the same (product quality, perhaps) and on which of these dimensions we are going to be surprisingly different, either permanently different or temporarily different through in-and-out acts of Thought Leadership.

At the very center of the map is the meaning of our Challenger brand—the product rock or brand truth on which everything we do is based, and the Lighthouse Identity we have wrapped around it. The four agendas coming from this, then, are the four areas of impact on which we see Challengers today most commonly using to spearhead their challenge to the market, as forms of expression for their Lighthouse Identity, their differentiated offer to the consumer.

Let us discuss each of them in turn.[3]

The Ease and Convenience Agenda

The first agenda centers on how convenient it is for the consumer to access us, and how easy we are to use or navigate when they do. Although these pragmatic dimensions are often overlooked in brands, we see rapidly growing Challengers profiting from Overcommitting in exactly these areas. The convenience of the early Amazon, the reassuring simplicity of the early Google (and it is easy to forget now how cluttered some of its competitors became), the simple accessibility of ING Direct, the wrapping of Kodak's digital camera benefit in the whole concept of

EasyShare—all of these clearly point to opportunity if we choose genuinely to see this agenda for what it might represent in our category.

Just so we are clear about the difference between terms, *convenience* has to do with the ease of *access* we give our consumers (at their fingertips, put in their path, don't have to leave the car to buy it, everything they need aggregated in one place for them). *Ease of use* has to do with how easy it is to use the service or product *when I have accessed it* (liberatingly easy technology, like the Flip video camera or insurance services that make it easy to file claims). And *speed of use* has to do with how little time it takes to access the benefit (Virgin Atlantic's "Limo to Lounge in 10 minutes," for example).

The Product Agenda: The Different Dimensions of Our Product Experience

Researching the first edition of this book in the late 1990s, it was voguish in marketing circles to talk about the unimportance of product—that all products had effectively reached parity in most categories (even ones as historically product-led as cars) and the only real connection to be made in every category was an emotional one. (You have to bear in mind that at that time this was essentially a packaged goods or superbenchmarked service world, which perhaps accounts for the nod to the zeitgeist of "product superiority is dead; it's all about emotional branding now.") In the past 10 years, however, the marketing emphasis has very much swung back again to product. Apple and Jonathan Ive have led the way in reminding us that products have the ability to fill us with wonder again. The digital world has shown us extraordinary functionality in Google and Wikipedia (anything we could want to know, and more, in 0.23 seconds), and we see a more recent generation of Challengers beyond the digital domain also changing the game through the product functionality and experience: Dyson, Lush, Wii. So product performance is back, though back with a difference. Because in the post-iMac-/iPod-/iPhone world, the focus on product development is not *simply* about a better functionality (although that is a key dimension), but often about being accompanied by a more enticingly polysensory relationship with the brand—whether you are talking about malt whisky (Glenmorangie), fabric conditioner (Snuggle) or chewing gum (5, from Wrigley).

Sometimes this polysensuality is real, sometimes cued (the sensuality of the posters on the walls of American Apparel). And a key part of this experiential element lies also in the aesthetic/design appeal of the packaging or product form, which is why it has been given its own vector here in Figure 14.1. method is just one brand to recognize the opportunity to market oneself through an exceptional design aesthetic, even at a mass market level. One might argue there are now a number of categories where the distinction between product and package is in reality now an entirely blurred one. And it is no accident that method started its mainstream life in Target, which is doing so much to democratize design in the United States.

So there are three dimensions to the way we can pursue the product agenda: product performance, polysensory experience, and design aesthetic. All key, all obviously interrelated. So understanding our Lighthouse Identity as we do, where are we going to simply compete within these, and where are we going to surprise? Where are we going to be Thought Leaders? Where are we constrained by consumers' complacencies about the limits of the category—which, in other words, might require Symbols of Re-evaluation to break through?

The Participative Agenda

Everything is social: The world is one of increasing interactivity between networks of people. It always was—such is the nature of man as a social animal—but the combination of technology, Web 2.0, and the change in our trusted source of authority (from being public figures, institutions, and experts to more of a peer-based authority model) means this interactivity is now able to, and in some areas needs to, enter the brand-buyer relationship as well. This will require us to consciously "Break the plane" (remembering Chapter 7) and create not just a *closer* relationship with the consumer, but a more *deliberately interactive* one.

There are three dimensions to this agenda. First, we need to distinguish between *basic interactivity* and *deep participation*. Basic interactivity and participation between consumers and brands are now becoming key dynamics in every category around us. Even the most historically quiet and static of experiences—museums, for instance—are deliberately moving away from being frozen places of exhibition and becoming much more two-way and interactive, not simply in terms of online interactivity (the best museums, which post everything from knitting to video art on the Internet, have 7 to 10 times as many online visitors as they do in-person visitors), but in the museum experience itself. This evolving sense of the social nature of the experience is echoed in the world's leading retailers. Virgin's Vice President of Marketing for its Entertainment Group, which includes the US Virgin Megastores, notes: "I think that even with everything we have online, the most interactive of experiences is shopping in the store . . . . Our customers have come to expect a really dynamic environment. Retail space is now less about inventory management and more of a *social* experience."[4] The emphasis here is obviously on *social*—we all understand the importance of experience in itself. This is the vector labeled *Basic Interactivity*.

But there will also be a group of people who will offer the chance of much deeper participation here—communities built around the social object that the brand represents. Communities who will help do each of the four activities we saw earlier: (1) communities that will want to engage, (2) communities that will be prepared to co-create, (3) communities that will oppose, (4) communities that will look to improve. method is, in its own words, "People against Dirty." And that does not mean method is simply a company consisting of "people working on the brand who are against dirty," but that method is deliberately trying to create a community of users of the brand, all of whom represent the brand in this way. (We note again that if you are trying to create a community, it is useful for them to have something to rally *against*—in this case, dirt.).

We have been noting throughout the book that this new world we are moving into will force us to reexamine some of our basic vocabulary. We might extend this now to the phrase *heavy user* of a brand. Historically, the phrase has meant someone who simply bought a lot of our product. Now, perhaps, we are seeing a different kind of heavy user—one who *participates heavily* with us. Traditionally, heavy users in terms of consumption were small in number, but they accounted for a disproportionately large volume of sales; heavy users in this new, secondary sense are also small in number, but they carry a disproportionately strong amount of influence. Perhaps as we go forward we should be looking at, and tracking, heavy buyers and heavy/deep participators equally seriously.

And the third dimension on the participative agenda is that of the degree to which we make it possible for people to personalize or customize their use of us and our product or service—that is, participate and interact not just with the brand, but also with the product. The future will be personal, after all, as well as social, and Challengers from Scion to Facebook, via Burger King's "Have it your way," should be stretching our own understanding and imagination for what might be possible on our own brand here.

The Social and Environmental Agenda

There would be many who would argue that the environmental issue is the Big Fish that every brand and every person needs to eat, and there is an increased expectation from consumers that brands should play an active part in putting this right. Some brands might lead the way (Whole Foods and San Francisco putting a stop to plastic bags, for example), but every brand will need to play its part. This broader awareness of one's responsibility is becoming hardwired into many of the newer generation of Challengers we see emerging, and it will need to be hardwired into us as well; the more successful those new Challengers in other categories are in getting their own narratives heard in this regard, the more they will necessarily influence our position as a Challenger in ours.

The other of the two areas of impact in this quadrant has to do with creating a better society. This can clearly take a number of different forms. In the United States, for example, we see American Apparel not simply making sweatshop-free clothing or basing all its production within the United States, but actively lobbying consumers on its e-mail database to vote for particular candidates because of their position on labor laws. In Hong Kong, on the other hand, *Apple Daily* has consistently named and shamed local businesspeople and politicians for offenses ranging from tax evasion to conflicts of interest. More significantly (given the initial government clampdown that forced Jimmy Lai to close his first business) *Apple Daily* in 2003 encouraged the people of Hong Kong to take to the streets to protest against the government—and even went so far as to give them front pages that they could use as banners and messages to hold up and wave on the march. At half a million protestors, it became one of the largest demonstrations in the history of the island. We can see here again that the word *agenda* needs to be taken very literally: It is what a Challenger *does* rather than says or intends in this area that makes the difference.

We should note, however, that for most of our Challengers the role of this agenda—across both dimensions—is carefully managed, in that it is rare for it to be positioned to the consumer as the dominant reason to buy the brand, however deeply the social or ethical cause might be championed within the company. Such companies are (in the words of one of them) "deep green on the inside, light green on the outside"[5]— that is to say that they ensure that their principles, though genuinely and deeply held, are not thrust down the consumer's throat as the paramount reason to buy the brand. Instead, they recognize that the promise of superior performance, quality, utility, or desire will be underpinned by this agenda rather than replaced by it. The early Body Shop aside, perhaps the most celebrated recent case of this recognition is that of Green & Black's, a high-quality organic chocolate brand. Originally marketed on an organic platform with a niche position in the UK market, it then repositioned the same product as a luxury dark chocolate, *underpinned* by its organic backstory. Sales rose from $8 million to $100 million, and international expansion under its new owner, Cadbury, followed. Dave Hieatt, of howies, argues articulately that when it comes to the sustainable side of a brand, for instance, one has to consider it not as a separate dynamic to be thought about in and of itself, but as one whose success is intimately related to the product appeal and aesthetic—there is no point in making a piece of sustainable clothing if it is not attractive enough to tempt someone into buying it. That is, in fact, *worse* than not producing a sustainable product at all—for in creating a product that you cannot sell, you will simply have created more waste.

These four agendas, then, taken together, make up the four agendas that one sees Challengers most commonly regarding as the *scope* of the Lighthouse Keeper. Channels, communications, promotion, packaging, even price—*all these can be used across any of these agendas as a part of implementing them.* For instance, innocent enlists participation partly through the way it uses its packaging copy, while Lush's lack of packaging is used to dramatize both its sensory experience and its environmental agenda. And we should also note that we are deliberately not mapping here agendas for trends such as health, taste, premiumization, or ethnicity. This is because, as Challengers, our preoccupation with delivering a Challenger offer against these trends will not be *whether* we deliver them, but *how we can deliver them in a different way from everyone else* along one of these dimensions. How, for example, can we make health much more convenient, or easy, or more sensually delicious, or less of a lonely road, or something that benefits others at the same time as ourselves (to take a roughly clockwise tour of our four agendas)? And, of course, as Challengers, we may want to swim *against* some trends and currents in any case (remember Burger King), rather than be carried along by them. So let us map these other macrotrends on these four agendas to see where the opportunities within them may lie for a Challenger, rather than attempt to add them as separate ones on their own.

So, having carefully separated each dimension of these four agendas, let's put them back together again, and look first at how we are going to use the Credos to plan our challenge to the market, and then how they might work together to help us in that challenge.

PUTTING ALL THE AGENDAS TOGETHER

In starting to use this model as a way of assessing our own brand, and how it currently delivers across these agendas, the question for us is going to be not simply which dimensions on which agendas we are going to play out our Lighthouse Identity, but also the degree to which we are really pushing out across one or more of these agendas.

As we do so, bear in mind this is a holistic map. Challengers are not looking to play in just one or another of these four areas. Some Challengers have started with their roots very much in just one (Facebook's starting point was all about community participation, and innocent was all about a really delicious product that made it easy to be good to yourself), but as they have grown, they have started to strategically expand their footprint across some or all of the other three as well (innocent, for example, is moving into 100 percent recycled bottles, and has built up a community of some 230,000 people annually knitting little woolen hats for the bottles on behalf of Age Concern's "Fight the Freeze" campaign). But be clear where you will Sacrifice and where you will Overcommit.

PUSHING BEYOND BRILLIANT BASICS: USING THE CREDOS ON THIS MAP

While all brands at some level will need to have a sense of this kind of map and this kind of scope for what they do, as Challengers we will need to be very clear idea about *where we will simply do what everyone else is doing and where we will be different or exceptional*. Where, in particular, are we going to choose to express our core challenge to the market? Where are we going to aim to be Thought Leaders? Where on this map are the kinds of complacencies that the world has about our category and how brands behave in it, and where do we need to break through to change it?

It is helpful, then, to introduce one more very simple dimension to this map: the notion of *Brilliant Basics*. Brilliant Basics are what, in each of these areas of impact, we are going to need to do well, but will not in themselves be a point of difference for us. If we overlay this refinement on the map, then it is delineated by the circle that lies just beyond the Lighthouse Identity at the center (see Figure 14.2). Everything that is shaded *within* that circle is a Brilliant Basic, that is to say, an area in which we'll need to perform to some degree on, simply to be an active part of the modern world, but not something that will make us different from anyone else in the category around us.

So here is the question for us: Where are we going to push beyond just the Brilliant Basics? Where on these agendas is our Challenger story, our Lighthouse Identity primarily going to be manifested and experienced? We will not be able to do this everywhere, certainly initially: We will need to make choices. Lush, for instance, could be represented by Figure 14.3. It has Overcommitted on two primary ways of engaging us within its overall offer of "Fresh, Handmade Cosmetics." First, it delivers an extraordinary polysensory pleasure. Second, it is an activist for sustainability and animal rights, with a series of acts of Thought Leadership and Symbols of Re-evaluation, such as sending its staff naked into the streets (well, wearing only an apron) to promote awareness that more products should be naked—because packaging accounts for 2 percent of greenhouse gases—and attempting to pile a truck full of manure outside the European Parliament to create a stink about animal testing.[6]

FIGURE 14.2　The Four Agendas—pushing beyond the brilliant basics.

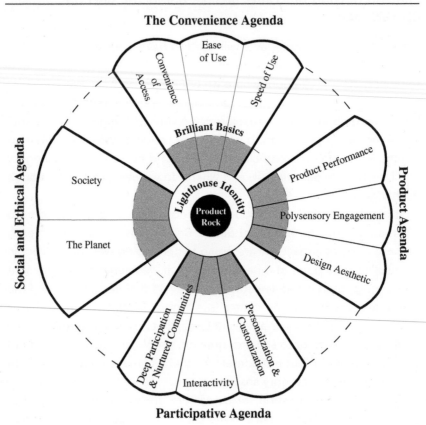

So, it is easy to see, were you a fledgling Lush, where your key areas of impact would need to be, the ones you would Overcommit on—and also the ones you would deliberately Sacrifice.

How would Red Bull fit? It would have little or nothing in the social and environmental areas and a great deal in the participative and performance areas. Dove would have a strong performance in the social (though not the environmental) and participative areas, with a little in product performance but not pushing beyond Brilliant Basics in design aesthetic and polysensory experience. If you were running Dove, then, you would be regarding polysensory experience as either Sacrifice, thus allowing you to focus on other areas (e.g., deeper participation) or as an area to commit innovation against.

FIGURE 14.3   The four agendas—Lush as an example.

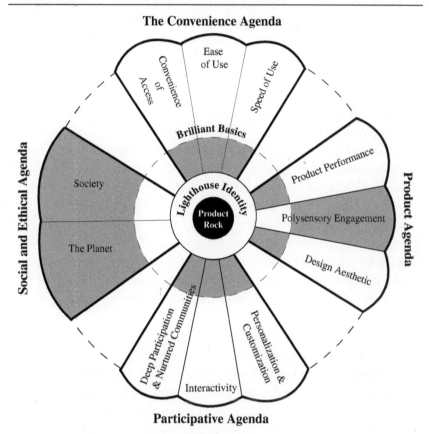

The Convenience Agenda

Ease of Use

Convenience of Access

Speed of Use

Brilliant Basics

Product Performance

Social and Ethical Agenda

Society

Lighthouse Identity

Product Rock

Polysensory Engagement

Product Agenda

The Planet

Design Aesthetic

Deep Participation & Nurtured Communities

Personalization & Customization

Interactivity

Participative Agenda

USING THE MAP TO PLOT YOUR OUTPUTS FROM THE CHALLENGER PROGRAM

This is not intended to be a map of profound insight; rather, it is intended to be a useful tool to help achieve real clarity and simplicity, particularly as we pivot between strategy and implementation.

As a tool, then, it has four different kinds of value to us:

1. The first is to generate possibilities. As a mapped aggregate of all categories, it can be overlaid onto a category that normally wouldn't think in these terms—insurance, for instance. Insurance wouldn't really figure even in Brilliant Basics on any of these. Were we a Challenger in insurance, then, it would be stimulating to use this map

to ask ourselves questions about what the potential might be for a Challenger in insurance on these dimensions. What would be the smell of security, for instance? How would you touch it? If you as an insurance company wanted to make people *feel* safe in their homes, how would you really make them *feel* it as a polysensory experience? How would you then create acts of Thought Leadership around that? What would you want consumers to reevaluate, and how? What stance would that prompt you to take?

2. The second, more important use for us here is the way that we have been using it in the chapter so far—as a tool to take our identity, and help us understand where we are going to express that identity; to force us to be very clear as a team on where we are going to Sacrifice and where we need to Overcommit to genuinely break through as the Challenger we need to be. For this, we will collectively use the map to help us all be really honest that in each chosen action we are *genuinely* delivering more than "Brilliant Basics with a little dash of lipstick"—that we are *genuinely* creating a significant point of difference in our chosen challenge to the market or Market Leader.

3. The third use of the map is to help us then *push* our ambition and thinking in those chosen areas. For this use, regard each of these agendas as vectors, each having within them a scale from 1 to 10, with 1 lying at the center and 10 at the outer edge. So, even if we think we have a product, action, or service along one of these agendas that is indeed beyond Brilliant Basics and is indeed the basis of a Challenger point of difference, what would it mean to push it *much further* in this same direction? Say you have a good little community, some deep participation. What would you have to do to double the size of that community, or triple it? You have some basic interactivity? What would it mean to turn that into a key part of your relationship—how would you brief packaging, for instance, to help increase that much further? What if you treated packaging as Direct Marketing, and made the brief to your packaging partners to achieve a 15 percent response rate in terms of interacting with your community in some way?[7] What would that stimulate their creative team to do with the packaging to make that actually happen? And what other kinds of categories could you and they learn from that would help you understand how to do that?

4. And the fourth use of the map will obviously be to help us think about how we are going to use the channels and marketing tools at our disposal to deliver against the areas we are going to Overcommit on, recognizing that the way we use the channel will always follow the agenda we need to deliver in it. How could we use packaging to deliver against each of these, for instance? Or what would you have to do in each of these areas to get a headline in the National Newspapers the next day?

USING THIS: A FINAL OBSERVATION

These agendas are interdependent, and need to be. As we think about how to be Thought Leaders in our chosen area in particular, in many ways it is the *interdynamics* between these vectors, in the way that Dave Hieatt describes above, that creates a lot of the energy in these Challengers. When you wander into Lush, this wonderful polysensory experience, and see it has a new product called Guantanamo Garden (to draw attention to the Guantanamo detainees), which smells wonderful yet is bright orange (to represent the jumpsuits), and which then dissolves to release hidden photos of a couple of those detainees, it is the *combination of the sensory experience and the ethical stance* against the detention center that creates a richer, multidimensional relationship between us and the brand, rather than just either one or the other on its own. To take another example, a perfect instance of a brand using the intersection between design aesthetic and deep participation can be seen in the Scion Owners Clubs: organized events where owners show each other how they have customized their cars and where they share experiences and tips. Plotting fertile intersections, then, will be a fifth potential of such a map.

These intersections can be big ambitions and actions (Dove's Self-Esteem Fund), or they can be little ones. So Kashi (now part of Kellogg's), the brand that is "7 whole grains on a mission," is grounded in a belief that "Wellness isn't a place, it's a journey . . . and every day is an opportunity to live life a little healthier than the day before."[8] Kashi challenges its users to make little changes in their lives, from trying yoga to using natural headache remedies to experimenting with "slow laundry."

And as the agendas are interdependent, so we need one Lighthouse team working across all four of them. Within a large company 15 years ago, these agendas would have represented four different departments. You would have had a CSR department, a product development group, a customer feedback team, and a brand team. But now, as Challengers, the key is not simply to lean into the emergence and nature of the agendas themselves, but to change the responsibility for those agendas. Today they have to be placed holistically under one team—not least because they are so necessarily interrelated in the way they will express the uniquely different manifestation of our Lighthouse Identity, and use of the subsequent Credos.[9]

PART 4

MIND-SET, CULTURE, AND RISK

15

CHALLENGER AS A STATE OF MIND: STAYING NUMBER ONE MEANS THINKING LIKE A NUMBER TWO

How do you fight like a hungry man, when your refrigerator's full?
Bernard Hopkins, World light heavyweight boxing champion[1]

THE BROADER RELEVANCE OF CHALLENGER THINKING

The premise so far has been that Challengers need their own models of strategy and behavior; that we are entirely unlike the Brand Leader in position and resource and, consequently, need to find an entirely different set of rules of engagement.

It is possible, however, that certain other kinds of brands in certain other kinds of situations may also find the Challenger model of value. While the focus of this book is naturally on Challengers themselves, this chapter briefly dwells on two other applications of Challenger thinking: brands facing a kind of "Big Fish" other than a larger competitive player, and Brand Leaders themselves.

What Is the Big Fish?

As we have seen throughout the book, while the Establishment brand is often a threat, it is not always our Big Fish, the key threat that will eat us if we don't eat it first. As the Eighth Credo started to indicate, the Big Fish is in fact more usefully defined as the central issue facing the growth, transformation, or survival of any given brand: the one critical point of focus that needs to be identified before any useful strategic conversation can be had. Insofar as there are six basic marketing challenges that marketeers can find themselves up against, a larger competitive player represents only one of these threats, although it is usually the most compelling one for a Challenger brand.

The six basic marketing challenges are:

1. A brand threatened by the superior competitive position or overt aggression of a larger, better-placed competitor. Pepsi, for example.
2. An established brand facing a situation where the social context or popular opinion has moved against it. Examples of a social context moving against it would be whiskey in a white spirits world, high-fat products such as cheese in a low-fat world, or a brand caught up in a bigger social debate such as child labor or human rights in China. An example of a brand that popular opinion has moved against might be Spam, or a utility with negative equity, such as a gas or telephone provider, which the consumer perceives to hold a monopolistic grip on the market.
3. A brand in a category where the rules of that category are capable of constant and rapid change, or are about to rapidly change. Examples of this kind of challenge might include most high-tech and Web 2.0 categories. We might also include brands facing the consumer and business implications of a recession, for instance.
4. A brand threatened with new kinds of competition. For example, traditional leisure shoe manufacturers coming to terms with the explosion of the sport and fashion sneaker, or information and knowledge retailers facing the explosion of wikis and other kinds of accessible information on the net.
5. A brand faced with a declining retail role for traditional brands, either through category commoditization (i.e., consumer

indifference) or a dominant stance or aggressive pursuit of private label by the retailer.

6. A brand whose apparent dominance has caused it to relax (Microsoft, perhaps).

These are, strictly speaking, brands with challenges, rather than Challenger brands, at a key transitional moment in their lives. As such, though, they may need to consider some or all of the thinking and behavior normally associated with Challengers (e.g., assuming Thought Leadership, or Creating Symbols of Re-evaluation), for defensive as much as for offensive reasons. That is to say, the instant goal may be as much about staying in the game and neutralizing the single dominant threat as it is about generating rapid growth. In the new marketing era, the Challenger brand—and the underlying strategic approach it embodies—may in fact prove to be an infinitely more powerful, and more far reaching, model than the historical model of the Brand Leader.

Brand Leaders and the Big Fish

The confidence, the arrogance, of the Brand Leader, strutting through the marketplace as if there were no other, no longer applies. Today, to stay Number One you have to think like a Number Two.

If we are the Number One brand, the Big Fish that threatens to eat us is ourselves—our own success. Our new size makes it difficult to be as nimble, as proactive as we once were. As Chinese journalist George Zhibin Gu notes, commenting on the changing world order: "The great powers in the past have all been pulled down more by their own weight than anything else. Should the future be any different?"[2] The apparent security and real profitability lent by being Number One in the market makes us loss-averse and protective: We cease to behave in the way that made us successful and took our brand to leadership in the first place.

Yet the reason Nike has up to now continued to dominate the footwear market is that it reinvents not just its advertising imagery, but the way it communicates with and engages a broad community of sports lovers around the world every year in order to stay ahead. It always surprises—not just because of its creativity but its restlessness: Its internal mantra is, "Do it once, and move on." Although it is now the

Establishment brand in terms of brand share, and although it is no longer subversive in the way it used to be, Nike has until recently continued to act like the hungriest and most imaginative brand, setting the pace in its category, at least, in engaging the consumer. Nike has aimed to be the Thought Leader as well as the Market Leader. Phil Knight has been very clear about the reason for this, famously remarking that though Nike is the industry Goliath, it will only succeed by thinking and acting like the industry David.

And there are clearly some good reasons why any ambitious Market Leader might want to think like this:

- To overcome the dangers of complacency
- To realize the genuine opportunity for further growth if one still thinks and acts like a Challenger
- To lean into the need for the leader to be the change agent, not the status quo—or risk another player being the change agent to that leader's disadvantage
- To keep consumer empathy and identification on their side ("Nobody roots for Goliath")
- To embrace the need to energize and rally their organization/the consumer community against a bigger enemy or goal

So while the purpose of this book is not primarily to address the needs of Brand Leaders, this chapter does look briefly at how and why a number of leading brands, from Nike to Oprah, have redefined what it means to be a Brand Leader in directly addressing some of these issues, principally because they looked to stay Market Leaders by thinking and behaving like the Challengers they used to be.

SUCCESS IS A VERY DANGEROUS THING

Warren Buffett recently revealed that when he plays online bridge against Bill Gates, the founder of Microsoft assumes the nom de guerre of "Challenger X." As we see Microsoft, after years of being a hugely successful, product-led Market Leader, having to stir itself to think like a Challenger again to face a range of new threats posed by Google, Apple, and the gaming giants, it is striking to see how some of the largest and most significant leaders around us are living up to Phil Knight's belief about Market Leadership, and continuing to think like the Challengers they once were. Look at Dell: The company is now 40,000 strong, with $57 billion in sales, and Michael Dell's personal fortune currently worth $17 billion—it would be natural to assume a maturation of his mind-set at the helm of his extraordinary success. One would have thought that his refrigerator was full, to echo the quote from Bernard Hopkins at the beginning of this chapter. Yet that is not what Michael Dell says—quite the opposite. How does he see his brand and company? "I still think of us as a Challenger," he says. "I still think of us attacking." He has still, and wants Dell to have, the big appetite and sharp teeth of the hungry entrepreneur he started as in Austin, Texas. He is fighting against the complacency that naturally sets in as you become Number One.[3] And the key, in many ways, is just this—to remember that being a Challenger is primarily a state of mind, not a state of market. And to always maintain that state of mind.

And we can see that other Market Leaders are very explicitly addressing this within their organizations. Lexus's market supremacy in the U.S. automotive luxury market in 2004, for example, was an extraordinary achievement for a still relatively new Japanese brand in a category (i.e., luxury) where convention would have said history and pedigree are everything. An achievement of which Lexus was both extraordinarily proud—and yet astutely wary at the same time. And which is why, the year after they became Market Leader, Lexus organized a three-day meeting for all its dealers, with the theme "To stay Number One, we need to think like a Number Two." The premise was a very simple one: For Lexus and its dealers to relax now would risk leaving them and the brand vulnerable to Mercedes and BMW, whom they had just left in their wake. To remain Number One they needed to make Lexus even better, even more differentiated. So Mike Wells, then Lexus's VP of Marketing, stimulated the brand team and the dealers to look beyond the automotive category to find their path to continued superiority and differentiation. He and his team laid out a ballroom in the Four Seasons in Aviara, Southern California, to replicate the experience of visiting an Apple Store (then still relatively new to the world), invited the dealers into further narrative and video "tours" of a Virgin Atlantic first-class lounge, a Dean and Deluca, and a Nordstrom, and enabled them all to go on a long and detailed exploration of the Four Seasons Hotel itself, to see how every department within this very different kind of service business was trained to deliver exceptional service to its customers. Why do this now, when Lexus already had a proven model that could get it to Number One? Rightly wary of relaxation, of the dangers of complacency that going Number One could precipitate, Lexus continued to want to *think and act like the Challenger it once was.*

So clearly being a Challenger is primarily about a mind-set. And one of the primary signatures of this mind-set as a Market Leader, one of the most powerful ways to prevent oneself falling prey to complacency, is to continue to lead that market, continue to be the agent of change. In 2006, Bill Clinton came to address the British Labour Party Conference, the party that was still, in effect, the Market Leader in British politics at the time, and then still helmed by Tony Blair. There had been a lot of conversation in the media leading up to the conference about the public's restlessness with the Labour Party's relatively long tenure in government, and Clinton spoke to this, referencing a recent poll that indicated 70 percent of the British people thought it was now time for change. What should the incumbent say in response to this, Clinton asked? "You should say: Of course it is," he said. "It's always time for change in a great and dynamic nation." They should not allow anyone, he continued, neither the media nor another political party to frame future choice as being "change versus more of the same." He concluded: "You are the change agents in this great nation. You have been and you will be."[4]

Being an agent of change if you are Market Leader often appears counter-intuitive. The natural gravitational pull for a Market Leader (certainly a nondigital or nontechnology Market Leader) is in the opposite direction: Protect what you have: Preserve the current criteria for choice and suppress the upstart change agents. Oh, and, maybe launch a new niche brand now and again to occupy some emerging space that it looks as if you can't extend into. Dieter Mateschitz of Red Bull has taken inspiration from the world of American football to structure his organization, at one stage having "offensive" and "defensive" divisions in his marketing department, and his ambition to continue to be the change agent obviously delivers both of these ways of thinking about one's task. It protects you against a fresh Challenger becoming, in turn, the change agent against you. And it recognizes that there is in reality plenty of growth and opportunity for most leaders if they are prepared to seek what is ahead, rather than simply protect what lies behind. At time of writing, it is too early to say whether Google's push into phones with Android or Amazon's attempt to reinvent the book with the Kindle are going to be successful. But it is clear that the considerable investment both have made in these new technologies represents a desire to continue to be at the leading edge of category change, if not to be the change agents themselves—in Google's case at least for defensive as well as offensive reasons.

CHALLENGING SOMETHING BIGGER THAN ALL OF US

Historically, then, we have seen Market Leaders who have sought to maintain leadership by thinking like the Number Two they once were two key dimensions. Like Intel's Andy Grove, by being "paranoid" and in your mind restlessly looking for the next inflection point that will threaten the category and your leadership with it. And like Phil Knight, by looking to appear to the world "smaller" on the outside than you are in reality on the inside. And we see both of these manifested in such leaders evidencing a continued determination to be the agent of change, rather than simply enforcers of the status quo.

But perhaps the digital age is amplifying a new kind of reason why Market Leaders need to be very careful not to be seen as Goliaths, and indeed throwing up a new way in which we see "leaders as Challengers" manifested. In the 1960s, the first modern Challenger, Avis, was almost strangled at birth: Some of the advertising account team tried to block the initial presentation of the "We Try Harder" campaign, because the thought of celebrating the idea that one was anything other than a winner was almost "un-American"—something that ran so counter, they felt, to American culture that it would inevitably be rejected. Yet 45 years later, we see a complete cultural volte face: In a recent interview, John Grisham, the most successful storyteller in the world in the 1990s, observed with amusement that it was now "the American way" to look for the person at the top to fail.[5] And this cultural desire to identify and topple Goliaths seems to become ever more central to that skeptical and combative dimension to our media and social culture that we noted in Chapter 6. A recent commentator on what drives social media and social networking noted that unity against a perceived corporate Goliath is a characteristic of a relatively high amount of activity on sites such as Digg or Reddit: "On many sites . . . and in many social media savvy communities . . . the key motivating factor is often an 'us versus them' approach, with the users as the underdog battling a giant corporation or politician or social structure."[6] We saw earlier that communities and social groups often need to create *monsters* to rally around, that this will be one of the ways that they form that identity and recruit others to it. And clearly, in the networked digital world, one practical reason to be the best possible corporate citizen is to avoid becoming one of those giants that the community unifies itself by rallying against (or indeed finding yourself unwittingly attached to the bigger threat that is the point of focus).*

And one could argue that there is a very small group of Challengers-turned-Market-Leaders who are teaching us that the best immunity *against* being turned into a monster *is to identify or create a monster oneself*—something that transcends the market or category, something that becomes a bigger issue for the community and one we, as champions of that community, can stand up to on their behalf. And key among that small group of Market Leaders we can learn most from here are successful media personalities. Especially Oprah.

Oprah Winfrey was a startlingly successful Challenger—her show's ability to overturn Donahue (and a host of other talk shows also run by white males) is a fascinating Challenger study in itself (how she put a

---

* A friend recently ran a workshop on branding at an NGO in Switzerland for a group of principled 20- and 30-year-olds. The first exercise was to ask them for first impressions of well-known brands. The conversation went like this:
Moderator: "Let's look at Coke. What's the first thing that comes to mind?"
The Room: "Red." "Evil." "Ubiquity."
Moderator: "Starbucks?"
The Room: "American imperialism."
Moderator: "Nike?"
The Room: "Sweatshops. Exploiting children."
Moderator: "Just curious—did anybody think: "Shoes?"
For this group there were no global brands any more; only global monsters. And this was one of the key forces that unified the group.[7]

new emotion, a genuinely warm and personal empathy, into the category, for instance). And it would have been natural for Oprah, as for all the other talk show hosts in U.S. media history, to have her hour in the sun and then fall in turn to a newer, fresher competitor again. But she hasn't. When briefly threatened by a new Challenger in Jerry Springer, whose new agenda for talk shows cheerfully and theatrically plumbed the depths of human interactions, prompting a host of rivals to follow suit, Oprah could have responded by going the same way—perhaps this was simply the way that the American public wanted their talk show hosts to behave, these days.

But she didn't: She responded by being the change agent, and in fact elevating the ambition and spirituality of her show. Alongside this, she introduced new forms of media (a magazine), new *applications* (Dr. Phil), and new ways for her community to participate with her (a book club). And she has gone on to become a billionaire, with a show that still tops the ratings, by continuing to challenge. Her challenges are now not to the other talk show hosts, but to the bigger monsters she sees threatening her chosen community (American women)—notably domestic violence, child abuse, and weight loss and self-esteem issues among women. Oprah is not a Goliath, both because she is smaller and visibly vulnerable to these larger monsters in the eyes of her community, and also because she uses all her strength and size to fight them on her community's behalf. And her community eternally loves her for it.

If we need then, more than ever as Market Leaders, to beware of finding ourselves positioned or depositioned as Goliaths, then let us turn ourselves into Challengers again; perhaps we need to find monsters bigger than ourselves to challenge on the community's behalf. In Oprah's case, her monsters are usually, of course, anything but manufactured—they are issues that are deeply and genuinely meaningful from her own past and present life. We should not be manufacturing our concern about these monsters, especially if they are social issues or environmental issues (and at one level the environment is of course the entire world's Big Fish). If we genuinely care about these kinds of macro issues, let us by all means lean into them. And if we don't, there are all sorts of everyday monsters worthy of attack, from The DVD Rental Process to The Hideous Tyranny of Chardonnay.[8]

SUMMARY

Our understanding of what it means to be a dynamic Market Leader has been transformed over the past 20 years by a small clutch of brands such as Nike, Lexus in North America, and Oprah. We see these brands retaining Market Leadership in three ways. First, by continuing to think like the Challengers they once were—recognizing that being a Challenger is primarily a mindset, not a state of market. Second, by ingraining that restless urge to continually evolve, and continue to be the change agent into their broader culture. And third, we see some of them deliberately evolving their stance, transcending their category and positioning themselves instead as fighting against something larger and more significant as a threat on behalf of their chosen "community." We discussed in Chapter 12 the evolution of Challenger stances as a means of maintaining appeal and interest with the consumer, both through finding a new way to be seen to champion the consumer, and by refreshing consumer interest in the narrative "conflict" between the brand and the category (or another player in that category); perhaps this last stance, as the slayer of monsters rather than just the slayer of larger enemies, is therefore one of the most potent Challenger stances of all.

16

RISK, WILL, AND THE CIRCLE OF ROPE

Guts! Guts! Life! Life! That is my technique.

George Luks

When Channel 4 launched in the United Kingdom as the fourth network channel, it enjoyed some success in showing for the first time sports from other countries—American football, cycling from France, Australian rules football, and so on. Shortly after launch, the channel tentatively added sumo wrestling to this cosmopolitan lineup, and (as it had with each of the other sports unfamiliar to the British armchair sports fan) prefaced the beginning of the sumo season with an hour's introduction to the rules, history, and vocabulary of the spectacle in store. Reviewing the great sumo champions of the previous decade, the *yokozuna* (all of whom reveled in popular nicknames like "The Dumptruck" and "The Ox"), Channel 4 interviewed the aging trainer of the then current titleholder (called, I think, "The Tiger"), an occupation known in sumo parlance as a *stable master*, and asked him the secret of his protégé's success.

The old man was very clear. There were, he said, three things that were important to be a great sumo wrestler. The first was physical strength—and yet, he observed, while The Tiger was strong, there were other fighters who were stronger. And they cut to film of the champion, no bantam himself, being towered over by others twice his bulk.

The second important requirement, said the stable master, is excellent technique; but if The Tiger was strong on technique, he noted, there were other *yokozuna* as good or better. And there followed film of our champion gamely holding his own in an intricate barrage of hand slaps with an opponent.

However, the third requirement, said the stable master, is *shin*—Japanese for *spirit*. It is this that makes The Tiger the champion: He never gives up. He never loses the will to win. And they showed an extended clip of the champion, seemingly about to be propelled beyond the circle of rope that delineates the sumo fighting area, yet always somehow recovering, fighting back, and twisting his opponent's strength to his own advantage until he was the one left inside the ring while his adversary toppled gigantically out of frame.

Now there are actually a number of important dimensions to Challenger brands that we haven't touched on at all so far. Chance, for instance: Marketing is not a science, not a matter of plot and counterplot, like a game of chess. Being lucky, and being able to exploit that luck when it falls one's way, can be a critical part of a Challenger's ascent. It was only by complete chance, for instance, that Target discovered Michael Graves had some designs for a line of cookware in a drawer in his filing cabinet, but the way Target responded to that discovery—launching what became the first of a series of designer cookware—has been at the heart of its recent success. And it may have been lucky to discover that 50 Cent liked VitaminWater, but was it not brilliant opportunism to ride that fortune by making him both an investor in the brand, and a flavor of his own?

But the more I interviewed the people behind Challenger brands, the more that particular image of the circle of sumo rope came back to me—the sense of spirit being the true delineator. While I had set out to write a book that would identify how Challengers use a more intelligent technique, if you like, to overcome an opponent's superior strength, I realized increasingly that I had failed to discuss the real differentiator, which was something far harder to define. *Shin*. Spirit. The emotions of those I talked to, the way they expressed themselves, rather than what they actually said. The medium, not the apparent message.

It is hard, of course, to write about these sorts of emotions without opening oneself up to charges of penning the business equivalent of a

Hallmark card. The reader may feel that we are veering horribly off course from the territory of case study and analysis into the world of self-improvement aids: They envisage any moment the onset of soft focus shots of eagles or Labrador puppies, and italicized quotes from famous Native Americans about the potential that lurks in every human heart.

Yet, at the same time, how does one leave unmentioned the extraordinary moment when the founder of a company, retelling for the thousandth time the story of his own company's journey to a complete stranger, still finds himself so moved in the storytelling that he literally has goose bumps on his arm? (He was as startled as I was. "Look," he kept repeating as he rose to his feet and shook one shaggy forearm repeatedly at the PR director and myself, as if we doubted him, "*goose bumps*.")

How does one omit the propensity to embrace risk, the love of unequal competition, the obsession with quality or innovation, the intense desire to win, the certainty of superiority, the sense of *fun*—qualities that so strongly color the way these people talked about the business they are in? How, in fact, does one leave out talk of all these qualities without oneself falling into (God forbid) the fear of emotion, the "zero-defect" philosophy characteristic of the Establishment brand? It is not just that spirit is inspiring; at a more pragmatic level, it is that it seems to be the driver in the difference between Challenger intent and Challenger behavior. And we are not interested in intent; we desire a whole new way of thinking and behaving. So it might, in principle, be possible to summarize the strategic approach by listing the Eight Credos and the four-stage Challenger process they represent, in Figure 16.1.

And we might, for instance, essay a summarizing table of the differences in mindset and ambition between the Brand Leader and the Challenger brand in table form such as Figure 16.2.

Yet these kinds of conclusions, whether the reader finds them valuable or not, are missing something crucial. Herb Kelleher put it well. When asked about Southwest's impending battle in California against Shuttle by United, he replied that what would keep them on top was their "hearts and their guts."

Very little is written about the role of emotion in organizations and business. It is as if, now that IBM has defined itself as being about solutions, it is we humans who have become the International Business Machines. Yet emotion is a key variable. Whether it is a positive desire (such

FIGURE 16.1 The Challenger Strategic Approach: A four-stage process.

Stage 1: Attitude & Preparation

Stage 2: Challenger Strategy

Stage 3: Challenger Behaviour

Stage 4: Sustaining Challenger Momentum

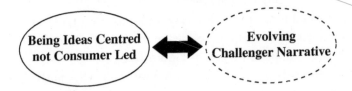

as the idealism of a method or innocent) or a robust paranoia (such as the one that has apparently driven Samsung's successful innovation culture) doesn't seem to really matter, but you need a healthy dose of one or the other.[1]

This goes beyond the old truth of people doing well what they love to do. It is about how you develop the personal impetus to fight through

FIGURE 16.2 Challengers versus Market Leaders: The difference in mindset and ambition.

Market Leader	Challengers
Dominant share	Perceived momentum
Maintain status quo	Agent of change
Reinforce behaviour	Redefine behavior
Trusted competence	Admired intent
Ubiquitous acceptance	Strong preference
Innovation functionality	. . . and ideas that inspire
Addresses many challenges	Overcome central challenge
Perceived professionalism	Perceived cause
Consumer-led	Consumer-intimate, but Lighthouse Identity
Satisfaction	Advocacy

the moments when you feel you are about to be thrown out of the circle of rope. A story will serve to illustrate this.

It is Quebec, a winter's morning. Four people are sitting in a room with a phone bill they can't pay.

The four make up all but one of the executive group of Cirque du Soleil, a new circus made up predominantly of ex–stilt walkers, which has just finished the first year of its new life. The company is heavily in the red, and it is their money. They are discussing hard practicalities—not least the bill on the table from the telephone company, which their overdraft will not cover. As they talk, the phone rings. Ironically, it is a collect call. From Italy.

They accept it. At the other end is Guy Laliberté, the fifth member and founding partner of the group, and he is in a state of some excitement. Great news, he tells them—he has just bought a new Big Top from a man he has struck up a friendship with in his travels in northern Italy. A huge tent, much bigger than the one they have now.

The room in Quebec is appalled: This is a disaster. The overdraft, they remind him. The bank, the debts. Even the wretched phone bill, for God's sake.

But the excitement from Italy is undiminished; they are looking at this the wrong way around, Laliberté tells them. This has been a year of just establishing themselves. Next year they will be better and better known: In order to recoup the money they owe, they will need a bigger seating capacity at each show. This Big Top is almost double the size of the old one: It will seat 1,200 people. It is, in fact, the only sensible way forward.

Guy Laliberté is a very persuasive man, and at last the four in the room in Quebec allow themselves to be persuaded. They agree to buy the Big Top in Italy with money that they do not have. Within a year they are back in the black.

This pattern repeats itself. Three years later the group argues again about expansion—should they move outside Canada, try the U.S. market? Many vote no: They have dabbled just across the border in Niagara Falls, and it was at best a mixed success. Laliberté pushes for yes—they should go to the United States. They have to keep moving.

There is considerable disagreement: After years of financial difficulty, many of them now have families, mortgages, pension plans. The founding partners win the vote, but at a cost—some members of the company part ways.

They open the Los Angeles festival. By the time the opening night comes, they have exhausted all their available funds in preparing for the show. If it goes badly, they do not even have enough money to pay for the gas to get the trucks back to Canada.

It is a success.

And so it goes on.

What the Cirque du Soleil story illustrates is that being a successful Challenger is not simply a question of taking one initial, enormous risk; a Challenger will flourish only if it has the courage to *continue* to take risks—even in the face of adversity. Indeed, it needs to foster within it a risk-taking culture that will continue to remain bold as it achieves higher levels of success, rather than falling back into conservative self-protection, forgetting the very reasons for its initial success. Fostering this culture is one of the primary responsibilities of a leader in a Challenger organization—for the culture as well as vision have to be exemplified at the top.

Jonathan Warburton, owner-driver of Warburton's bakery, observes: "One of the great responsibilities of owner-drivers is to stick their necks out and be seen to take risks, because they're fireproof. What chance is there of the hired help taking risks if the guys at the top they are looking up to, who are fireproof, won't stick their necks out?" Tourism New Zealand's CEO echoes this need, as a sponsor of risk, for a Challenger leader to be prepared for a certain "carelessness with self."

And this preparedness to take risks—informed, educated risks—throughout the organization is important not simply because it is a vital part of an idea culture (where the courage to champion and pursue a new idea is as important to its success as the ability to have the idea in the first place), but because the old methods of reducing risk and putting copper bottoms on marketing decisions are looking ever more unsound. The Hollywood screenwriter William Goldman is given to remark that in show business, "Nobody knows anything," meaning that no one can predict what is and isn't going to work; one could be forgiven for thinking that, at the speed at which our markets and marketing world are changing, the same could be true for Challenger brands.

Now one of the purposes for creating a structure, a sort of systematized approach in the way we have been trying to do through the book such as we have is precisely because we are not Dieter Mateschitz, or Steve Jobs, or James Dyson. As Challenger individuals and teams working on second-tier brands, but who are for the most part not the founders of their own companies, we need entrepreneurialism, but structured entrepreneurialism—entrepreneurialism on a set of guiding rails. And that all the individual examples we have discussed have been transposed into a system that is a postrationalization, rather than the path that anyone deliberately wrote for him- or herself from the beginning, is in fact something that makes us *more confident* in the approach, because it spans the learning from a number of different categories, from launches to relaunches, from luxury to mass-market brands. We said at the beginning that if the old marketing model was broken, and yet to be replaced by a proven new one, we could at least identify some timeless Challenger principles to live by, one that we could throw around the worlds of physical brands, digital brands, and service brands alike, and which would allow us to take any Challenger brand from any of these worlds, and create clarity about how to think about building success for it in the future. And it is these principles and this approach that we have been exploring throughout the book.

But all the principles and examples and tools in the world do not replace the need for some aspect of *shin*. Even if we may not possess the apparent fearlessness in the face of risk that one sees in the great entrepreneurs, at the very least there is the need for will. (I have long been fascinated by the power of will: For instance, among the Jewish community in New York, death rates decline before Passover and rise afterward—people have *kept themselves alive*, through will alone, to attend an important event.) This, at least, we must have; behavior will be difficult to implement, and it will take time.

How much time? It depends on the business you are in, and how much of the organization you will take with you—but it will almost always be much longer than you think. It took the two leaders of the Unilever team on Dove four years to realize what became Dove's "Campaign for Real Beauty": a year to develop the strategy and put an internal stake in the ground, a year to get to the right creative idea that would genuinely deliver that strategy, a year to find a country that would run the work and prove it to the doubters elsewhere, and a year to roll the initial advertising out and then develop the more concrete ideas and behaviors that would become the all-important proof points, such as the Self-Esteem Fund. Clearly Dove is a story of powerful thinking, and brilliant internal engagement, but also, at heart, it is a story of an enormous act of will, and tenacity over time. The Marketing Director of one brand we worked with led his team to develop the Lighthouse Identity, and then presented the resulting red-blooded communications idea to his Chairman. The Chairman was appalled—he told his Marketing Director that it would go into research "over his dead body." The Marketing Director took the "refusal" as a request for further information. After a number of further conversations, the idea did indeed find itself in research. Consumers loved it, and the idea ran. Sales tripled. Another act of will.[2]

And the demands on this personal and emotional side of ourselves is not something that ever finishes, for once you have started being a Challenger, you cannot stop. Once you have started to create momentum within the eyes of your own company, let alone in the eyes of the consumer, to stop moving suggests death: better to have never started moving at all. All of which is why, if we are looking to become genuinely idea-centered and to genuinely maintain momentum, we will need to practice *regularly* a kind of analysis entirely different from the kind we do now. At the moment, our tendency is to look regularly inward: We seek strategic direction every year from competitive analysis *within* our own category.

But what the examples contained in this book suggest, if nothing else, is that while such analysis of our own category is obviously an important prerequisite for thinking about how to defend our business, if we wish to gain a genuine competitive advantage we should be looking *outward*. What we should, in fact, be doing is the systematic and frequent analysis of:

- Number Two brands
- Outside our category
- Demonstrating rapid growth

This analysis will look for three things. The first is, of course, individual ideas that we can simply appropriate and transpose into our own category. (Who says using entertaining narrative techniques taken from comics, as *Apple Daily* used, couldn't make a whole group of other areas of written matter something people were interested in reading—such as how an Index Tracker works, or how to productively use the other 80 percent of your mobile phone's functionality?) The second thing such analysis will look for is insights into how brands have achieved breakthroughs in an individual category, and then attempt to translate the results into implications for our own category by using the kinds of exercises presented in Chapter 13. So, for instance, when we discover there is an outdoor clothing retailer that offers a shower room in which consumers are able to test rainproof clothing, two thoughts immediately begin to occur: How can *we* make the retail experience match the pleasure of the usage experience? And then, how can we turn trial, and the experience it offers, at our point of purchase into a source of differentiation? If we read that in the past six months, half of the best-selling novels in Japan were originally released as page-per-day serials sent to mobile phones, the question is not, "What are the opportunities for the U.S. phone manufacturers in that?" but "How could we, in an entirely different category, turn some element of our brand relationship into a compelling daily story that people would want to follow on their way into work every day?" And clearly the intersection between the digital world and the real world will be a hugely stimulating one to participate in for a Challenger in any category over the next 10 years—though it is striking, of course, how much this rapidly changing new digital domain is itself being built around meeting very old and enduring human concepts, such as community, societal sharing, the importance of storytelling, and simply being able to see where all our friends are all the time. I showed an eminent anthropologist, Bob Deutsch, around a (then) bleeding edge "virtual" office I worked in a few years ago in Los Angeles (no assigned desks, latest wireless technology, playful common space, dramatic meeting rooms) and asked him his reaction. "Fascinating," he said, "it reminds me of my work among primitive tribes." Startled, I asked him why. He found my astonishment odd—he thought it was very obvious: no individually owned space, an emphasis on common meeting areas, all of the group constantly aware of where everyone else was, the most important conversations happening at common points of need, such as where the water (or latte) was drawn and the food prepared. What made the future work was a deep understanding of the past, and in particular the fundamental frameworks that bring us as humans together or drive us apart.

So in looking across categories in this way, we will defy those who tell us that the learning is all in one direction, that it is what the new generation of digital Challenger brands can teach physical brands that is the future; instead, we will look at very new concepts such as how brands build communities, and ask ourselves what we can learn not just from the new generation of community-based brands, but also from brands that have built their entire businesses around successful communities for years—such as local newspapers, or radio stations (What would be the equivalent of a DJ within our digital community, for instance? How would they behave differently from just a "community manager"?).

And in looking outward, we don't just mean outside our category. We mean outside our culture, in all the meanings of that concept. It doesn't matter where these brands come from—Bangalore, Tokyo, Boulder, Tel Aviv, Helsinki, Shanghai—we must create the time and space to immerse ourselves in, and look all over the physical and digital worlds for, inspiration, for the inspiration to ideas and inspiration that can help us change gear within our own category. Eat the Big Fish. Alibaba's Jack Ma says, "China is a place where miracles are made." Why?

And what can we learn from that if we wish to create miracles of our own in Minneapolis or Munich?[3]

And critical to all of this searching, too, this expansion of our peripheral vision, will be retaining and rooting it in our sense of self, our own Lighthouse Identity. Being inspired by what we find, but not a slave to it, and finding in that inspiration a way to selectively re-express what we stand for and why we stand for it in a way that is ever more relevant and engaging to our consumers and our communities of interest.

Which leads us back to Apple again. Looking beyond our category, a will that refuses to give up, the continual possibility of change—all these bring us back to the brand that made being number two an icon again for today's generation of managers. Things famously went adrift at Apple for a while after 1984: Losing the hunger and single-mindedness that had made them the successful iconoclasts, they also lost sight of their core values and who they were. By 1997, analysts said they were way outside the circle of rope.

But Steve Jobs knew better. The launch of the iMac, in particular, famously marked a return not just to innovation, but to the kind of revolutionary user experience that had given Apple its initial following. At its launch, both founder and inventor commented on it in vocabulary entirely new to the computer industry—because that vocabulary came from two entirely different categories altogether. Jonathan Ive, the senior director of Apple's Industrial Design group, noted in an interview that the language people were using to describe the translucent iMac was not the language of high-tech industry, but the language of food. And Steve Jobs himself unveiled the iMac in May 1998 with the words "Today we brought romance and innovation back into the industry." Romance? Food? In the computer industry? At last Apple was thinking and behaving like a Challenger again.

However, the first piece of mass communication that appeared from Apple when Jobs returned, a 60-second television commercial, was not an advertisement about product, or speed, or design at all. It was about something far more fundamental—a restatement to the world and to itself of Apple's identity and purpose. This decision was a risk—with time to turn the company around slipping away, many commentators felt Apple should have been spending its limited advertising resources on more direct, pragmatic product communication—but the emotional declaration of the brand's identity set the foundation among Apple users and staff alike for everything that was to follow. Over a black-and-white montage of people who famously broke the mold in their individual fields, from the arts (Martha Graham, John Lennon, Maria Callas) to business (Henry Ford, Ted Turner) to science and sport (Albert Einstein, Muhammad Ali), a voice celebrates their greatness, in terms of their ability to see things differently, the scale of their ambition, and their absolute self-belief:

Here's to the crazy ones. The misfits. The rebels. The trouble-makers. The round pegs in the square holes.

The ones who see things differently.

They're not fond of rules. And they have no respect for status quo.

You can quote them, disagree with them, glorify, or vilify them. About the only thing you can't do is ignore them.

Because they change things. They push the human race forward.

And while some may see them as the crazy ones, we see genius. Because the people who are crazy enough to think they can change the world, are the ones who do.

It ended very simply, with the Apple logo above the two words "Think Different."

And although in this piece of communication Apple was speaking single-mindedly for and about itself, its spirit epitomized, just as in 1984, that of Challengers all around the world. As we look at the questions and issues we will have to face in the future as citizens of the world and not simply as brand owners, whether they are how to reverse our environmental impact or how to feed the world, one can only believe this spirit will be more necessary than ever before.

References and Sources

Preface

1. www.thinkexist.com.

Chapter 1:   The Law of Increasing Returns

1. This is one part (Figure 1.2) of a greater body of unpublished work into this area by Udo van de Sandt, whose thinking this is.
2. I owe this observation—and graph—to Cindy Scott.
3. A.S.C. Ehrenberg and M.D. Uncles, "Dirichlet-type Markets: A Position Paper," 1998. I am grateful to Professor Ehrenberg for allowing me to reproduce this from the publications of the R&D Initiative.
4. Kurt Badenhausen, "Blind Faith," *Financial World*, July 8th, 1996.

Chapter 2:   The Consumer Isn't

1. Donald J Trump and Meredith McIver, *How to Get Rich* (New York: Ballantine Books, 2004).
2. Constance M. Lewallen and Steve Seid, *Ant Farm 1968-1978* (Berkeley: University of California Press, 2004).
3. My thanks to David Weisfelner and OMD for allowing me to print this study, and the other materials of theirs used in the book.
4. Emily Bryson York, "We Want to Be Pepsi to Subway's Coke—Steve Provost Aims to Boost Sales by Wooing Women," www.adage.com, January 29, 2008.
5. I owe much of this line of thinking to original observations by Marty Cooke and Sally Reinman, and some of the substance to subsequent work by Anne Truscott and Fred Sattler.
6. My thanks to Christy Liu and Simon Sylvester of Y&R for allowing me to reprint these data.
7. Virginia Valentine and Malcolm Evans, "The Dark Side of the Onion: Rethinking the Meanings of Rational and Emotional Responses," JMRS 35.2 (1993).
8. http://blog.highlandbusinessresearch.com/2007/10/01/how-social-media-like-flickr-and-you-tube-has-become-an-influence-on-destination-selection/.

Chapter 4: The First Credo: Intelligent Naivety

1. Twyla Tharp, *The Creative Habit* (New York: Simon and Schuster, 2003).
2. Susan Casey, "Blueprint for Green Business," *Fortune,* May 29, 2007.
3. Interview with Mark Simon, COO, Next Media Interactive/Apple Daily Newspapers.
4. Lovefoxxx by Jessica Brinton, The *Sunday Times,* November 18, 2007; http://women .timesonline.co.uk/tol/life_and_style/women/celebrity/article2851270.ece.
5. Viv Groslop, "Shocking Pink," The *Guardian,* June 2, 2008.
6. Keith Naughton, "Out of the Box Thinking," *Newsweek,* May 12, 2003.
7. Julie Treumann, "A Brand-New Brew," *Time,* January 9, 2007.
8. "About Mii," www.brandweek.com, October 8, 2007.
9. Twyla Tharp, *The Creative Habit* (New York: Simon and Schuster, 2003).

Chapter 5: Monsters and Other Challengers: Gaining Clarity on the Center

1. Perez Hilton, The Piers Morgan Interview, *GQ,* June 2008.
2. Sheena S. Iyengar and Mark R. Lepper, "When Choice is Demotivating: Can One Desire Too Much of a Good Thing?" *Journal of Personality and Social Psychology*, 79, 995–1006 (2000).
3. Stephen Armstrong, "Kind of Blue," *High Life,* June 2007.
4. Jeffrey M. O'Brien, "Wii Will Rock You," *Fortune,* June 11 2007.
5. www.lesserevil.com.
6. Joel Stein, "Two Buck Chuck Takes a Bite out of Napa," *Business 2.0,* September 7, 2007.
7. Christopher Booker, *The Seven Basic Plots: Why We Tell Stories* (London: Continuum International Publishing Group, 2006).
8. "The Practical Joker Who Turned Business Green," Anita Roddick obituary, *The Week,* September 15, 2007.
9. My thanks to Sarah Newman for the original question that provoked this chapter.

Chapter 6: The Second Credo: Build a Lighthouse Identity

1. Tom Patty influenced much of my thinking about identity. Kate Edwards helped develop the concept of Lighthouse Brands.
2. "From Heroes to Losers," by Professor David Marc, speech to the APG conference 1996, Los Angeles.
3. Marianne Macdonald, "The Most Powerful Woman in Television—That You've Never Seen," *Observer Woman,* June 2007.
4. "The Best in Your Bag," *Sky Magazine,* August 2000.
5. Sholto Byrnes, "Raging Bull," *Independent Review,* January 6, 2005.
6. Barry Mansfield, "Web Slinger," CNBC European Business, April 2008.

7. Jemima Kiss, "Twitter of Success," *The Guardian,* October 8, 2008.
8. Jack Schofield, "Wrangling the Web into an Open Future," The *Guardian,* February 28, 2008.
9. Susan Casey, "Blueprint for Green Business," *Fortune,* May 29, 2007.
10. Much of this section came from an interview with Robin Wight, and his own thinking on Icon Brands.

Chapter 7: The Third Credo: Take Thought Leadership of the Category

1. http://middlestage.blogspot.com/2005_10_01_archive.html.
2. The whole concept of Thought Leadership came from Matt Shattock.
3. Lucas Hollweg, "He's Cooking," *Sunday Times,* July 3, 2005.
4. Gavanndra Hodge, "Kissy Kissy," *Girl About Town,* September 23, 2002.

Chapter 8: The Fourth Credo: Create Symbols of Reevaluation

1. http://findarticles.com/p/articles/mi_m3092/is_1999_Feb_8/ai_53904922.
2. David Smith, "YouTube Goes Live to Take on TV," *Observer,* March 2, 2008.
3. Alice Park, "Top-Flite Gets Macho," *Time,* September 10, 2007.
4. "About Mii," www.brandweek.com, October 8, 2007.
5. www.capital.com.au/html/events02.htm.
6. "Message and Muscle: An Interview with Swatch Titan Nicholas Hayek," *Harvard Business Review,* March/April 1993.
7. Dan Glaister, "Nice Sweater. Here's One Just Like It. Only £4.40," *The Guardian,* January 21, 2006.
8. Ibid.

Chapter 9: The Fifth Credo: Sacrifice

1. Ryan Underwood, "Jonesing for Soda," *Fast Company,* March 2005; www.fastcompany.com.
2. Susan Casey, "Blueprint for Green Business," *Fortune,* May 29, 2007.
3. My thanks to Dawn Ahmed for her insights into the Scion case history.
4. Betsy Morris, "What Makes Apple Golden?" *Fortune,* March 17, 2008.

Chapter 10: The Sixth Credo: Overcommitment

1. Ernest Rutherford: "We don't have the money, so we will have to think."
2. Edward J. Noha, CNA Insurance, address to Professional Insurance Agents of Connecticut, 1990. I am grateful to Bob Ceurworst for drawing my attention to this.

Chapter 11: The Seventh Credo: Using Communications and Publicity to Enter Social Culture

1. Rachel Cooke, "Be My Guest, Please," *Condé Nast Traveler,* December 2007.
2. Elizabeth Bumiller, "Counterculture shock," *New York Times,* February 13, 1997.
3. My thanks to Thomas Falck for his help in this study.
4. Conversations with John Stuart and Megan Kent were a considerable influence on this section.
5. From an interview with Emily Liu of Cadbury Adams.
6. Mireya Navarro, "His Way Meets a Highway Called Court," *New York Times,* July 10, 2005.
7. "Show Biz News," *Costa Calida Informer,* issue 113.
8. Barbara Kiviat, "How One Man on a Harley Reinvented Banking," *Time,* July 16, 2007.
9. Ryszard Kapuscinski, *Travels with Herodotus* (New York: Knopf, 2007), p. 51.
10. Les Binet and Peter Field, "Marketing in the Era of Accountability," IPA dataMINE.

Chapter 12: The Eighth Credo: Become Idea-Centered, Not Consumer-Centered

1. www.notcot.com.
2. Interview with Geoff Ross.
3. Interview with Dawn Ahmed.
4. This section was prompted by an initial question from—and subsequent conversation with—Donna Neal of SAB Miller.

Chapter 14: The Scope of the Lighthouse Keeper

1. www.fastcompany.com.
2. Joanna Weiss, "In a Year of Fragmentation, No Easy Fix," *Boston Globe,* December 30, 2007.
3. Conversations with Antonio Lucio inspired and influenced much of this section and chapter.
4. "Born Again Virgin," *The Hub,* January/February 2008.
5. The company is method.
6. Jonathan Guthrie, "Bath Bomber Makes a Splash," *Financial Times,* October 24, 2007.
7. A brilliant idea of Ron Coughlin's.
8. www.kashi.com.
9. I am grateful to Russell Davies for his thoughts and builds on this chapter.

Chapter 15:   Challenger as a State of Mind: Staying Number One Means Thinking Like a Number Two

1. Richard Williams, "Battle to Be the Greatest of Them All," the *Guardian,* December 8, 2007.

2. www.portland.indymedia.org.

3. BusinessWeek, *Strategy Powerplays* (New York: McGraw-Hill, 2006); www.expresspharmaonline.com.

4. www.newsbbc.co.uk. The link with "Challenger leaders" was by Ian Leslie.

5. "10 Questions," *Time,* February 25, 2008.

6. www.danzarella.com.

7. Interview with Marie McNeely.

8. My thanks to Chris Riley for helping develop this line of thinking.

Chapter 16:   Risk, Will, and the Circle of Rope

1. Peter Lewis, "A Perpetual Crisis Machine," *Fortune,* September 19, 2005.

2. The Marketing Director was Graeme Lindsay

3. Robin Kwong and Tom Mitchell, "Alibaba Shares Soar on First Day of Trading," *Financial Times,* November 7, 2007.

Acknowledgments for the Second Edition

This book has had three lives to date: the original process of writing it, the use I and others have put it to in working with it, and the researching and writing of the second edition. In each of those lives, my debt to others has been considerable.

In the first of its lives, it benefitted from hugely from four main influences. The first and most important debt was to Kate Marber. It was Kate who came up with the initial concept of Challenger Brands, and who was instrumental in developing the early research and thinking that gave the whole idea impetus and life. Alasdair Ritchie supported and championed the idea when many around him didn't, and nurtured me personally through the emotional roller-coaster that inevitably accompanies the creation of something new. Key figures in two agencies I worked in, Chiat/Day Los Angeles and TBWA Europe, opened my eyes to what it meant to really be a challenger, and the potent pleasures of Piracy. I cannot overstate the influence they have had on my thinking and attitude to business. And a great group of planners and information experts in both agencies (later to become one) profoundly shaped the thinking and views expressed in the book.

From 1999 onwards, the book has been a part of a small company astride the Atlantic (and now beyond), and the underlying thinking has been a cornerstone of our approach to the strategic work we do with clients. In a small company, everybody challenges, and everybody adds—that is the pleasure of working with people you like, admire, and trust. In eatbigfish that pleasure and challenge has come from the people we are, and have been, namely Teresa Murphy, Mark Barden, Hugh Derrick, Chad Dick, Peter Field, Jude Jarvis, Olivia Knight, Kate Smith, Bella Acton, Helen Redstone, Toby Brown, Jude Bliss, Katy Clift, Helen Murphy Rob Poynton, Pam Scott, Diane Simpson, Robin Hafitz, Eve Noiret Ryan and Lily Double. And the group of us have, over the last nine years, had the pleasure of working with some extraordinary clients on some wonderful brands: it would be invidious to single out some over others, but I for one have learnt more from those clients and brands in the last few years of my working life than I have in the previous 20. Quite apart from their contributions here, the second and third books in particular have been largely inspired by them. It has been a privilege. And it also gives me huge pleasure that the book has had a working life outside the company, for those who have applied the working principles to their own brands, from Colombia to the Ukraine. My thanks to all who have written and shared their stories and results.

Now the book finishes the end of the third stage of its life: the researching and writing of the second edition. I hope it will be clear from the text itself the debt I owe to all the interviewees, but my thanks in particular to Eric Ryan, Richard Reed, Dan Germain, Pierre Schaeffer, George Hickton, Tom Birk, Mike Wells, Geoff Ross, Dawn Ahmed, Emily Liu, Lynne Vanderveer, Doğan Kaşikçi, Jim Hytner, Dave Hieatt, Graeme Lindsay, Kevin George, Russell Taylor, Mark Boot, Keir Cooper, Mark Simon, Rory Sutherland, Alessandro Manfredi, Silvia Lagnado, Thomas Falck, Peter Eckhardt, Thomas Aakjær Jensen, Greg Nugent, Rich Field, Renzo Rosso, Robin Wight, Jean-Laurent Ingles, Paul English, Peter Field, Donna Neal, Ray Davis and Lani Hayward. David Weisfelner and OMD were generous in sharing their data and arranging one of the interviews on my behalf, and our colleagues at angriffslust—Thomas Holt, Jens Vogt and Dorothea Meyer—hugely helpful in the insights into the German cases. Jackie Cooper and her colleagues at Edelman shared their thinking on the new media world with me, and Russell Davies gently but brilliantly pointed out two of the more glaring oversights in an earlier version of one of the chapters. Antonio Lucio has been a continual and invigorating impetus to push the thinking further when I have been tempted to let up and rest a little; he remains the youngest and freshest thinker one can share a breakfast table with. My thanks to him for the foreword to this book.

For John Wiley & Sons, Inc., Richard Narramore commissioned the second edition, and has adroitly combined a firm hand between the shoulder blades when it was necessary, with a sympathetic ear when I needed it.

Mark and Liv from eatbigfish shared the interviews with me, and Jude, Helen and Toby filmed and edited them; it is embarrassing to admit how excited a good interview still gets me. Mark and Peter also read key chapters at critical stages, when I was least certain of them.

And of course there are always the wild cards—the people in one's professional life that just make it much more interesting. Richard, Ofer and Gal, Nikolaj and Rasmus, here's to you.

Throughout these three lives of the book, there have been key friends who have seen it through from first to last—chief amongst them Matt Shattock and Graham Wells. Thank you, both.

Finally, it is funny how in acknowledgements one always leaves one's family to last; perhaps it is because throughout the writing process it seems all too often that one is, indeed, leaving them till last. The dedication at the front of this book to my wife Ruth, for her own sacrifice in letting me write a third. The dedication is at once only two words and at the same time an absurd amount more. Finally, my thanks to my two 13-year-old boys, who have just moved onto the next stage of my education. Social networking, content creation, digital broadcasting—there is so much I have to learn.

Book's over, boys; let's get started.

Photo Credits

Illustration	Page	Company	Credits
Avis ad.	xii	Avis	Avis Rent A Car
method's range of products.	42	method	With permission of method.
Bionade bottle.	53	Bionade GmbH	With permission of Bionade.
Blue Man's funeral for the 1980s.	64	Blue Man Productions	Courtesy of Blue Man Productions, Inc.
Surf packaging.	66	Surf Packaging	With permission of Surf.
method text.	95	method	With permission of method.
howies' long label.	106	howies	howies
Bang & Olufsen's BeoLab 5 speakers with BeoSound 9000.	121	Bang & Olufsen	Courtesy of Bang & Olufsen Media
Swatch launches large.	148	Swatch	Swatch Ltd.
Customized Scion xB.	174	Scion	Courtesy of Scion, a division of Toyota Motor Sales, USA, Inc.
Umpqua store.	224	Umpqua Bank	Basil Childers

Index